When Toys Come Alive

Lois Rostow Kuznets

When Toys Come Alive

Narratives of
Animation,
Metamorphosis,
and Development

Yale University Press
New Haven and London

Designed by Nancy Ovedovitz. Set in Berkeley Medium type by The Composing Room of Michigan, Inc. Printed in the United States of America by BookCrafters, Inc., Chelsea, Michigan.

Library of Congress Cataloging-in-Publication Data

Kuznets, Lois R.
    When toys come alive : narratives of animation, metamorphosis, and development / Lois Rostow Kuznets.
        p.   cm.
    Includes bibliographical references and index.
    ISBN 0-300-05645-1
    1. Metamorphosis in literature.   2. Toys in literature.   3. Children's literature—History and criticism.   4. Fantastic literature—History and criticism.   I. Title.
    PN56.M53K89   1994
    809' 927—dc20   93-40849
                                                                        CIP

10   9   8   7   6   5   4   3   2   1

To those significant ones with whom I have lived
intimately and who have taught me what it means to
be alive and become real: especially Jim, Naomi, and
Miriam.
　And to the dear friends, former teachers, and
students who continue also to contribute to the
human joys I experience—which toys taste only in
fantasy.

"Get up! Get up, dear Sarah Jane!
Now strikes the midnight hour,
    When dolls and toys
    Taste human joys
And revel in their power."
—Florence and Bertha Upton, *The Adventures of Two*
Dutch Dolls—And a Golliwog, 1895

This crazy world whirled about her, men and women
dwarfed by toys and puppets, where even the birds were
mechanical and the few human figures went masked and
played musical instruments in the small and terrible hours
of the night into which again she had been thrust. She was
in the night again, and the doll was herself.
—Angela Carter, *The Magic Toyshop,* 1967

"I often wonder why you toys are all so eager to go down
to earth. It's a toss up what sort of children you'll belong
to—you don't even know whether they'll be kind to you—
but here you come, year after year, like the trusting little
creatures you are—clamouring to be chosen. Up here you
are at least your own masters and happy enough. But still
I suppose it's what toys are for, when all's said and done."
—Katherine Tozer, *The Wanderings of Mumfie,* 1935

Contents

Illustrations

Frontispiece and title page from *The Adventures of a Doll,* by Mary Mister. Artist unknown. Frontispiece and title page from *Memoirs of a London Doll,* by Mrs Fairstar [Richard Horne]. Artist unknown. Photo courtesy of the Osborne Collection of Early Children's Books, Toronto Public Library, Toronto, Canada.

"I begin my memoirs." From *Hitty: Her First Hundred Years,* by Rachel Field. Illustrated by Dorothy Lathrop. Reprinted by permission of Macmillan Publishing Company. Copyright © 1929 Macmillan Publishing Company; copyright renewed © 1957 Arthur Pedersen.

D. W. Winnicott. Drawing by David Levine. Copyright © 1978 Nyrev, Inc. Reprinted by permission from *New York Review of Books.*

"At the word Three! the two boys pulled off their caps—." From *The Adventures of Pinocchio,* by Carlo Collodi, translated by Carol Della Chiesa. Illustrated by Attilio Mussino. Copyright © 1969 Macmillan Publishing Company. Illustration © 1969 Giunti Marzocco S. P. A., Firenze. Reprinted by permission of Macmillan Publishing Company.

"The Feast at Sandwich." From *The Return of the Twelves,* by Pauline Clarke. Illustrated by Bernarda Bryson. Reprinted by permission of Putnam Publishing Company.

"Their fears allayed—each takes an arm." From *The Adventures of Two Dutch Dolls— And a Golliwog,* by Florence Upton. Illustrated by Bertha Upton. Photo courtesy of the Osborne Collection of Early Children's Books, Toronto Public Library, Toronto, Canada.

"'Lor', ain't it pretty!' said the parlour-maid." From *The Magic City,* by E. Nesbit. Illustrated by H. R. Millar. Photo courtesy of the Osborne Collection of Early Children's Books, Toronto Public Library, Toronto, Canada.

"The leader of the rats held out a folded yellow paper. 'Sign on the dotted line, please,' he said." From *Poor Cecco,* by Margery Williams Bianco. Illustrated by Arthur Rackham. Copyright © 1925 George H. Doran Company. Reprinted by permission of Doubleday, a division of Bantam Doubleday Dell Publishing Group.

"And with that final bitter remark Squirrel took off Miss Hickory's head." From *Miss Hickory,* by Carolyn Sherwin Bailey. Illustrated by Ruth Gannett. Copyright © 1946 Carolyn Sherwin Bailey, copyright renewed © 1973 Rebecca Davies Ryan. Reprinted by permission of Viking Penguin, a division of Penguin Books USA.

"A large rat crept out of the shadows of the girders into the light of the overhead lamps, and stood up suddenly on his hind legs before the mouse and his child." From *The Mouse and His Child,* by Russell Hoban. Illustrated by Lillian Hoban. Reprinted by permission of HarperCollins and Faber and Faber.

"The golem went into the cheder and sat on a bench. The children gazed with amazement at the giant who sat among them." From *The Golem,* by Isaac B. Singer. Illustrated by Uri Shulevitz. Illustrations copyright © 1982 Uri Shulevitz. Reprinted by permission of Farrar, Straus, and Giroux and Andre Deutsch.

Preface

Once upon a time, about half past twelve, the gingham dog and the calico cat ate each other up. I learned in early childhood of this violent episode in the secret lives of toys, duly witnessed by the venerable Old Dutch Clock and the Chinese Plate and faithfully reported in Eugene Field's "The Duel." Even then I puzzled over the event's defiance of the laws of conservation of matter. But storytellers, ballet performances, and reading initiated me further into toy mysteries similar to this strange internecine clash. Long buried deep in my consciousness, such nocturnal toy adventures were animated only later by my own imagination.

Nor did these intriguing associations resurface even when for several years I studied and wrote about Edwardian author and toy collector Kenneth Grahame, whose early essays and stories often brought forth marvelously intricate descriptions of toys. Although I noted Grahame's toys as evocatively charming, they did not attract my principal attention for they were rarely animated in a viable narrative of their own. They paled beside the woodland creatures he created in *The Wind in the Willows*. In the fall of 1986, however, about the time I was finishing my study of Grahame, I was invited to give a talk at the opening of the Elizabeth Ball Collection of Children's Books at the Lilly Library of Indiana University. I discovered that among the treasures of the Ball Collection were many toy books and harlequinades. I cannot trace the paths of association that led from Grahame's toy descriptions and my notions of toy books to the topic on which I finally talked, "From Andersen to Hoban: Toys as Characters in Literature." Nevertheless, that talk became the basis of this study. Everything I have always known about the secret lives of toys in literature began to emerge then.

At first, I hardly realized the multidisciplinary ramifications of my interest in toy characters. My scholarly and imaginative reading led me into not only fiction but history, psychology, anthropology, literary theory, and finally computer science's struggles with artificial intelligence. Fringe benefits abounded also. I enjoyed the luxury of working in a rare-book library, where fragile items were placed on tiny pillows, their pages held down by beanbag snakes (though in one such collection, despite the giant magnifying glass provided me, I could not read Branwell Brontë's tiny script). I browsed and bargained in jumbled, dusty, secondhand bookstores and book-fair kiosks. I visited noisy toy shops, quiet museums, and basement collections of child-hood toys. I clipped items from the newspaper about sandbox play in Jungian therapy and the latest dollar totals of the toy market. My friends sent me clippings about traumatized children drowning their dolls after they them-selves had survived floods. I sat through scary movies and sentimental or provocative television shows. I watched Russell Hoban wind up the tin mouse and mouse child that inspired his book. All in the name of research!

Many people aided me in this endeavor. Although they are almost too many to name, I would like to give special thanks at least to some, hoping that they will understand when I do not come up to their expectations of excel-lence (and that those whom I inadvertently neglect to name will be com-forted by my obvious inadequacies).

Mary Alice Burgan, then chair of the Department of English, Indiana University, invited me to give my original talk, and Diane Bauerle, cataloger of Children's Literature, informed me about the contents of the Elizabeth Ball Collection of the Lilly Library. Fred Harris at San Diego State University showed me his large private collection of toys and lent me books. Especially helpful to me in gathering historical material were Margaret Crawford Ma-loney, director, and Dana Tenny, librarian, of the Osborne and Smith Collec-tions of the Toronto Public Library. On one occasion, Lissa Paul of the University of New Brunswick not only entertained me but read my first chapter while I consulted the Osborne Collection; on several other occa-sions, David Townsend of the University of Toronto did the same. A whole group of people in Great Britain made my research trip in May 1991 success-ful: the list of toy books in the Renier Collection of the Bethnal Green Museum compiled by Tessa Rose Chester inspired me to go there; Nancy and Aidan Chambers of Thimble Press gave me encouragement to come; Clive Hurst, head of Bodleian Special Collections, set things in motion; Gillian Avery and Andrea Immel gathered cartloads of books to await me in the Bodleian reading room; Naomi Lewis spent an afternoon talking with me about her own interest in doll stories, and Elspeth Aubrey took me to toy museums in Stratford and Bangor, Wales.

That trip to Great Britain took place during a year in Ann Arbor made possible by a sabbatical granted by San Diego State University (and sup-ported by my chair, Carey Wall), as well as by generous visiting-scholar privileges through the University of Michigan Graduate School. While I worked at the children's room at the Ann Arbor Public Library, Marcia Shafer often gave a helping hand. Fred and Diana Peters have always helped with materials in German, and Tom Buckley did some urgent translation at the end. Anne Lundin and Dee Jones at the DeGrummond Collection of the University of Southern Mississippi made their resources accessible to me.

Many other colleagues in children's literature gave me general encouragement. In my own department, Alida Allison, Jerry Griswold, and Peter Neumeyer supported my efforts (while collegial literary theorists Emily Hicks and William Nericco gave me much needed direction). Barbara Rosen and Margaret Higonnet of the University of Connecticut so conscientiously edited one of my articles that they inspired me to write a book instead. The "Austin Triumvirate" of Mary Agnes Taylor, Gillian Adams, and Marilyn Olsen were helpfully hospitable in many ways. Francelia Butler's collection of toy narratives in *Sharing Literature with Children* gave me many pointers. Althea Helbig of Eastern Michigan University invited me to speak and found books. Suzanne Rahn's interest in my work on *Hitty* brought forth an article. Priscilla Ord, at Longwood College, sent me clippings galore. Anita Moss of the University of North Carolina, Charlotte, always raises my scholarly morale. Jack Zipes, of the University of Minnesota, Twin Cities, provided me with much helpful direction.

My professional writing group, consisting at various times of Joanne Cornwell, Dorothea Kehler, Sherry Little, Sue McLeod, and Susan Wyche-Smith, listened constructively and helped me shape several chapters, and Jeanie Grant Moore, of the University of California, Riverside, reread the manuscript as a whole. The enthusiasm of Ellen Graham, Senior Editor at Yale University Press, now retired, spurred me from first contact, and editors Jonathan Brent and Susan Laity followed the book through production. My psychiatrist cousin-in-law, Merton Kahne, encouraged me to explore the area and should not be held responsible for my blunders in his field. Barbara Shollar, of the City University of New York, generously spent part of her vacation in San Diego helping to edit the last draft. On occasion my writer daughter, Miriam Kuznets, turned tables and read my manuscript, while Jim Dowling, my husband, often listened to rough first drafts over dinner and kept rescuing my hapless computer from my wrath.

I cannot imagine having brought this book to fruition without the help of these people, and multitudes of others, several of whom I put to sleep by my readings from this text.

1 An Introduction to My World of Literary Toys

 The fantasy world in which literary toys come alive overlaps but does not duplicate the material, mundane universe, where, in all known cultures, toys are concrete inanimate objects made from whatever materials are available to children, parents, and other adults and designated for imaginative, imitative, motor, or group play.

Toylike objects have other general societal uses, the first of which may even precede any recognized use in play. Such artifacts originally appeared as ritual objects in adult ceremonies of fertility, funeral, and ancestor-worship rites and as sacrificial substitutes or fetishes. They have also been crafted as mercantile models meant to advertise skill in fashion design, furniture making, and early technological prowess, and they function in turn as displays of conspicuous consumption. In them can be recognized educational tools meant to train the young in such orthodox societal roles as mother- and soldierhood or to exercise specific motor skills. Finally, these artifacts have often become collectible items, stimulating private or public nostalgia or historical and anthropological research, representing in miniature certain cultural artifacts, or simply existing as works of art for aesthetic contemplation.

Animated toys as characters in literature transcend these "real-world" uses in significant ways, representing not only human hopes, needs, and desires but human anxieties and terrors as well. Both developmental and existential concerns emerge in toy stories. Even before I began my serious investigation into toy literature, I recognized that one or more of the following motifs usually appears in its narratives:

1. Toys, when they are shown as inanimate objects developing into live beings, embody human anxiety about what it means to be "real"—an independent subject or self rather than an object or other submitting to the gaze of more powerfully real and potentially rejecting live beings.

2. Toy characters embody the secrets of the night: they inhabit a secret, sexual, sensual world, one that exists in closed toy shops, under Christmas trees, and behind the doors of dollhouses—and those of our parents' bedrooms. This is an *uncanny* (in Freudian terms) world of adult mysteries and domestic intrigue.[1] It can be a marginal, liminal, potentially carnival world.

3. When manipulated by human beings—adults or children—toys embody all the temptations and responsibilities of power. As characters with whom humans identify, they also suggest the relatively powerless relationship of human beings to known or unseen forces: their dreadful vulnerability.

4. And when toys come alive as beings created by humans (usually male), they replicate "divine" creation and imply vital possibilities for human creativity while arousing concomitant anxiety about human competition with the divine. These creations also threaten human hegemony.

When I turned to toy texts previously unfamiliar to me, other aspects common to many of them demanded attention as well. For instance, the competition between adults and children for the control of toys loomed large. I realized that I had underrated the extent to which toys play out anxieties about violent mutilation, deformity, and rejection by loved ones and reveal the anger and depression that pervades the survivors of such suffering, even when those feelings are masked by self-sacrificial protestations. As I became aware of developing relationships between animated toys and anthropomorphized animals in toy narratives, the persistence of animistic, paganistic longings beyond the Judeo-Christian system also assumed great importance. With regard to form, I had to pay more attention to the nature of verbal play in toy dialogue: it frequently depends on "naive" punning or literal misreadings of figurative language, significant in calling into question conventional notions of the relation between language and "reality," signifier and signified.

In this book, I place my observations into a wider social and literary context, viewed from an eclectic, but clearly feminist, theoretical perspective. As an adult female, I find that Barbie and Ken dolls cast a large shadow over my work. Societal uses of toylike objects in human culture and the place of toys in Western developmental psychology constitute the important background for this text. Within this context, and concentrating on British and American literature or texts that have been translated into English, I focus my study on toys as characters in eighteenth-, nineteenth-, and twentieth-century literature for children and adults. I make no claims to survey toy stories in toto, cover the field chronologically, or argue one particular theory throughout. I consider Newbery Medal winners and comic strips, beloved texts from the late nineteenth- and early twentieth-century Golden Age of children's literature, and literary fairy tales. I sometimes group texts on the basis of the nature of the coming-alive experience and sometimes on the kind of toy represented.

Indeed, choices of both topics and texts owe much to my own tastes and fancies, since toys, on shelves or in books, refuse to come alive if handled in a heavy-handed fashion, without a certain playful enthusiasm—an enthusiasm that I am unable to summon up for every toy narrative and every kind of toy character. Certain ideas and texts seem destined to play off each other as they did when in the midst of the Gulf War I sat down to write my polemic chapter on toy soldiers, "Where Have All the Young Men Gone?" In contrast, although I have visited the teddy-bear museum in Stratford-upon-Avon and seem to bump into a teddy bear every place I turn (having more than one good friend who regards the bear as serious totem), I have not managed to devote a whole chapter to these creatures that occupy such a special place in literature as well as life. Winnie the Pooh, of course, is not neglected, but the host of his species that come alive in later books are, for the most part, missing here. Other, less obvious, lacunae appear at in my omission of some species of toy—rocking horses, for example—or in my glancing only in passing at beloved texts like Lewis Carroll's two Wonderland books or Johnny Gruelle's Raggedy Ann series.

Some readers may find me either more or less theoretical in my approach than they would wish, especially when dealing with certain classic texts beloved since childhood. This study owes much to my training as a New Critic and the experience in formal close reading of texts that it gave me. But philosophically I have moved a long way from Monroe Beardsley's class in aesthetics at Swarthmore College in the late fifties, where I was taught to shun critical "fallacies" in order to adopt aesthetic tenets designed to keep criticism objective and definitive. Gradually, through life experience, teaching, and a relatively recent introduction to feminism and the associated literary theories gathered under its wing, I have changed into a different reader of literary texts.

I am still interested in formal literary traditions, conventions, and practices. But I am now convinced that no definitive, objective reading will emerge and that no pure interpretation exists. Moreover, perhaps "phallacies" are unavoidable. The task of establishing the political purity of the aesthetic approach no longer interests me. I once searched for a closed unity of interpretation, a universal reading. Now I discover from self-examination that, like the authors, characters, and other readers of the texts I read, I am caught in the tangled mesh of situation, intertwined with texts that no longer seem to me the well-woven and tied-off tapestries whose warp and woof I once tried to discern.

What this means for my critical practice is that I have continued to do what I was first trained to do: close readings of individual texts. But like those postmodern theorists who attend to individual texts, I neither consider my responses privileged or universal readings nor do I attempt to keep one text pure and separate from another. I choose an intertextual approach, one that takes into account my experiences, literary and otherwise, and theories developed in diverse fields of study. I am indebted to recent assimilative or critical studies like Toril Moi's *Sexual, Textual Politics,* Susan Stewart's *On Longing: Narratives of the Miniature, the Gigantic, the Souvenir, the Collection,* Brian Sutton-Smith's *Toys as Culture,* and Leonard Barkan's *The Gods Made Flesh* for giving new insights into the ways information from various fields can be applied. When it suits me, I am ready to use Dorothy Dinnerstein and Erik Erikson, as well as Jacques Lacan, among the neo-Freudians, or Jean Piaget, D. W. Winnicott, and Sutton-Smith together as play theorists; moreover, Marxist leanings find themselves in close juxtaposition with individualistic humanist longings. My sense of character in the novel derives as much from Northrop Frye's generic categories as from Mikhail Bakhtin's ideas of the dialogic imagination. I want to play with imagery at the same time as I recognize, with Jacques Derrida, the importance of the silenced, unimaged negation behind the imaged. In fantasy theory, I am attracted to both William Robert Irwin's "game of the impossible" and Tsvetan Todorov's structuralist "fantastic."

Nevertheless, in considering both toys and toy characters, I find certain theoretical stances especially apt and useful. Take, for instance, the Freudian concept of the gaze. As I was working on Chapter 2, I came across a gorgeous coffee-table book entitled *The Doll* (1972). The text was written by Carl Fox, former director of the museum shops of the Smithsonian Institution and the Brooklyn Museum, and a doll collector himself. The stunning photographs, which dominate the work, were taken by H. Landshoff. For me, Fox's commentary is extremely provocative. He ends his introduction with the following: "We offer you a gallery of doll portraits drawn in time, place, and cultural history. *They are images of mankind that confront you with unblinking eyes, wherein you may find the mirror of beauty, memory, and childhood grace. The reflections are multiple, pleasant, and even perverse.* What we strive for is a talisman for memories, a conjuration to evoke for you some feeling of innocence, delight, and mystery. *Perhaps the greatest single attraction of the doll is its almost magical power to engulf the viewer and lift him out of himself into the doll's world—whatever it may be"* (emphasis mine, 13).

In this quotation from an adult male collector of dolls, I am first struck by the singular inappropriateness of using the signifier *mankind* with regard to the largely female or at least asexual world of dolls and male pronouns for the viewer, who is likely to be female. Given that clue to Fox's masculinist viewpoint, however, I am even more dazzled by how well this quotation fits psychoanalytic theory of the gaze, emphasized in particular by Lacan. This theory considers such looking to be an aggressively phallic, even sadistic, if not necessarily male, visual activity.

According to theories of the gaze, mastery over objects of desire, people as well as things, is achieved by looking at them without acknowledging their independent power of looking back. At most, the object or person is simply assumed to mirror the viewer's own perceptions and desires. This idea is certainly reflected in Fox's concept of the doll as a "mirror of beauty, memory, and childhood grace." More interesting still is Fox's last sentence, in which the author expresses some of the attraction to, as well as possible fear of, engulfment by the viewed object. Feminists like Luce Irigaray and Jane Gallop apply the theory of the gaze to gender relations. They hypothesize not only the male desire to be lifted "out of himself" but the fear of engulfment that lies behind this vision, a fear that requires the gazed-upon object or person to be unalterably "other."

These terms, too—*self* and *other, subject* and *object*—belong to that part of Freudian theory taken up by Lacan and feminist theorists who recognize the ways a patriarchal view of the world has fostered a concept of an individual, conscious selfhood that necessarily defines itself in separation from other selves: in opposition to the communal, the female, and those of diverse races, creeds, and classes conceived of as other and treated as objects with no self-consciousness. When the unconscious objects that are toys become self-consciously alive, they blur the lines between self and other, subject and object, and require the reader to note those blurred dividing lines, imaginatively if not analytically.

Experience of the toy outside the world of books as quintessential other and object heightens our awareness of what it means for a toy character to attempt to become a conscious self and a subject, often the protagonist, within the text. This same experience of physical toys also alerts us to the difference between biologically determined sex and socially constructed gender—a difference vital to feminist theories of psychological development.[2] How does one determine the gender of a toy? Rarely by its genitalia, mostly by its clothing, hairstyle, and the language used to signify it.[3] This absence of biological sexual markers in most toys calls attention to the arbitrary assertion of constructed gender differences in the depiction of toys as characters, especially in those texts that reflect gender roles from the world outside the text.[4]

Dominant ideas not only of gender but of race and class penetrate the texts in which toy characters appear. The fact that toy narratives belong to the fantastic mode does not blind me to the ways they are mimetic. For instance, typical dollhouse stories for children begin by showing Mama Doll in the nursery or kitchen (or in the parlor if there is a Maid Doll or Black "Mammy" Doll in the kitchen), Papa Doll in the library, and Brother and Sister Doll playing with their gender-linked playthings wherever they are allowed to play, while Intruder Toys of various sorts try to break into this cozy-bourgeois-nuclear-family world (see Chapter 6). Such texts can subvert or enhance the values of the mimicked world through the working out of conflicts and struggles.

Of course, toys as objects are created in imitation of many other living (and nonliving) things besides human beings and frequently come alive as, say, anthropomorphized animals, so that boundaries between species are both blurred and called to the attention. In considering the kind of toy narrative where, among other "live" things, dolls, toy animals, and sometimes humans interact, I have found apt the concept of "liminal" or threshold behavior postulated by anthropologists like Victor Turner, which describes the occasions provided in many societies for otherwise forbidden crossing of social boundaries to take place. Concepts of borderland and marginal space where insiders and outsiders meet are valuable for engaging these texts.

Finally, character, both in fantastic and realistic fiction, depends upon reader and text playing a game of draw-the-lines-between-the-dots in order to image a being from the words printed on the page. To take an early and striking instance: the "living being" who emerges from a text like the prologue to Chaucer's Wife of Bath's Tale—the gap-toothed, half-deaf Wife, who seemingly creates herself from snips and snatches of antifeminist dogma beginning with the Church Father Jerome in his tirade against the unorthodox Jovinian—is a mutual creation of reader and text. From such experience of reader response it is no great leap to the willing suspension of disbelief that accepts as a being or subject Hitty, the wooden doll who writes her life story with a pen almost as big as she. Toy characters are no more or less real than human characters in literature (and I think they may be even as "true," in the sense that Michael Riffaterre defines "fictional truth"). Certainly, both types of character depend upon the reader to respond to the words that inscribe them.

When I began this study, I was most aware of how toy characters in literature, like many other characters in fantasy, often function as *subversive* forces acting out crises of individual development generally repressed by modern society. This function, shared by toys in life, is familiar to child psychology as well as to psychoanalysis and to philosophers and intellectual historians who discuss the creative role of play in the lives of human beings in general. Those who have studied individual literary works about toys recognize the ways toy characters both disguise and express suppressed desires, helping to evade individual and societal censors. Critics have also examined how play and art belong to the same realm, a realm in which human beings have the power to create a whole world and the creatures that inhabit it.

Moving beyond the social sphere to the cosmic, we find another motif common to toy narratives: the anxiety that this creativity—in competition with the gods—entails. This anxiety reflects concerns about the nature of human existence and what it means to be or, alternatively, not to be real. These works can bring out the ways mortals feel themselves to be playthings of the gods or, worse, abandoned by a careless owner. They can also depict our fear that technologically sophisticated human creations may take on a life that will outlast human life.

When adult readers come to existential depictions of toys in literature, the anxieties those toys act out perhaps bring the readers full circle to their own childhood needs: when a faithful, comforting, and all-suffering playmate created from a rag, a bone, and a hank of hair may have helped them through life's early unavoidable traumas. From adult memories of such consolation comes a human nostalgia for what A. A. Milne in *The House at Pooh Corner* calls "that enchanted place on the top of the Forest" (178), where living toys wait patiently for human return. Such adult remembrances of consolation also permeate Kenneth Grahame's story "A Departure." In it two young children, watched over by a sympathetic older brother and the benevolent Man-in-the-Moon, sneak out into a moonlit garden to bury a doll and a toy bull, thus commemorating the involuntary but unavoidable transfer of all their other toys to a children's hospital. This nocturnal excursion is clearly a subversive act on the part of the children, in which they both protest their lack of power over the destination of their toys and take a step on their own initiative toward adult independence. The adult participants, who include Grahame's narrator/persona, seem dominated, however, by a nostalgic, romantic longing for a past and a childhood that never existed, as implied by the title of Grahame's collection, *Dream Days* (1898). The two children solemnly performing for themselves a necessary rite of passage were less likely to dig up those toys again and again than was the adult narrator.

I recognize that my own interest in digging up toy narratives was begun under the influence of a similar adult nostalgia. As readers of my study will discover, this nostalgia diminished upon my reading and rereading these texts, which with a few notable exceptions seem to me to have missed many opportunities that objects becoming subjects offer for going beyond simple mimesis of prevailing cultural constructs. Thus, I frequently ask my readers to take a good hard revisionist look at longings of and for the past excited by many toy texts, and to consider whom such longings really benefit.[5]

Moreover, in the process of digging deeper into the texts as well as of introspection, I have found myself trying to discern the nature of the subversion I frequently discover in these texts. Throughout this book I shall note an individualistic, nonconformist, "shock the bourgeois," antiauthoritarian rebellion rooted in such nostalgic romanticism (subversion of the kind noted by Rosemary Jackson in her study of fantasy); in toy narratives, this kind of subversion of familial and institutional restraint may attractively aid the young in their individual struggles to become "real."

Goals that might, however, have thrilled the child-me as a projection of my egocentric needs and desires are not necessarily what a woman with threescore years of experience in this world still finds fulfilling. I see myself now searching these texts for signs of another, more radical, subversion— subversion of the elitism, racism, sexism, and androcentrism in a pervasively patriarchal culture. This is the future-, other-oriented subversion that I now feel necessary for human survival on a shrinking, polluted planet. Literature that raises the kind of questions raised by toy narratives can play a role in fostering this more radical subversion, just as it has in fostering individualistic subversion.[6]

For the most part, signs of such future-, other-oriented subversion are lacking in these texts. I have found toy stories to be generally conservative in dealing with the givens of a patriarchal culture and subversive largely in the individualistic sense. Only occasionally, in breaking down barriers among various "creatures," will a toy fantasy go beyond communal status quo and in doing so seem to deny the centrality of human concerns—concerns that dominated those ancient burial rites in which humans tried to take into the underworld toylike representations of the creatures and appurtenances that added meaning and a sense of individual power to their brief lives.[7]

I do not wish to be buried with my toys. Literature for children and adults cannot, it seems to me now, turn only to the past for solutions and to childhood or funereal consolations in order to help survive the traumas of the future. For this reason, I have in the last chapter of this study gone beyond the toy narrative to the speculative fiction of robot and cyborg. Some of the latter narratives, which are usually categorized as that brand of fantasy known as science fiction, seem to me occasionally to take giant steps forward in confronting present existentialist concerns suggested by toy fantasies but addressed by those fantasies largely in traditional, limited—if often seductively charming—ways.

In this very personalized tour of the literary world of animated toys, therefore, I guide readers to the entrance of Toyland and usher them through its gates, but then keep asking the members of my tour group to consider whether, having found it an attractive and exciting place to visit, they would really want to live there forever.

2 Toys: Their First Ten Thousand Years

The English word *toy*—which first crops up in Robert Brunne's *Handling Sinne* (1303) and then disappears from surviving recorded vocabulary for two centuries—boasts no proper etymology according to the *Oxford English Dictionary*. *Toy* has been associated throughout its history in the English language with triviality, vanity, delusion, and lustful practices, and only since the late sixteenth century has the word also been used to designate children's playthings. Children have, nevertheless, been playing with toys for a long time, all over the globe. And toys and toylike objects historically have had loftier, weightier associations than the English word suggests. As I noted in Chapter 1, they are connected not only with the amusement and education of the young but with religious ritual, social mores and values, gender definition, commerce, technological experimentation, and artistic expression.

Strangely enough, when I began studying the history of toys, I realized that the roles toys play in literature truly reflect these associations and that I had subconsciously understood them from my own childhood imaginings about the secret lives of toys. Upon rereading a book that informed my own childhood, Rachel Field's Newbery Award-winning *Hitty: Her First Hundred Years* (1929), I discovered an important source of those early musings. In general, the history of the doll Hitty seems so much one of ontogeny recapitulating phylogeny that I have chosen her book to demonstrate the intriguingly ambiguous position of toys in the human psyche and society. In addition, *Hitty* illustrates something else fundamental to the history of toys: that adults, rather than finding toys trivial, are involved in a sometimes buried, sometimes obvious, struggle with children to keep control over them.

Toys in Human Society

In *A History of Toys,* Antonia Fraser notes the universality of certain types of playthings of early childhood. Like others who deal with the subject, she is careful to distinguish primitive toys from objects of ornament or ritual. Yet she still finds yo-yos (sometimes used as weapons), balls (made from bladders and string), tops (perhaps having originated in spindles but evolved into both whipped and string variety), kites, and pull-along animals and dolls available to children for play in ancient Egypt and the Orient. Various materials were used for these toys, among them ivory, gold, and bronze, as well as clay, wood, and fabric (the last both easily accessible and ephemeral).

Whether the primitive replicas of living things, human and animal, that survive were dolls used for play is indeed hard to determine. Many of these figures may not have been playthings but idols, fetishes for protection or fertility (the predominance of female images supports the latter), or substitutes for human and animal sacrifices placed on altars and in graves (Boehn 69). Historians of toys try, therefore, to avoid "confusing ritual figures with toys proper," for, as Fraser notes, "no dolls have been discovered in children's graves of the prehistoric period and [it is] unlikely that at a time when men believed in the magical properties of the artificial human figure, mere children should have been permitted to play with objects so wrapped in mystery" (31). Still, like Max von Boehn in *Dolls and Puppets,* she can also conceive of the lines becoming blurred.[1] Fraser points out that toys given to Japanese children throughout the ages seem to have had "a double function—almost every one of them has some magic attribute as well as its function as a plaything," an attribute meant to ward off specific illnesses and the like (39). Dolls never have completely lost their ritualistic nature in the Japanese culture, as indicated by the doll ceremonies celebrated on 3 March for girls and 5 May for boys. The root word for doll in two other Asian cultures, Chinese and Korean, is the same as that for idol and fetish (Fraser 39).

Some historians of toys would like to derive the English word from *idol* as well (Freeman 19). According to the *OED,* however, *doll,* not unlike *toy,* has origins and uses that trivialize their object and seem deliberately to ignore such ritualistic connections: apparently the word, first recorded in 1700, is simply derived from the diminutive of Dorothy (at one time *Doroty* also signified a puppet), and has associations with littleness, triviality, and vanity. In Latin and French, the words for doll are the same as those for puppet; in

German, the word essentially identifies a block of wood. *Pandora,* used to designate a particular type of fashion doll that came from France in the seventeenth century, is considerably more mythically suggestive than *doll.*

Greek and Roman vases and reliefs show children playing with many different types of toys, among them hoops (suggesting classical emphasis on physical fitness and body development). Even Socrates was so undignified as to mount his children's hobbyhorse, according to Alcibiades (Fraser 44). And Plutarch writes mournfully about his dead daughter's dolls (Fraser 50). An interesting blurring of doll and ritual object occurs during this era. A Greek or Roman girl marked her transition from virgin to married woman by dedicating her dolls to the goddesses (Boehn 107). Dolls also begin to show up in graves of children—even those of young Christians buried in the catacombs—thus suggesting their status as favored toys. Perhaps the original sacrificial nature of such objects has also been continued in the act of burying these figures with their young owners.

The part children played in providing themselves with playthings can be imagined but not explicitly documented by historians of toys. Certainly those toys that children fashion for themselves out of natural objects and bits and pieces of human-made discards are likely to be far more ephemeral than those fashioned by artisans. These objects, often treasured talismans, again blur the distinction between toy and ritual object—from the viewpoint of a child psychologist, if not that of a historian of toys or religion.[2]

Historically, the presence and survival of a variety of toys seems connected with affluent and/or technologically sophisticated societies: Fraser indicates that the number and variety of toys surviving from the European Middle Ages declined compared with that of toys left from the Greek and Roman era, although clay figures and metal soldiers on horseback date from that time, and hobbyhorses and paper windmills are commonly illustrated in medieval wood-block prints. Moreover, the medieval guilds for certain crafts encouraged the development of famous toy workshops in Nuremberg and elsewhere. Traveling fairs kept toys in circulation. Again, human and animal figures were fashioned for religious observance as well as childish pleasure: medieval guilds commonly produced crèches for nativity scenes, providing images of living creatures that, like those of earlier ages, were endowed with special spiritual meaning and to some extent forbidden to children as playthings.

The Renaissance seems, however, to mark the point at which blurring between playthings and ritual objects became unacceptable among Western adults. Toylike objects became secularized and to some extent trivialized. The increasing complexity of civilization—in which "childhood," at least among the upper classes, became prolonged—along with technological advances gave toys provided by adults for their children other social purposes. Among those classes of society that could allow their children leisure time, toys became an instrument of "socialization": dolls substituted for or supplemented younger siblings in preparing young girls for traditional nurturing roles; toy soldiers and toy weapons taught boys the arts of war, replacing to some extent earlier initiatory warring and hunting expeditions with real spears, slingshots, or bows and arrows. Games of skill had from very early times employed toys of various kinds in a competitive manner, developing group as well as individual pride in accomplishment. (Actually, games too had often been associated with ritual in early times, but their secular social nature eventually became predominant.)

In the late eighteenth and early nineteenth centuries, the social and educational purposes of toys were clearly articulated in educational movements based on the theories of John Locke. Christina Hardyment, in *Dream Babies from Locke to Spock,* points out that the didactic potential of toys is explicitly considered in books like Richard and Maria Edgeworth's *Practical Education* (1798), in which a "rational toyshop" is proposed (65). With both strong supporters and detractors, this didactic view of toys was argued throughout the nineteenth century. Among the detractors, notes Hardyment, was Isaac Taylor, who begs in *Home Education* (1838), "Let play be play and nothing else," and Charlotte Yonge, who in *Womankind* (1876) criticizes the Edgeworths for "their want of poetry and failure to perceive the way in which toys deal with the imaginative, the tender, and aesthetic sides of children's minds, as well as the intelligent and mechanical ones" (75, 143). The debate continues in the twentieth century: first Friedrich Froebel's, then Maria Montessori's educational toys fueled the cause of didacticism at the turn of century, and later progressive educators like the followers of John Dewey and the founders of the Bank Street School in New York took mixed positions with regard to educational toys—sometimes emphasizing their didactic practicality and sometimes pointing out their potential for stimulating the imagination—but always showing concern about their socializing potential.

Throughout world history, mechanization has been used to create toys and automata as well as more "adult" objects. Pre-Christian treatises like Hero of Alexandria's *Epivitalia* focused on self-moving statues and other experiments with mechanical objects.[3] And mechanized figures have appeared in India since ancient times. Wind, water, mercury, sand, and, later, clockworks all powered early automata.

The attitude of the European medieval church toward mechanical objects was ambivalent, however, when not simply censorious. Although elaborate clocks with mechanized figures striking the hours had begun to appear in churches, Thomas Aquinas (1215?–74) used his authority to speak against mechanical toys. He associated them with the devil because of their "magical" abilities. By the late fifteenth century, however, mechanical figures were considered appropriate gifts for Christian kings: Leonardo da Vinci (1452–1519), scientist as well as artist, constructed a lion automaton for Francis I. And books like *Epivitalia* found a new audience among Italian Renaissance scientists. Still, suspicion lingered on. In what may be an apocryphal story, René Descartes (1596–1650), to prove some of his theories on mechanics, is reputed to have built a life-size figure of a young woman, "Ma Fille Franchina," which accompanied him on a sea voyage only to be thrown overboard by the frightened ship's captain (115).

The attitudes of the medieval church and of Descartes's distrustful captain toward automated figures underline a more widespread suspicion of animism: for many centuries objects shaped like people or animals were associated with paganism or the "devilish" practice of magic. Possession of dolls was considered evidence of guilt, for instance, during the seventeenth-century witch hunts in New England. These issues faded into the background in the eighteenth century as Western societies became increasingly secularized, technologically sophisticated, and concerned with both individual flowering and social engineering.

Indeed, as Fraser points out, the eighteenth and nineteenth centuries, during what has become known as the Industrial Revolution, were the "heyday of fine automata" (113), as a result of heightened interest in scientific experimentation and technological innovation. The nineteenth century also took from Renaissance science a fascination with optics, which led to the construction of optical toys using light, motion, and mirrors in ingenious ways. And other nineteenth-century technological developments, like the use of steam for locomotion, were applied to model trains and boats that functioned as toys.

To the extent that such toys do not replicate human or animal images but appear simply to be machines they hardly raise questions of animism; suspicion of competition with the divine creator, however, apparently did not simply disappear when more "lifelike" human or animal toys, endowed with movement simulating life, were concerned. Promethean issues, associated with human creativity in both science and art in early Judeo-Christian theology (rife in sixteenth and seventeenth-century golem legends, for instance), become evident once again in nineteenth-century tales of evil toy makers or "mad scientists" like Victor Frankenstein, who built himself a monstrous, bigger-than-life-size toy and then felt forced to hunt it down to kill it. Popular late twentieth-century narratives centering on robotry and biological engineering—the android or cyborg problem, so to speak—revive this anxiety about animism (see Chapter 10).

Like science, economics has always played a role in the acceptance of and attitudes toward toys. Colonizing and imperialistic explorers of the New World included cheap toys among the gimcracks that they used to establish trade relations with the natives. The official historian of the English expedition that arrived in 1585 on Roanoke Island, North Carolina, notes: "Offered them our wares, as glasses, knives, babies (or dolls) and other trifles [in] which we thought they delighted" (quoted in Fraser 77). Fraser includes a striking sketch from this expedition in which a near-naked Amerind child holds a fully clothed Elizabethan doll. By the seventeenth century the commercial value of toys had become clear.

Large dolls (about two and a half feet tall) were regularly sent to England, Germany, Spain, and Italy to advertise French fashions—an extension of an aristocratic practice that had begun as early as the late fourteenth century of sending elaborately dressed dolls as gifts to royalty. Even the lengthy War of the Spanish Succession (1701–14) did not stop the fashion-doll trade to England. And the "Pandoras" led a charmed life in this period: according to Abbé Prévost (1697–1763), "both courts granted a special pass to the mannequin" (quoted in Fraser 103). The pacific—and mercantile—ends of trade were also furthered by miniature samples of goods, furniture, and rooms. Certainly the development of these objects again blurs the line between toys created as playthings for children and replicas created for adult purposes. These "toys" were too valuable to play with, just as earlier objects had been too sacred. Nevertheless, according to an early anonymous rhyme celebrating both trade and play, children did get their hands on them: "The children of England take pleasure in breaking / What the children of Holland take pleasure in making."

Expensive toys serve class hierarchies as well. In an economically stratified society the toy becomes a sign of wealth—hence, of social status. The rich child will have more, and fancier, toys than the poor one; the doll of the young princess will be clad and accoutered as richly as her mistress; the young prince will be provided with a virtual army of toy soldiers to practice on before he commands the real thing.

Indeed, toy soldiers have a fascinating history, the most opulent period of which was the seventeenth century. Louis XIV inherited a model army from Louis XIII, who as dauphin had ordered soldiers cast to accompany a German-made set. As the Sun King augmented his war toys with silver figures, they also were made more mechanically ingenious. Ironically, however, these silver toys had to be melted down to pay for real military campaigns. Families justified giving their sons elaborate sets of toy soldiers by claiming the toys were training tools for future commanders of troops. Of course, they were also indicators of wealth and status—a fact that was less frequently admitted. Today they are collectors' items (see the discussion of toy-soldier narratives in Chapter 5).

The toy soldier and the doll symbolize most clearly the division society makes between girls and boys at play—as well as the gender separation assigned to nurturing and aggressive instincts. Toys thus become ideal tools for societal gender modeling. Here, too, despite society's drive to emphasize such distinctions, ambiguity and blurring of lines has probably always existed. It is unlikely that dolls given to girls to play with—and not reserved by their parents as "too good" for children—were regarded by children themselves simply as objects of nurture. Interestingly, although dolls seem to have been called "babies" at least since the age of exploration (as revealed by lines quoted above), the baby doll—dressed in infant clothes and residing in a cradle—dates only from the early nineteenth century. And even after baby dolls made their appearance, young girls played with dolls that while not anatomically correct were nonetheless dressed as adults and resembled adults, just as children themselves, up to nearly that period, were dressed as adults. The relationship between a child and an adult doll is more complex than a simple microcosm of the mother-child paradigm. In *Cavalcade of Toys,* Ruth and Larry Freeman observe that a doll is often used as "companion and confidante" of its owner (18; see also my Chapter 6). The illustrations appended here from two early nineteenth-century toy narratives show the ways dolls appeared to be as adult, or more adult, than their "mistresses."

Seemingly, early toy makers did not go out of their way to make their human or animal figures as tactually attractive to children as these objects were visually attractive. As noted earlier, flexible and huggable rag figures certainly existed from early times, but simply did not survive. But commercial development of completely soft figures in either animal or human shape came surprisingly late—in the early nineteenth century. Nurturing instincts can be more comfortably fostered by cuddly stuffed figures than they can by human or animal creatures made of metal, clay, ceramic, or even wood. But here again gender roles become blurred, for boys' (unacknowledged) nurturing feelings are more clearly permissible toward animals—and more likely to be evoked by stuffed animals—than toward dolls made in the image of adults or even babies from china, wax, or wood.

The ubiquitous teddy bear is an early twentieth-century toy sometimes wrongly attributed to a bedridden German needlewoman, who was approached by an American buyer carrying Clifford Berryman's cartoon of Teddy Roosevelt bear hunting. In fact, the cartoon first inspired an American manufacturer (Voss 62), who transformed an awesomely dangerous creature into a cute, tame one.[4] The Freemans dub the now well-tamed teddy bear "a

Frontispiece and title page from *The Adventures of a Doll*; frontispiece and title page from *Memoirs of a London Doll*.

boys' doll" (24). The twentieth-century boy may be thus encouraged to develop his nurturing instincts or express his emotions through such cuddly bears. His sister is given an equally huggable baby doll, which may require some of the less attractive aspects of child care, like changing wet diapers, traditionally relegated to women. But boys are still more likely to receive

those socializing toys that prepare them for so-called manly pursuits—
nowadays these toys include cars, trucks, and tools, along with the more
traditional soldiers and weapons, when the family permits "war toys."

My own consciousness of the ways children are socialized through toys—
negatively as well as positively—helps me to understand mid-to-late
twentieth-century attitudes toward toys among the Western middle classes,
attitudes that carry with them some of the same fervor that sparked medieval
condemnations of devilish mechanical toys. These attitudes have been
shaped by two centuries of theorizing about children and toys that began
with the Lockean educational movements. These movements were an important part of the general, ongoing concern with childhood that social historians like Philippe Ariès identify as first engaging the eighteenth century. I
was brought up among a generation of American middle-class intellectuals
that saw toys as capable of inculcating ethical values and shaping racial and
sexual attitudes—for good or bad.

I also believe that toys help shape aesthetic vision. Toys have been subject
to aesthetic judgment ever since artisans of costly and elegant toys become
recognized artists. And the aesthetics of toys, especially as a moral issue,
concerns adults more than children, at least consciously. True to my aesthetic
modernism, I prefer plain, sturdy, tasteful "crafted" wooden toys to plastic,
factory-molded ones, whether children like them or not. My taste is shared by
Roland Barthes, who in an essay in *Mythologies* extols the wooden toy over
the plastic because the former gives more range to the individual imagination
and generally does not replicate commercial products. Like many of my
contemporaries, I deplore the Madison Avenue hype of "junk" toys on Saturday morning television, which encourages consumerism. But toys are big
business in our society (according to the *Ann Arbor News* of 9 April 1991,
some fourteen billion dollars were spent on toys in the United States in
1990): commercialism and my didacticism are frequently not in accord. Toys
as objects are, as already suggested, fraught with controversy that reflects
adult values and anxieties in diverse ways, as much as it does the young toy
owners' needs, loves, and hostilities.

Aesthetics do not always involve moral concerns, however. Here, they
bring me back to one of my initial propositions: that adults and children have
always been engaged in a struggle over the proprietorship of toys and their
definition and use as playthings. The most seductive toys are not always the
simplest or the sturdiest. Many an adult has withdrawn toys from children
claiming that the latter do not know how to use them properly or treat them
gently. Making toys "collectible"—that is, valuable property—is one obvious
aspect of that struggle. The scarcity, the artistry, or the antiquity of the item
(or all three at once) dictate that mere children will not be allowed to touch,

only to look. Children, of course, have rarely lacked the means to carry on both open and stealthy battle over toys, even though in their economic powerlessness they have usually lost the war.

Toys have been recognized as valuable property since the beginning of the toy trade. Antonia Fraser, perhaps euphemistically, calls some of the more intricate and fragile early toys (including elaborately miniaturized furnished rooms and houses) "toys of contemplation." She points out that until the nineteenth century dollhouses boasted locks rather than easily manipulated hooks on their doors and were usually the wrong size for dolls (171). As we approach the twenty-first century, the number and fervor of the collectors of toys, as well as of other items, seem to be growing. Lust for antiquarian objects can be understood—if not necessarily admired—as a need to hold onto the past in a century of rapid change. Toy collection in particular appears to signify adult nostalgia for the simplicity and delights of childhood. Like all nostalgia, this emotion is based partly on a past, a childhood, that never was. But antique toys, unreachable as they are in museums and behind glass, can still evoke nostalgic fantasy.

Beyond being collected, toys have played a part in the world of graphic arts. Since the Renaissance, portraits of children have frequently included toys, which provide an atmospheric and perhaps symbolic background for the sitters (Hitty serves as an artist's model for this purpose). Contemporary art, however, has begun to feature toys: they enter a foreground likely to mock nostalgic fantasy by playing upon the theme that "Toys ' Я ' Us." In the spring of 1990 the *New Yorker* reviewed a show by Los Angeles artist Mike Kelley, who uses toys among other "found" objects. The clearly intrigued reviewer finds the atmosphere in the main exhibit to be that "of an abandoned found-lings' ward in which shabby playthings, now animated, have taken over." Here, the reviewer considers that these toys "fully realize their destinies as fetishes and objects of psychosexual parody. . . . The toys themselves, in their original states, pandered to infant and senescent lusts. Kelley, however, is a hotly pursued grownup artist, and this show is an inspired challenge to the collecting drives of adults" ("Art" 13). And, in a postmodern age, Barbie dolls have inspired a variety of graphic artists catering to adult tastes. In a *New York Times* article entitled "A Onetime Bimbo Becomes a Muse," Alice Kahn describes how Andy Warhol and many others, including the photographers in a 1991 New York Museum of Modern Art exhibit entitled "Pleasures and Terrors of Domesticity," have helped Barbie to break "out of Toyland and into Artville" (2:1).

In animated film too, toys have become actors. The film critic Terrence Rafferty, in a 1988 review, defines the world of toys as uncanny not just in the eyes of the artist or animator, but universally:

In "Alice" the Czech animator Jan Svankmajer plays with objects the way Lewis Carroll played with words, and creates out of Carroll's Wonderland a world of more ambiguous, more unsettling nonsense. Svankmajer, who animates household items and worn-looking dolls, makes nonsense physical, palpable, and thus gives Alice's adventures in illogic an undertone of menace. Things that won't behave normally are scarier than words that won't, and when these things are the material of our ordinary lives, the stuff we manipulate happily everyday, the favorite toys we surround ourselves with for comfort, the effect is chilling, claustrophobic. (77)

A literary critic might point out that playing with physical objects was already part of Carroll's existential vision. Nevertheless, the animator's use of toys heightens the sense of unreality in a piece already replete with uncannily fantastic twists and turns.

As in this animated film, toys can be associated with children's literature not just as characters but in concrete and physical ways. Starting with John Newbery's mid-eighteenth-century shop—from which came the very books now associated with the beginnings of children's literature as such—toys and other objects have frequently been used as marketing ploys for books. Newbery, with his sharp eye for the market, used them as come-on devices. He paired "fans, pincushions, spinning tops, whips and dolls" with his books, advertising, for instance, "book alone—sixpence—book and pincushion together[—]eightpence" (quoted in Quayle 212).

Also in the mid-eighteenth century came an even more physical conjunction of toys and books: the toy book. In *Early Children's Books,* Eric Quayle describes the variety and ingenuity of books that are themselves objects of play, starting with "turn up" books. Because their original subject matter concerned harlequin pantomimes, these turn up books came to be known as "harlequinades."[5] This particular type of inexpensive toy book has mostly passed from common manufacture; books for cutting and building, however, often associated with theatrical productions and including both stage and actors, as well as books that ingeniously incorporate flaps for moving characters around, or open out stereoscopically, continue to be part of the children's book trade.

Text in books that are also playthings tends to be simple, when it exists at all. Theatrical books are more literary—like one sent me from Pollock's Toy Museum in London: it includes various versions of traditional mumming plays about Saint George and the Dragon (one by the nineteenth-century writer for children Mrs. Ewing), as well as a buildable stage and characters to act on it. One can see how a certain coming alive from the book was embodied in such productions in a very literal way—a coming alive that continues to fascinate even in the day of television, for toy books provide tactually active pleasures, as well as visual ones.[6] Moreover, they act as stimuli to imaginative play. Toy books, when directly connected with the idea of the theatrical stage and characters, can function as puppets do, for both naturally suggest drama, helping develop a concept of sustained narrative and dialogue in role-playing.

Toys and books also come together in illustrations, which, beginning with crude woodcuts, have always been associated with texts for children. Actual toys lend themselves as models for illustration and often seem to inspire illustrators to write books about them. The illustrations in several early twentieth-century series books, like Florence and Bertha Upton's Dutch dolls and the golliwog stories, are based on actual childhood toys (see Chapter 6). Beginning in 1914 illustrator Johnny Gruelle (1880–1938) brought to life in the Raggedy Ann and Andy series the toys belonging to his daughter Marcella, who died at the age of fourteen. Gruelle's colorful illustrations of a variety of dolls as well as of other creations—like the camel with the wrinkled knees and the paper dragon—have entered into the American consciousness, even when his less original narratives are forgotten.[7] Even *Hitty: Her First Hundred Years* was inspired by an antique doll that animated both Dorothy Lathrop's illustrations and Rachel Field's text.

Authors have less frequently, but with interesting effect, used photographs to illustrate toy narratives. Dare Wright's *Lonely Doll* series (1950s), concerning a doll and two teddy bears, shows toys in provocative poses, sometimes with live animals like kittens. And Brooke Goffstein ingeniously photographs dolls of all types in miniature settings to illustrate such offbeat texts as her *Our Prairie Home: A Picture Album* (1988). Illustrations can offer images contrary to an imaginative reader's notions of character and setting. But they clearly help establish a substantiality for fictional characters in general and for toy characters in particular. Illustrations thus serve to stimulate the reader's receptivity to the "coming-alive" fantasy, taking it beyond the text and linking it visually to the experience of toys as playthings.

Toys and Literature

I am not attempting here an authoritative or complete history of toys: rather, I wish to emphasize the connection between how toys appear as characters in narrative and how they have appeared as objects throughout their long history. Literature, after all, is embedded in culture and engaged in a continual, multivalent interaction with it. Turning now to toy narratives, we can see that they embody many of the same ambiguities of role and audience as do toys themselves.

In an oral culture, "literature" is generally shared by adults and children, and it is often characterized by tales involving animism, beginning with genesis stories. These tales offer differing accounts of the origin of the cosmos, the gods, and finally human beings, but some of their motifs seem to be echoed in descriptions in later literature of the genesis of toys. One pattern that appears in many genesis stories, a divine creator shaping tribal ancestors from preexisting materials and breathing life into these inanimate beings, seems particularly pertinent here. Take, for instance, oceanic myths of creation:

The first men were made from grass according to the Ata of Mindanao, with two rushes according to the Igorot of Luzon, with the dirt on skin elsewhere in the Philippines, with excrement in Borneo. . . . They were carved from stones (Toredjas of Celebes) or from the trunk of a tree (Admiralty and Banks Islands). According to different tribes of Borneo the creating gods made several successive attempts with different materials. But by far the most frequent explanation is that men were modelled from clay. . . .

   After forming human beings, the god gives them life in various ways. Sometimes it is by incantation. . . . Sometimes the god breathes in the vital principle, considered to be either his own breath . . . or a fluid or liquid the god goes to heaven to find. (Luquet 468)

In these accounts, the creator clearly performs work similar to that of human image makers, who discovered how to use base materials to model the creatures around them. These figures are the likely ancestors of toys. From a secular standpoint, I might postulate that toylike objects inspired the creators of the mythic narratives to imagine divine creation as analogous to toy making and the gods as the first toy makers. But although games of diverse kinds also appear in various mythologies—usually played for high stakes between humans and gods—objects identifiable as toys, especially in human or animal forms, are not common.

   Fraser does cite one Inuit legend that alludes to doll making in the lower Yukon: "A doll-being who cut the gut skin which had formerly covered the holes in the sky, and thus enabled the winds to blow across the earth through the openings," did other good deeds as well, which made the Inuit create miniature dolls for their children in her honor (34). In her collection *The Silent Playmate* Naomi Lewis includes what appears to be a Japanese fairy tale about a doll that comes alive to help a childless old couple; she introduces it as an unusual version of the conventional motif of "a wanted child arriving in some strange way" (120). A Russian fairy tale, "The Beautiful Wassilissa" (also included in Lewis), is one of the few traditional tales to mention toys: it is a version of the Cinderella story in which a child receives not only a blessing from her dying mother but a doll that acts in some ways as a protective fetish.

Two stories from Greek mythology, the Pygmalion-Galatea and the Pandora-Prometheus tales, concern the metamorphosis of a woman fashioned from basic materials. Both show a misogyny that will continue to appear in "living doll" narratives through Hoffmann's "The Sandman" (which inspired the ballet "Coppélia") to *The Stepford Wives*.[8] Metamorphosis also pervades the golem legends of Eastern European Jewry of the sixteenth and seventeenth century. Metamorphoses of such figures are discussed in Chapter 10, and metamorphosis also plays a part in the toy narratives investigated in Chapter 4. A few narrative traces of the ancestry of characters and themes of toy narratives are thus discernible in creation stories and other myths, legends, and fairy tales.

One type of toy narrative seems to have its formal roots in a more obscure early genre that also frequently involved animism: the riddle. I refer not to the one-liners of modern times that often depend on wordplay ("What's black and white and red [read] all over?") but to the intricate ancient riddles that appear in such important manuscripts as the Old English codex known as the Exeter Book. Such riddles were probably first recorded in the eighth century. For my purposes, their importance lies in their point of view, and in this regard they fall into two main categories: riddles told by a viewer who describes the various attributes of the object of the riddle using the words "I saw"; and those narrated in the first person, in which the object of the riddle speaks. This second category is of great interest here in its expression of the subjectivity of a natural phenomenon (a storm), an act of god (creation), an animal (jay, bull) or, most significant, an inanimate object.

One of these Old English riddles, for instance, is the story of a sword (an item which in heroic and romantic literature often has a personal name) in which the weapon describes how it shares the warrior's glory, but not his domestic pleasures and loves. Sometimes bawdy with double entendre, the Old English riddle is more frequently philosophical in its observation of humans; the first-person voice of the ancient riddle tends as well to be cautionary about human behavior. Perhaps the most exalted relative of this riddle form is the Old English *Dream of the Rood,* in which the cross on which Christ was crucified speaks in a dream vision. The voices of the animated objects in early children's literature, like Mary Ann Kilner's pincushion and peg top in *The Adventures of a Pincushion* (c. 1780) and *Memoirs of a Peg-Top* (1783), are, if humbly, related to the voices in ancient riddles.

But Kilner's didactic stories and others like them were also products of their own time and the fashionable, sometimes risqué, biographies of animate and inanimate creatures that, as Mary V. Jackson observes, "came into vogue very early in the history of the novel and were admirable vehicles for the leisurely picaresque plot and trenchant social satire so loved in the age"

(138). These were not intended for children alone.[9] Although Kilner's stories were much more circumspect and certainly attempted to inculcate ladylike virtues in their presumably female readers, her Pincushion is permitted by circumstances—its young owner's carelessness—to begin a series of travels on which no lady would go. And in the realm of the toy story proper are her *Peg-Top* and *Adventures of a Whipping Top* (1784), by her sister-in-law Dorothy Kilner, which are praised by Jackson as "superb miniature sagas" (141).[10]

The formal relation between the Kilners' works and Rachel Field's *Hitty* has not gone unnoticed (see *The Oxford Companion to Children's Literature* 253). Two other early works tally even more closely in the nature of their protagonists, the length of their narratives, and certain common experiences with Field's story: Mary Mister's *Adventures of Doll* (1816) and Richard Henry Horne's *Memoirs of a London Doll Written by Herself* (pseudonymously "edited" by "Mrs. Fairstar"; 1846). Mister's text is fond of didactic contrasts between good and bad children and also serves as a travelogue for Wales; Horne's work moves among social classes in nineteenth-century London. In spite of these obvious differences, the voices that emerge from these books sound like Hitty's—"very prim yet spicy," as Rachel Field herself describes it (quoted in *Something about the Author* 112).[11]

In my analysis of *Hitty,* I will make more than has previously been made of the nature of the autobiographical discourse in all these accounts of the secret lives of inanimate objects, including the riddle. Since, unlike toy characters in most other forms of fantastic narrative, these talking objects are rarely endowed with much automobility, the contrast between their active minds and feelings and their passive matter generates a special subjectivity not unlike that of the oppressed human being (who is usually condemned to silence). But in these stories the act of telling and the achievement of picaresque adventures—albeit through the agency and at the whim of others—in some ways subvert the oppression of being treated like an object rather than a subject. They invite the reader to identify with the "other." When the speaker is female, like Hitty, Pincushion, and the dolls in Mister's and Horne's texts, an added resonance is given to this autobiographical discourse even when, as seems probable in most of these cases, feminist subversion is not consciously intended.

Hitty: Her First Hundred Years

At the Newbery Award ceremony in 1930, the doll that inspired Rachel Lyman Field (1894–1942) to write and Dorothy Lathrop to illustrate (in a heavily collaborative venture) the winning book looked on at the festivities in her usual "pleasant" but impassive fashion. Field's many other books for children written before and after *Hitty*—both realistic historical novels like *The Calico Bush* (1931) and whimsical miscellanies of verse and story like *Eliza and Elves* (1929)—would win her no such lasting fame as this book, although Field became temporarily successful as a writer of romantic novels, several of which were made into movies.[12]

At the beginning of the book Hitty introduces herself to the reader from her place in a New York antique shop—the spot, presumably, where Field and Lathrop first recognized her as a valuable and interesting object from the early nineteenth century, with a history just waiting to be imagined. Largely through its narrative stance the book establishes itself from the beginning as one of those fantasies described by William Robert Irwin in *The Game of the Impossible* in which little "overt violation of what is generally accepted as possibility" (4) and few departures occur from what another fantasy theorist, Kathryn Hume, calls "consensus reality." And those departures into fantasy also develop "with all under the control of logic and rhetoric" (Irwin 9). What readers are to accept is that Hitty has been conscious from the time that her face was carved by an Old Peddler, has picked up reading and writing from one of her several young owners, and now—given the opportunity to reach "a perfect snow bank of bills and papers" (2) on her owner's desk where she is placed at night—is inspired by an easily reachable quill pen to take up writing her memoirs.

Hitty's high level of physical activity in manipulating this pen (which in the illustration establishes scale by being about as large as she) is uncharacteristic of her abilities throughout the rest of her story. She is usually restrained from most voluntary movement by her inability to bend her unjointed limbs. But the reader, having once suspended disbelief with regard to Hitty's consciousness and physical activity, will not find credulity further strained, for this book is Hitty's first and only attempt to communicate in all of her hundred years. (None of the other characters recognizes her vital consciousness: even her young owners are never let into the secret, as they are in some doll fantasies.) To be sure, her passive but not entirely objective observation is shown against a backdrop of adventure and coincidence common to picaresque: strange things do happen to Hitty, but both her vulnerability to the will and carelessness of others and her relative immortality as a wooden object lend an air of authenticity to her saga that would not attend the story of a human being in like perils. Such authenticity is enforced by Field's attention to historical and geographical detail in describing Hitty's journey from the Preble family farm in Maine to the South Sea Islands, India, Philadelphia, New Orleans, and other points along the Atlantic Coast—including back to Maine—before she lands in the New York antique shop.

In one other regard, however, Hitty might be said to have powers beyond

"I begin my memoirs." From *Hitty: Her First Hundred Years.*

the ordinary, and these tie in with what has been discerned about the significance of objects created from natural materials in the image of human beings.
In his *Dolls and Puppets,* Boehn describes how magic powers are attributed to
mandrake roots, which sometimes appear to take human form, and are, by
legend, supposed to come from "the last seminal infusion of a man hanging
on the gallows" (65). The material from which Hitty is made does not have
quite such flamboyantly grotesque associations; she is carved from a small
piece of mountain-ash wood brought by her creator, the Old Peddler, from
Ireland to America. Says Hitty, in describing her origins, "A piece of
mountain-ash wood is a good thing to keep close at hand, for it brings luck
besides having power against witchcraft and evil" (3–4).[13]

Whenever the power of mountain-ash wood is brought up, Mrs. Preble, the
mother of Hitty's first owner, is careful to argue against such superstitions. Yet
events in Hitty's narrative seem to prove these powers, as well as illustrate the
potency of such beliefs and the ways distinctions between ritual objects and
playthings are continually being blurred, even as recently as the nineteenth
century, throughout the world. In one instance Hitty and the Preble family
go whaling with Captain Preble so that Mrs. Preble can serve as ship's cook
and are shipwrecked on a South Sea Island. Hitty saves the family—albeit
passively—because a local chieftain regards her as a venerable object. She

graces his shrine for a spell, after which she is rescued and brought to India. There she is finally lost to the Prebles and serves another stint as fetish, this time to a Indian fakir and snake charmer, before being rescued again by missionaries. They, after "cleansing" her properly, give her to their young daughter, who is eventually sent to school in Philadelphia and takes Hitty "home" with her.

Hitty's comments about these transformations in status are curiously ambiguous, contributing a like ambiguity to how conventional Western religion is presented in the book. Hitty, like her original human owners, tends to be patronizing toward the practitioners of paganism. Yet in the course of the novel many conventional attitudes are subtly subverted, and the subversion seems to stem from the very material from which this seemingly conscious being is made. Far more importance is attached to Hitty's origin as a piece of mountain-ash wood than to the artistry of her human creator. Field does not tap such mythic sources explicitly, but Hitty's origin connects her with pagan stories of souls imprisoned in trees waiting for some instrument of release. Although Hitty's existence before being carved is not postulated, consciousness comes "naturally" to this seminatural creature; no inspiration or infusion of spirit is necessary, and Hitty records no special filial relationship with the Old Peddler. Moreover, Hitty's long existence before she tells her story gives her a worldly as well as philosophical vantage point that excludes mere mortals. Unlike toys in some other narratives examined here—*Pinocchio* is the classic case—Hitty shows no desire to be human, and the terms in which she asserts her complacency concerning her own state of being are interesting.

One of Hitty's first experiences in the world, for example, comes about through Phoebe Preble's disobedience in taking her to church.[14] Field supports a conventionally religious view of life on this earth by having Hitty present to hear the doxology, which she repeats without comment for the benefit of the reader: "Praise God from whom all blessings flow, / Praise Him all creatures here below" (7). Yet shortly thereafter we find Hitty making the following observation on Phoebe's punishment for disobedience—cross-stitching an apothegm on conscience before she can play with Hitty again— "This was to be a lesson to the little girl, and after hearing all the things Mrs. Preble told Phoebe about consciences and how careful one must be to listen and do as they said, *I began to feel glad that dolls do not have them*" (emphasis mine, 12).

Hitty's distance not only from her putative "father," the Old Peddler, but from her "maternal" child owners can also be discerned from this quotation. Although dependent on humans for locomotion and showing some loyalty, she never recounts games of playing child to her owners' mothering, nor does she develop much emotional dependency on them. True, when she is rescued from the South Sea shrine, she says that "I would not have exchanged my place in Phoebe Preble's lap for the most beautiful temple of ivory and sandalwood ever fashioned by the most admiring tribe of savages. But I suppose that is the nature of dolls" (77). But her attitude here seems that of a "professional" doll—that is, she sees her "dollhood" as a role entailing certain duties, services, and privileges. And even toward Phoebe, who named her Mehitabel and stitched "Hitty" on the chemise that miraculously accompanied her on all her travels and thus gave her a proper name, Hitty can summon up only slight sadness on their accidental parting in India.[15] Looking back on that moment, she states in an *inhuman* fashion, as if in answer to the reader's unspoken need for some faithfulness to her original owner: "No, I never saw Phoebe or any of the Preble family again, though once I did hear news of them in a roundabout fashion. . . . She must be dead a good many years now, even if she lived to be a very old lady, for that was over a hundred years ago and *she was not made of mountain-ash wood*" (emphasis mine, 85).

Hitty's comments on the missionaries who retrieve her from the snake charmer emphasize not only her origins but her self-satisfaction in them, which challenges conventional religion. "But once again Providence or *the power of the mountain-ash wood intervened.* . . . To this day I shall always believe they did as much good by restoring me to my proper place as a doll as *they did by all their baptizing and hymn-singing*" (emphasis mine, 91). The missionaries' constant teaching of the Bible, the catechism, and hymns "made [her] a little uneasy at first": she recalls, "There was a part about remembering 'our frame, that we are dust,' which rather alarmed me until I remembered that this did not apply to me, since I was made not of dust at all but of good solid ash wood" (94). She quotes the hymn sung at the missionaries' service, *"In vain with lavish kindness / The Gifts of God are strown, / The heathen in his blindness / Bows down to wood and stone,"* and comments, "But I felt that this hymn could teach me little after my experiences on the Island." She further muses in a way that can only bring out the ironies of the situation: "I wondered what Little Thankful's parents would say if they knew that they were entertaining in their midst one who had been just such an idol?" (94).

Hitty also forms relationships with animals: young birds in a nest, monkeys in the South Sea shrine, fish in various waters, mice in the hay where she has been lost. (This is consistent with much that occurs in other toy stories; see Chapter 8.) Nearly all treat her as one of them, and with them she seems to feel an affinity and lack of distance that she does not experience with human beings—nor one might add, with the other dolls with whom she comes in contact but with whom she establishes no communication. Looking back on the monkeys in the South Sea shrine, she recalls, "The kindliness and delicacy of their hands reassured me in time and I came to enjoy the touch of their fingers when they stroked me curiously, as they sometimes did" (74). After her hayloft exile, she speaks in similarly sensuous terms, unlike those used to recollect her experiences with children: "Barn swallows and field mice were my only company. I came to be upon the most friendly terms with them, especially the latter. I saw whole generations of field mice grow from babyhood to maturity. . . . Sometimes the mice took pity on my sad state and when they were washing off their babies' faces, they would wash mine, too" (153). Combined with other elements in the story, Hitty's distance from humans and her sensuous closeness to animals align the book more in the tradition of paganistic animism than with an attempt to identify Hitty's "life" with the development of human ethical or emotional concerns or traumas. Nor do these elements encourage the reader to identify with Hitty's humanity but rather with her superior ability to survive, albeit without a conscience.

Field, of course, does not in this children's book lack the usual didactic concern with acceptable juvenile behavior. If the only moral of this story were the ostensible "Obey your parents, otherwise you will lose your doll for some period of time or forever," it would be well driven in by narrative events. Yet from the reader's point of view, which is Hitty's rather than that of the child owners, childish disobedience constantly acts subversively to bring about Hitty's freedom from the restraints of her physical immobility. It also on occasion provides the child owners with experiences they would not otherwise have had. So, although Hitty herself comments on her owners' actions in terms that echo adult censures of disobedient or erratic childish behavior, the narrative shows itself pro-adventure, whatever adventure's dubious source, and thus subverts adult strictures and attempts to control both children and their toys.

Among the mobilizing events are four notable examples of childish disobedience in addition to Phoebe's bringing Hitty to church. Shortly after that occasion, Phoebe and her brother Andy go berrying and disobediently wander out of the area their mother designated safe, where they are frightened away by the arrival of some Indians. They rush off, leaving Hitty behind to glimpse the nonthreatening appearance of "some five or six squaws." She notes: "I watched them filling their woven baskets and thought they looked very fat and kind, though rather brown and somewhat untidy as to hair" (20). She is not discovered by them, however, but by a crow, who picks her up and takes her back to its nest, which is, fortuitously, in the pine tree near the Prebles' house. She shares the nest with the baby crows until she is pushed out onto a branch from which she can be harpooned with a doughnut fork by Captain Preble.

This first adventure, like some of the subsequent ones, has a significant effect. Not only does it begin her intimacy with nonhuman living creatures, but it brings her closer to human beings considered other in the community that shaped her in its image and that has given her most of her linguistic vantage point. Like the picaresque hero of the bourgeois novel, she does not necessarily express a kinship with these "others," or even recognize her own "otherness," but she exists among human beings of all classes and colors in ways that subvert the lines conventionally drawn between them. In this case, the Indian danger postulated by Mrs. Preble is defused by Hitty's calm if somewhat characteristically prissy observation of the Indian squaws. Her stays with her South Sea Island worshipers and the Indian fakir similarly undercut conventional Eurocentrist fears.

After Little Thankful, the missionaries' naughty daughter, Hitty's next owner is a ten-year-old Quaker child, Clarissa Pryce. With Clarissa, Hitty spends the Civil War, and has an adventure of the sort that one would not have expected from this "quiet" child. Clarissa, however, like Hitty, gets something out of this disobedient adventure—a trip to hear Adelina Patti, the nineteen-year-old singer who was making her triumphant tour of the United States. Clarissa is tempted by her classmate, Paul Schneider, whose Uncle Hans is in the orchestra, to slip out of the house to attend the concert. This incident is replete with meetings with the "other": Paul, Clarissa's friend, is regarded as an alien in her school, where some of the girls "made fun of his rather shabby clothes and his slow foreign way of talking" (114), and he and his Uncle Hans speak with heavy German accents. Patti, herself, the young artist, is also a foreigner and thus an other.[16]

Clarissa's disobedient behavior is therefore finally advantageous to all concerned. For once, Hitty and her child owner are not separated by the owner's behavior, but they are parted by the exigencies of the passage of time and Hitty's inevitably "going into camphor" and, through a shipping mistake, ending up in the wrong attic, this one belonging to the Van Rensselaers of Washington Square in New York City. Here she is found and used as a dressmaker's model by a Miss Pinch, who contests with Isabella, the child of the house in which Miss Pinch is employed, for ownership of the doll. Isabella eventually gains control of Hitty, but she loses her to a group of "urchins" when, in boredom, the child slips out of her house on New Year's Day to visit a favorite family friend. A cautionary element dominates this third disobedient adventure, which ends in a frightening street fight from which Isabella is barely saved by the policeman's whistle and from which Hitty is borne off by the young boys in lieu of the pennies and souvenirs of clothing they had hoped to snatch from Isabella.

Still, this act sends Hitty off adventuring again. Indeed, at one point in the excitement of traveling with the gang, Hitty tells us, they "thrust me roughly on the end of a stick and carried me like an effigy at the head of their procession" (145), proving that the young boys are as alive to her fetishistic potential as the South Sea Island chief. Tim, a somewhat gentler child, takes her home to another type of other, his "Irish cabdriver's family." There he gives her to his sickly cousin Kate, whose lack of boisterousness Hitty applauds in comparison with the roughhousing in Tim's large family. Kate's quiet comes partly from her sickliness, however, and after she is sent to a farm to recuperate she manages to lose Hitty in the barn hay.

When Hitty is found there much later, an itinerant artist is staying at the farm. Hitty becomes a model for this Mr. Farley, who poses her with children sitting for their portraits. Hitty is now becoming old enough to be seen as an antique by the discerning eye. The struggle between adult and child foreshadowed by Miss Pinch's and Isabella's conflicting claims now begins in earnest. Childish disobedience hereafter assumes epic proportions in order to combat increasingly significant adult claims, and Hitty has only two more child "owners." The first of these is a "dark little girl" (165), the lonely daughter of a river steamboat captain. This Sally does not come by Hitty honestly—but then who truly has? For, in addition to recognizing those changes of ownership that might be attributed to chance and accident, we can see that Hitty has little sense of being an "owned object," although many have desired to define her as theirs.

Mr. Farley, who certainly thinks he owns her, lends her to two elderly New Orleans spinsters, who put her on display. Sally, a visitor to the exhibit, becomes obsessed with Hitty and manages, in this last episode of childish disobedience, to steal her and bring her back to the steamboat.

Sally is described by Hitty as showing a "certain fearlessness and spirit in her very motion. She was like an unbroken colt or a wild bird" (165).[17] But Sally is impressionable, and she is overwhelmed by a service in a church with a black congregation into which she wanders one Sunday when the steamboat is docked and her father off with friends. The preacher—who, I'm afraid, speaks the garbled dialect that has often falsely characterized African-American speech in books—has chosen the eighth commandment, "Thou shalt not steal," for his sermon. He seems to speak directly to Sally herself, preaching that the Lord can look into the heart of even the smallest child. Sally is badly shaken by the sermon and by the thunderstorm that follows, during which she crouches under a tree. Herself unbaptized, yet hoping to be spared, she prays that God take to heaven the newly baptized "'nigger children.'" Then she propitiates this god by throwing Hitty, whom she has been carrying in a basket (to hide her), into the Mississippi. Sally demonstrates that such burdensome human appendages as consciences may tame—but do not necessarily make charitable—unbroken colts and wild birds.

Sally's is the last example of childish disobedience in the narrative. The next child "owner" is the sister of the "Negro" children who fish Hitty out of the river (Hitty cannot forbear comparing herself to Moses in this incident). Although Car'line immediately claims Hitty, she is no more a match for adult white forces than Sally's conscience was for the minister's preaching. At the Christmas party given at the big house, Miss Hope, the daughter of the house, recognizes Hitty as the doll stolen from the exhibit, and gives Car'line a doll of her own, Mignonette from France, in exchange for Hitty.

With the best intentions, Miss Hope's attempt to return Hitty goes awry. From then on, not childish disobedience but the vagaries of the post office and the effects of adult human mortality as well as carelessness propel Hitty from place to place until she finally ends up in the New York antique shop. Toward the tale's end, the telescoping of time has the effect of making Hitty seem like the quiet center of a storm of human movement, especially as her owners become older and more likely to die, while she survives.

Hitty's immortal stability of character is expressed in a consistent style of slightly archaic formality appropriate to a retrospective memoir, a genre that to some extent attempts to capture the past like a fly in amber. History as memoir is also an egocentric form and one that attempts to create a self which is consistent through time. The adoption of this stable, egocentric auto-biographical voice seems singularly apt for a fantasy whose rhetorical thrust is to convince the reader of the subjectivity of an object. And the attempt to confirm and demonstrate such subjectivity is basically a subversive act with feminist implications, even if the latter are not explicitly so labeled by either Hitty or Field.

Such implications rest, I think, in Hitty's reversal of the gaze. Hitty, as a doll, is the quintessential object, displayed in the antique store window and open to the gaze of all passersby. Physically powerless, she still sees and attempts to express what she has seen, which in her story is not what those who have gazed upon her have been able to control and is certainly not a mirror of their desires. Of course, even in the primness of her discourse, her language has been tainted by those to whom she can only be an object.[18] Yet she seems, somehow, to have found a way to reverse the gaze. Rather than accepting the status of object, she achieves subjectivity. Like all human sub-jectivity, hers cannot be sure of its autonomy, yet it nevertheless feels itself to have survived against all odds. Moreover, although she herself has never rebelled against restraints, she has profited from her child "owners'" indul-gence in a disobedience that is at odds with the good-girl image adults assume to be fostered by dolls; the children thus to some extent act out for Hitty an unacknowledged rebellion.

But Hitty has not done all this without paying a price, a price that seems heavy in human terms, even if, unlike her human counterparts, she is inaccessible to hunger, guilt, death by drowning or freezing, sexual abuse, or any of the other taming/maiming effects that growing up, especially growing up female, may entail. A clue to that price is her silence about one catastrophe to which she, like humans, might be vulnerable—fire. Without belaboring the obvious, I note that fire is often a symbol of human passions: its absence is therefore a key to the self-censorship on which Hitty's survival is postulated. She is permitted to gaze only because she has so little desire, is so little bent on engulfing the reader, so much, finally, the "lady," who walks through mud unbesmirched, always with the same pleasant expression on her face. Like many well-schooled ladies, she demands so little.[19] For offensive weapons she is, however, permitted both irony and ambiguity, an irony similar in places to that of writers like Jane Austen. Therefore, Hitty does not, perhaps, offer the most personally fulfilling way of returning the gaze, but her limited success suggests possibilities that have been used by other women writers—or even virgin goddesses.

What an odd children's text *Hitty* is, one in which child readers are asked to identify with Hitty as an adult human female undergoing what begins to look like one hundred years of solitude—except when she encounters nurturing animals—and engulfed in a long silence that she suddenly breaks by taking up a very unwieldy pen. But in considering the paganism implicit in Hitty's insistence on the power of her mountain-ash origins, the reader has the means to transform this text. Let us, for instance, view her as a virgin goddess. Emphasis on Hitty's pagan powers permits a more attractive reading for the dependent child reader who needs to experience and identify with Hitty's strength rather than with her weakness. We thus note the deep satisfaction Hitty derives from *not* being human and therefore mortal. She can then contemplate further adventures and human watching with that eternal amusement of the pagan gods, as she writes these last lines: "I have never felt more hale and hearty in my life. . . . After all, what is a mere hundred years to well-seasoned mountain-ash wood?" (207).

3 On the Couch
with Calvin, Hobbes, and
Winnie the Pooh

Children . . . can speak to the issues of bonding by close affection for the toy; of autonomy by control over the toy; of heteronomy by following its schemes and suggestions; of education by discovering how it works; of entertainment by enjoying its marvels; of consumer pleasure by knowing it has public image or status and of novelty by discovering the unrevealed novelties it contains.
—Brian Sutton-Smith, *Toys as Culture*

Not all toy narratives are centered on child protagonists, but *Winnie the Pooh* (1926), *The House at Pooh Corner* (1928), and the comic-strip book *Calvin and Hobbes* (1987), featuring as they do young boys—Christopher Robin and Calvin—in imaginative relationships with living toys, depict child-toy relationships in ways that ask to be viewed in light not only of twentieth-century psychological and social practices and disciplines but also of the Western middle-class culture that produced the psychologist, the social scientist, the writers, and the readers.

Contemporary graphic artist Bill Watterson named his two comic-strip characters jokingly: six-year-old Calvin takes his name from the sixteenth-century Swiss Protestant theologian John Calvin, who is associated with the harshest puritan doctrines; and the child's animated stuffed tiger, Hobbes, has the name of the seventeenth-century English political philosopher Thomas Hobbes, who insisted that people require a social contract because without it life would be "nasty, brutish and short." Both men are linked with the grimmest views of humankind and its follies, as well as with the need for religious or secular controls. The two come from an age when children were thought to come into the world already guilty of sin, and to need, like adults, to spend the rest of their lives working off their guilt, with no time for frivolities like play and toys. Watterson, born in a small Ohio town perhaps prophetically named Chagrin Falls, may have come naturally to the dark streak within the apparent lightness of his vision. His choices of character names are certainly satiric: neither the original Calvin nor the original Hobbes can be considered playful or benevolently interested in the relationship of a boy to his toys.

Watterson's interest in the nature of the boy-toy relationship, like that of his readers, child or adult, represents a transformation of the Calvinist view of the child. Newer perceptions of children evolved through a succession of conceptual challenges that were complexly related to social and economic developments in the Western world: first the concept of the child as tainted by original sin was challenged by the eighteenth-century Lockean view of the child as a blank slate on which environment could make its mark; then *that* was challenged by the early nineteenth-century Romantic view of the child as naturally marvelously imaginative, if not totally innocent and pure; then *that* was challenged by the later nineteenth-, early twentieth-century Freudian revelations about the marvelously impure nature of the child's "polymorphously perverse" imagination. The modern or postmodern concept of the child on which adult guardians, liberal and conservative, operate today probably partakes of an odd, fluctuating amalgam of all these perceptions. (Indeed, I find a stubbornly lingering Calvinism in my own secular outlook.)

The late eighteenth and nineteenth centuries in particular saw a growing perception of children as different in important ways from adults. Not only different books and clothes but different objects became suitable for children's use. Those interested in training and education of the young considered seriously how to develop objects that would be of an appropriate size and nature for childish hands—objects that can indeed look like toys.[1] The Edgeworths' "rational toyshop," mentioned in the last chapter, is representative of this trend.

Taking Play Seriously

The earliest "scientific" theories of play as surplus energy, instinct, or recapitulation of the human heritage came about in association with nineteenth-century Darwinism and evolutionary theories concerning human development from "lower" forms of life.[2] A number of modern theories of play evolved from these ideas and from the animal research associated with them: play as education in survival strategies, as communication, as the precursor of art, and as ritualistic behavior. And both the meaning of play in human affairs and the nature of the relationships between toys and children have come under increasing scrutiny. Those interested in play and/or playthings come from many fields: intellectual historians like Johan Huizinga, social historians like Philippe Ariès, developmental psychologists like Jean Piaget, anthropologists like Margaret Mead, neo-Freudian analysts like Erik Erikson and D. W. Winnicott, and a host of late twentieth-century educational and experimental psychologists.[3] In 1982, for instance, D. J. Pepler and K. H. Rubin, the editors of *The Play of Children: Current Theory and Research,* noted a sizable upsurge in experimental studies of play since 1975. They explain this trend as follows: "We think it may be related to a rediscovery of how a phenomenon once thought to be developmentally trivial or psychologically irrelevant . . . actually can play a major role in development" (1).

In spite of extensive research, only twentieth-century experiments and theories seem concerned with play objects in a way useful to the perusal of toy narratives. As Brian Sutton-Smith states in *Toys as Culture:* "Any readings in the history of 'play' will quickly show that there is little mention of toys, either in earlier historical times or in cross-cultural studies. It is not that there were no playthings. . . . But, in general their uses of objects were social, a part of teaching by adults, or play with other children. . . . The predominant nature of play throughout history has been play with others, not play with toys" (26).

Jean Piaget's studies begun in the 1920s and reported in *Play, Dreams, and Imitation in Childhood* may signal that time when solitary play with objects becomes a central concern not only in experiments but in twentieth-century Western society. His distinctions between accommodation and assimilation in child behavior and his differentiation of stages of dramatic play are particularly helpful in considering A. A. Milne's and Watterson's texts. Also relevant are Winnicott's psychoanalytic theories outlining similar developmental stages and depicting similar developmental conflicts. Anthropological correctives like Sutton-Smith's and Mead's, however, set limits to the notions of the universality or timelessness of child-toy relationships that Piaget, Winnicott, Milne, and Watterson convey: anthropologists suggest cultural determinants of the role of toys.

Piaget's works, first translated from the French and published in English in 1951, were based largely on observation of his own young children in the 1920s—about the same time A. A. Milne was observing his son, Christopher, play with his toys. As David Cohen points out, Piaget's studies "tend to focus on what children do with objects, the point at which they use an object for something else (say, an eggshell to be a spoon) and the relationship between play and exploration" (6).

Piaget tried to fit the behavior he designated play into rather strict ideas about the twofold nature of the development of cognitive skills in the human child. He classified development into two types of activities (taking a cue from development as observed in animals and even invertebrates): accommodation and assimilation. In accommodation, the human organism alters itself in order to meet the demands of the external world—cognitively, for instance, developing new "schema," or internal maps, of external reality; in assimilation, external reality is transformed to fit into already operating psychic schema.

Play he found to be largely assimilative, conforming to inner needs rather than outer reality; since he tended to honor the intellect rather than the imagination, he was proud to report that the children he observed gradually stopped playing around with reality and learned to accommodate to it by enlarging and altering schema—for him an indication of cognitive growth. He notes: "Unlike objective thought, which seeks to adapt itself to the requirements of external reality, imaginative play is a symbolic transposition which subjects things to the child's activity, without rules or limitations. It is therefore almost pure assimilation, i. e., thought polarised by preoccupation with individual satisfaction" (87). His characterization of play as essentially egocentric is not complimentary.

Piaget's book on play is the third volume of a work on the first years of the child's development in which the first and second volumes were concerned, respectively, with the beginnings of intelligence and with the child's construction of reality. Piaget valued "objective" thought. Thus, he considered a child's trying to fit reality into its own inadequate schema to be a regressive act cognitively, even if assimilation satisfied emotional needs, in which he was much less interested. For instance, he observed his son's creation and use of model villages grow more historically accurate and interpreted this to mean that play had finally stopped and intellectual life had truly begun. Piaget would have approved of Christopher Robin's leaving his toys behind in "100 Aker Wood" and getting on to school.[4]

From Piaget too comes a sense of the stages of play and the points at which the child changes its behavior toward objects—moving from exploration through physical mastery of them and then using them symbolically to represent acts and persons. Piaget's observations of these stages are particularly relevant when looking at Calvin and Christopher Robin. Although subsequent investigators have refined his ideas, of special significance seem his observations of how a child first "plays" itself in pretend games, then projects its behavior (or that of others) onto toys or other objects, and finally pretends to be other human beings. In addition, Piaget's observations of animistic "thinking" on the part of young children are important in a study of toy narratives. I again note, however, that Piaget's value system—with its emphasis on rationality and scientific accuracy—seems to many theorists inadequate to capture the emotional or creative importance of play.[5] Nor, in his strict cutoff of play at early adolescence, does Piaget recognize, as does Erikson, the possible occurrence of play in adult problem solving.

Certainly modern psychoanalysts consider the role of imaginative play to be of more importance in emotional development than Piaget did. Freud himself, in *Beyond the Pleasure Principle*, gave several explanations for play-like behavior, noting the case of Little Hans, who made a repeated game—complete with repetitive sounds—of throwing his toys in all directions in order to cope with separation from his mother. Neo-Freudians have gone beyond him in elevating the importance of play.

Nowadays, child psychologists and psychiatrists routinely use toys and play as a substitute for or supplement to talk therapy, regarding them as instruments of symbolic representation of the disturbed child's problems in relating to family and environment. In Great Britain, Melanie Klein was especially associated with play therapy. She investigated how external objects represent internalized concepts in the problematically developing child. Play becomes a depiction of internal conflicts. Otto Weininger describes the role of toys in *The Clinical Psychology of Melanie Klein:* "Play psychotherapy invites the use of toys. Toys seem to be the natural means by which children express themselves. They are of considerable interest to most children at most times, but in play psychotherapy, the toys become bound with symbolic meaning and are used to express phantasies, wishes, fears, and actual experiences. . . . Each child will play with them in his own way" (119).[6] Of course, not unlike the writers of toy stories, the psychologist or psychoanalyst her- or himself makes the verbal interpretation for the young child.

Klein's ideas are associated with those of D. W. Winnicott, who is, however, particularly interested in how objects are used by children in general, not just disturbed ones. He investigates those objects to which children become notably, even obsessively, attached, in a manner that in an adult would be described as fetishistic. He postulates that objects like "security blankets" are used by children in their early experiences not just for sensual gratification, as some other psychoanalysts have postulated, but as a means of bridging the gap between the self and others, particularly the primary parent—usually the mother—who is responsible for the earliest care. Winnicott calls such objects "transitional objects." Transitional objects, which are not as yet toys proper (although some children use actual toys), are important developmental tools for children, recognized as such by most primary parents. According to Winnicott, while the primary parent is rapidly becoming "not me" in a way the child cannot control, the transitional object seems to the child paradox-

D. W. Winnicott.

ically to be both self, or "me," and other, or "not me." Thus, these objects make bearable the process of differentiation, creating the necessary boundaries between the child and the outside world without destroying all hopes of control over the latter.

These transitional objects, of which the most famous "literary" example is probably Linus's blanket in Charles Schulz's *Peanuts* comic strip, may seem only consoling substitutes for fading infantile hopes of perfect power. But they offer more help than that, in Winnicott's terms: "There is a direct development from transitional phenomena to playing and from playing to shared playing and from this to cultural experiences" (*Collected Papers* 59). In what may seem to some a great leap, Winnicott considers a successful transitional process involving such objects as paving the way for creative and imaginative use of external reality not only in play but in art, literature, religion, and all human endeavors that form a shared "higher" culture.[7] In order to make this leap, Winnicott postulates an intermediate area between "psychic reality which is personal and inner" and "external or shared reality"—a middle ground where he believes cultural experience takes place (*Playing and Reality* xi).[8]

Although Winnicott considers certain ritualistic sounds or motions to be equally efficacious "transitional phenomena," his work has significance for considering favorite toys—Silly Old Bears and stuffed tigers, for instance—as performing transitional functions and perhaps continuing to perform them for periods of stress and separation far longer in this mobile society than Winnicott at first imagined—past infancy and up to the school years, if not beyond.[9] I was not at all surprised to find a reference to Milne's work in Winnicott's introduction to *Playing and Reality,* where he notes, "In considering the place of these phenomena in the life of the child one must recognize the central place of Winnie the Pooh" (xi).

Among the neo-Freudians on this side of the Atlantic Erik Erikson is probably the psychoanalyst most involved with play and play objects. Like Winnicott, he uses play therapy to help disturbed children represent inner conflicts and considers the part play and play objects assume in everyday life outside of therapy. He sees as an important human capacity our ability "to use objects endowed with special and symbolic meanings for the representation of an imagined scene in a circumscribed sphere" (*Toys and Reasons* 43).[10]

Erikson considers playing with objects a source of emotional gratification, as well as a means of problem solving and conceptualization. Where other psychoanalysts might see play as a way of acting out only past and present conflicts, Erikson considers it to be more constructive. For him it also becomes a means of avoiding and solving problems likely to happen in the future and therefore of gradually strengthening the child's ability to deal with inner anxiety and outer demands—to develop ego strength. Erikson emphasizes the need for modeling with concrete objects as part of this problem solving. And he does not draw the line between child's play and adult's work as firmly as do many other investigators. Erikson's theories of problem solving through object play are more clearly applicable to texts about somewhat older children than to the works considered in this chapter. These theories will be considered in the discussions of Carlo Collodi's *Pinocchio* in Chapter 4 and of E. Nesbit's *The Magic City* and Sylvia Cassedy's *Lucie Babbidge's House* in Chapter 7.

Toys as objectification of internal needs, problems, and conflicts; toys acting as a bond between the "me" and the "not me"; toys as aids in problem solving: these are all insights yielded by psychoanalysis, although these ideas may be tainted by their derivation largely from case histories of disturbed children. Certainly their universality beyond the common culture of the interpreting psychoanalyst and the patient should be questioned. Their originators and practitioners share, however, a common Eurocentric culture with that of the writers considered here (whose universality beyond an audience of twentieth-century middle-class white children should also be questioned).

Play as a Cultural Phenomenon

Despite some statistical attempts to give "validity" and "reliability" to the observation of children's play, two later commentators in the field of play theory, Brian Sutton-Smith in 1986 and David Cohen in 1987, note the seemingly erratic nature of the studies of children's play and playthings, and they blame the lack of systematic progress on a lingering prejudice against play and playthings as serious subjects in the field of psychology. Both discern also a pervasive wrongheadedness about removing the study of toys (for Sutton-Smith) or play in general (for Cohen) from examination of the larger cultural environment of the young child, which they define in particular as the family and the institutions that impinge upon it.

In contrast to essentialist theories, Sutton-Smith's work of cultural anthropology *Toys as Culture* does not consider play with playthings to mean the same thing to all humans (and animals), at all times, and in all places. Sutton-Smith surveys the scene in late twentieth-century middle-class America, showing how important toys have become in this culture directed toward individual success. Deliberately limiting himself by time, place, and class, he finds that children are given more toys than they have ever been in Western history and that parents, in particular—sometimes subverting the notion of educators that toys should be used to encourage cooperation—use toys to reinforce the individualistic values prevalent in American culture. Parents try, through toy giving, to demonstrate their own love, but conversely they encourage children to use these toys in a solitary fashion, to exercise individualistic skills, so as not to bother their parents. Although this paradoxical behavior reveals parental anxiety about intimacy, Sutton-Smith finds it also practical in that it encourages the individualism favored in this society over communalism, perpetuating the association of isolation with problem solving and creativity.[11]

Solitary use of toys is not always play, however, for Sutton-Smith. For him, toys and play are really quite separate entities. He finds that most toys in our society fit into one of three types: "toys of acquaintance," or ephemeral signs of conspicuous consumption that are quickly discarded; "toys of identification," or consoling objects designed to help mitigate loneliness and separation from their givers (although the toys can sometimes be used creatively and idiosyncratically); and "age-and-sex stereotypical toys," which may be used for imaginative play but become socializing "tools" rather than true playthings (216). Christopher Robin's and Calvin's toys come in the second category: toys that console, while encouraging creativity.

In making these distinctions, Sutton-Smith not only emphasizes the consumer aspects of toys but questions the prevalent notion that "play is the child's work." This tag line has been in the twentieth century the excuse either to leave children alone to get on with play "naturally" (since they are not thereby wasting precious time) or, conversely, to intervene persistently with supposedly playful activities designed to train the child cognitively and emotionally for the future. Play theorists are aware of how, with the growth of "universal" public education from the mid-nineteenth century on, influential educators like Friedrich Froebel and Maria Montessori have interpreted the notion of play's being the child's work by attempting to exert more control over the type of play/work the child should be encouraged to do and the objects it should use. Theorists are also aware of the ways middle-class parents have been both in collusion with educators and in conflict with them, particularly in their choice of toys, which is influenced by pervasive media and market forces and by their own, not always conscious, needs.[12]

But Sutton-Smith would like more care taken in distinguishing that portion of the child's activities designated play from that designated work. He wants to limit rather than enlarge what is called play, although he would include adult activities in his definition. He is concerned to show play, with or without objects, as being limited to behavior having a "paradoxical" relation to reality. Play should be a means of expressing and communicating that is meant not to resolve conflicts but to keep generating them within definite boundaries—it should provoke "a constant succession of bipolar and disequilibrating structures which are recurrently equilibrated" (140). Play is exciting and fake dangerous because it tests the limits without meaning to break through them—although, by accident, it sometimes does (Sutton-Smith points out that play is not really "nice" and is often cruel). When play involves objects, it often requires the child first to master the object, find out how it works, then "work with it" before he or she can actually "play with it" in a free fashion that does not use the toy as a culturally determined tool. His definition resembles Piaget's assimilation theory, but Sutton-Smith values play more highly than Piaget does.

Sutton-Smith's definition of play also puts it for me in the area of liminal behavior discussed by anthropologists like Victor Turner, who point out that many older societies provide times and places for "carnival," at which an individual may cross the usual societal boundaries—sexual and otherwise—without danger of being cast out.[13] Such behavior does not involve exploratory learning or problem solving, nor even the use of the individual imagination. All these activities—for which children and adults use those objects

called toys—Sutton-Smith separates from play proper. Play certainly involves tensions and conflicts within the individual that may be helped (or
frustrated) by the kind of ritualization that society provides in play, which
Sutton-Smith calls a "primitive form of symbolization of underlying motivations" (141).

Much literature involving toy characters reflects the fact that when toys
themselves play liminally, rather than engage in the practical behavior usually encouraged by our culture—which is really work, in which toys are
tools—even socially approved play and playthings can become subversive of
society's directives. The violence and aggression often portrayed in doll play
rather than the maternal nurturing that some people naively assume will
ensue when children are given dolls can be considered a subversion of society's limiting schemes to prepare little girls for maternity. (Chapter 6 will
consider the appearance of this motif in doll literature.) A stronger type of
subversion is sometimes evident in stories where toys go their own way and
engage in liminal, carnival behavior. This behavior may allow the child reader
an otherwise forbidden identification—a safe form of acting out that has its
fascination and its terror. To some extent the texts considered here, in particular *Calvin and Hobbes,* walk this fine line, although the Pooh books blur it.[14]

Anthropological investigations confirm Sutton-Smith's notions that not
only is the kind of play/work encouraged by parents culture bound but that
even imaginative, liminal fantasy and activity may be as well. One characteristic of such activity—the very one that concerns us most when we consider fantasies involving toys—is animism. Shortly after Piaget first published his initial investigation of prelogical and animistic thinking in the
children with whom he worked, from which he and his followers generalized
to all children, Margaret Mead attempted to test the concept cross-culturally.
In a study conducted in 1928–29, she discerned a stunning *absence* of animistic projection among the children of the Manus tribe of the Admiralty Islands,
New Guinea—a finding made the more surprising because the religion of the
Manus was animistic.

Mead attempted to solicit animistic pronouncements from the Manus
children, both through verbal references to familiar daily happenings like
boats floating away from their moorings and through new experiences with
unfamiliar objects like Mead's typewriter or the crayons and paper she provided, with which the children could draw pictures they were later asked to
discuss. No animistic statements emerged except on the part of one child
who was considered deviant in the tribe—according to all the others, boats
floated away not on their own volition or through malice but because someone was careless. The gods of the adults did not appear in the children's
drawings nor were they described as working the unfamiliar typewriter. In

fact, spirits did not seem to these children to intervene often in human affairs, even though the children were furnished at birth with attendant spirits and were aware that their parents believed in these spirits. In short, all Mead's experiments suggest that the Manus children, completely matter-of-fact in their thinking, were less animistic than their parents. Mead attributes this finding to the following factors: "The Manus language is a bare simple language without figures of speech, sex gender or rich imagery"; "the Manus child is forced at a very early age to make physical adjustments to his environment, so that his entire attention is focussed upon cause and effect relationships, the neglect of which would result in immediate disaster in terms of severe punishment"; "the adults do not share the traditional material of their culture with their children" (234).

Mead goes on to point out how different these conditions are from the situation of children speaking Western languages and having little experience with how complex everyday objects in Western cultures work "for real." Mead maintains that, in supposedly nonanimistic Western cultures, animistic thinking is, nevertheless, embedded in language. Adults also neglect to give children the requisite technical information about cause and effect, either because they think the child does not really need it or because technology has become so complex that they themselves cannot understand it. Adults resort to animistic explanations themselves—despite wishes to raise technologically competent children in tune with the demands of Western cultures. Oddly enough both children in Western cultures and those in the Manus culture seem to be given a moratorium from deep adult concerns, although in Western cultures, and embedded in Western languages, are traditional myths, which adults pass on to children in place of technological explanations.

Mead's insight with regard to the Manus, apparently never confirmed by other studies, may seem suspect in light of revisionist anthropological works that criticize early twentieth-century studies by scholars who perhaps overemphasize the otherness of groups like the Manus. Nevertheless, Mead's research illuminates the lack of universality of Western culture while at the same time pointing to its peculiarities. Mead's insights also seem pertinent with regard to a certain type of literature for children that is discussed in Chapter 10, a type that is perceptively discussed in Joseph Schwarcz's "Machine Animism in Modern Children's Literature." Schwarcz's main concern is with children's books that anthropomorphize machines—trains, dirt movers, and, of course, computers and robots—in ways that suggest to him industrial society's anxiety about machines, as well as its failure to cope with that anxiety. He finds that certain literary attempts to come to terms with this anxiety are ultimately "dehumanizing." Schwarcz suggests that, in imag-

inatively animating machinery, writers blur the distinction for children between human beings and machines and create a vision of a mechanistic
society in which the human being is only a cog in a wheel. Schwarcz exempts
books about anthropomorphized animals and dolls because they ultimately
"represent" living beings and help the child learn to relate to them, fostering
human empathy.[15]

The popularity of Milne's fantasies and Watterson's comics among adults
as well as children seems to underline the encouragement of animism in
children and adults' adherence to animistic thought in the face of the complexities of modern technology. Indeed, in reading of experimental attempts
to make scientifically valid generalizations about child play with objects, I
was struck by examples that show adults' interest in two questions: What does
the kind of play that emerges when dealing with certain objects show about
children's psyches? and, Can children be influenced to be more or less ingenious or imaginative by our providing them with various kinds of play objects?[16] Strong concern with the second of these questions conveys the value
our society puts on imaginative thinking that is frequently animistic. Experiments designed to test imagination may indeed force children to be *less*
realistic than they feel comfortable being. David Cohen, who objects to the
artificiality of such studies, quotes one child, who was encouraged to enact
a scenario where she pretended to "feed" a "hungry baby" a pencil, for
want of a better object. She asked the experimenter: "Do you know this is
poison?" (53).

Play as Communication and Narrative

However it may conflict with desires to leave children at liberty to find their
own way or, conversely, to train them for later life, most intellectuals in this
society put a high value on the imagination, animistic or otherwise, and
nostalgically mourn its disappearance in adult life. This attitude seems to
stem from the late nineteenth century, when people who perhaps had little
actual contact with children themselves were inclined to idealize the differences between childhood and adulthood and to internalize a view of childhood promulgated by the Romantic poets.[17] These thinkers looked back with
longing on the pastimes associated with childhood—at least for that relatively small but growing portion of the young population that did not have to
labor in the fields, carry younger children on their backs, crawl into mine
shafts too small for adults, or pick up scraps under moving machines in
factories, but had leisure after school and on holiday to play and toys with
which to do it.[18] A. A. Milne's near-contemporary G. K. Chesterton, writing

in the early twentieth century, articulated this nostalgic point of view that finds not only youth but toys to be wasted on the young: "It is an old story, and for some a sad one, that in a sense childish toys are more to us than they can ever be to children. We never know how much of our after imaginations began with such a peepshow into paradise" (quoted in Gordon 4). Chesterton's underlying assumption, not only that the play world represents a lost Eden, but that toys stimulate the childish imagination and can lead to creative activity (as well as what I dub nostalgia) in adulthood, is indeed a generally popular one, and it arises from a period when many adults, like writer Kenneth Grahame, began collecting toys.

The value that those interested in play now put on fostering the imagination of the child may be unconsciously buttressed by such Romantic attitudes. Diana Kelly-Byrne, determined to base her theories on experience with at least one child, in an extremely interesting ethnographic study participated in imaginative play with a single seven-year-old for the period of nearly a year. In doing so, she confirms the role that imaginative play assumes in depicting emotional conflicts (at least for one gifted child and a few of the child's friends). She also observes the way players attempt not only to communicate with playmates but to gain control over them. Her study directly ties play to drama and narrative literature—the telling of stories that have a "rhetorical" or persuasive power.[19]

In the early stages of this play experience, Kelly-Byrne's subject, "Helen," dramatized and elaborately projected her fantasy plots using the toy animals that she collected. Later play involved the direct playing of parts—a progression from object play to dramatization similar to that observed by Piaget at an earlier stage. Helen's plots were taken from both television and books. The part that media—books, comics, movies, and television—play in stimulating imaginative play and providing the texts for it is to some extent considered by play theorists, who have discovered the complexity of the sources for such play (see Jerome L. Singer 234). Children are not mere passive consumers of canned imagination. As Watterson demonstrates in Calvin's daydreams, children can put their own twists even on material as thoroughly commercialized, played out, and formulaic as a television cartoon adventure (although children, like adults, are certainly limited in their assimilation by what is available in their culture).

No one in the disciplines I have briefly surveyed here seems yet to have attempted to discern "scientifically" what happens to the reader's imagination when playthings themselves come to life in a children's book. One would suspect that—like toys in imaginative play and like other characters in literature—toys as characters are objects of identification and projection on the reader's part. If the child owns a similar toy, he or she might then be likely to extend or copy the fictional plot in imaginative play with the toy. If that child happens to be like the child I remember being, she or he may be disappointed that toys as objects do not come to life for them as they do in literature—as child and as adult I have often been willing to let an author do my playing for me. On the dark side, as most critics are aware, Christopher Milne's toys were taken over and exploited as characters by his father, as to some extent was Christopher himself. As adolescent and adult, the son could hardly forgive either his father, for turning Pooh and Christopher Robin into household words, or his mother for aiding him. Christopher's loss of control over his playthings and the privacy of his childhood may, nevertheless, have been my and other children's gain [20]

Going to 100 Aker Wood

A number of critics have challenged the ostensible motivation of the Pooh books as a story for and about Milne's son, Christopher, and his relationships with his toys. What has emerged from critical studies is how much of the child within Alan Arthur, the father, rather than Christopher, the son, can be discerned in the books. Christopher Milne (who was emphatically *not* called Christopher Robin in his own home) quotes his father as saying that he was not "inordinately fond" of children. His father added: "'In as far as I understand [children], this understanding is based on observation, on imagination and on memories of my own childhood'" (*Enchanted Places* 13). Christopher Milne's own autobiographical comments make clear how much the setting of Cotchford Farm, where A. A. Milne and his family lived during Christopher's childhood, permeates the stories, yet the characters of the elder Milne's childhood and his own imaginatively heightened memories give added life to the toys with which his son played. But for me and for many others these stories seem more likely to find their source in the imaginative games played by the child within Alan Arthur. They are permeated by his nostalgia for his own childhood, in which he enjoyed an extremely happy relationship with his schoolmaster father and his older brother Ken but suffered from a distant relationship with his mother. A. A. Milne experienced a childhood different from that of his son, whose relationship with his nanny, as Christopher Milne notes, was central. In these stories, however, whatever their origin, Milne has been able to capture the relationship between child and toy in the early days of Piaget's assimilative play or Winnicott's use of objects to negotiate between the "me" of internal and the "not me" of external reality. Hundred Aker Wood operates as both a "peepshow into paradise" and a transitional country.[21]

In one of Milne's collections of poetry for children, *Now We Are Six* (1927), the poem "Us Two" appears. It ends thus:

> "What would I do?" I said to Pooh,
> "If it wasn't for you," and Pooh said: "True,
> It isn't much fun for One, but Two
> Can stick together," says Pooh, says he.
> "That's how it is," says Pooh. (37)

This verse points clearly to one reason for Pooh's popularity—the comforting recognition, on the part of both understanding adult and lonely child, of the pleasing part that the toy plays in consolation and companionship. I have already pointed out that Pooh is a transitional object: "the sticking together" of self with the not self of such an obliging Second helps ease the unfunness of feeling like a lonely, impotent One. This poem constitutes a celebration of "how it *is*" when "Wherever I am, there's always Pooh, / There's always Pooh and Me." It does not, however, get at, let alone resolve, the mystery of how such a transitional alliance *works,* not only in this poem but in the longer and more formally complex texts I am investigating, in which a third party—that of the narrator—initially looms.

Winnie the Pooh and *The House at Pooh Corner* are sophisticated texts created by an adult with a varied and long career behind him of editing for *Punch* and writing light essays, fiction, and plays.[22] As an adult, he no doubt had the usual complexity of feelings about himself (born in 1882) as long-term son of a father and mother, himself as relatively recent father of a son (born in 1920), and himself as relatively recent creator of literature for, and presumably about, that son (Christopher Robin first appeared as a character in *When We Were Very Young,* Milne's first volume of poems for children, published in 1924). As I have already noted, Milne's literary playing with his son's toys can invite biographical comment, but it can also help show something about the nature and versatility of toy narratives and about A. A. Milne as an artist in this genre.

Winnie the Pooh, unlike *Hitty,* is a framed narrative, a fact that has implications in terms of both point of view and time-space relations. With regard to time and space, the frame Milne establishes in the first two pages of chapter 1 has the child coming downstairs one evening dragging his toy friend, Edward Bear, to join a kindly adult "I."[23] The narrator intimates that this is a repeated scene, sometimes followed by a game and sometimes by a quiet sit in front of the fire to listen to a story, depending on Winnie the Pooh's mood. "This evening—" it is to be a story, requested by Christopher Robin on behalf of his friend Winnie the Pooh, who likes stories "about himself" (2). Chapter 1 also has an end frame, where Christopher Robin, eliciting a promise for more stories, so he won't just have to "remember" what happened, walks toward the door, asks the narrator to come see him have his bath, and ascends the stairs with Winnie the Pooh bumping behind him. Chapter 6 returns to the frame when Christopher Robin tries to remember what he gave Eeyore for his birthday. Chapter 9 ends with the narrator claiming to be tired. And the end frame of the final chapter duplicates the departure for the bath and the bumping ascension of Christopher Robin and Pooh.

The circumscribed indoor evening frame setting evokes "The Children's Hour" of Henry Wadsworth Longfellow's poem—a vision of what would now be called quality time, shared by the child and the middle-class adult (especially the father), with the child invading, with permission, the adult terri tory. In Milne's narrative the firelit room appears, and there the welcoming narrator (whose responsibility does not seem to extend to physical care since "I" only "might" visit the bathing child upstairs) uses the toy as an intermediary of communication between himself and the child. The narrator, in turn, invites the reader into the cozy scene as well.[24] The frame establishes two levels of reality in this fantasy. The indoor evening firelit scene of the story-telling encloses but does not really interact with the sunlit outdoor world of the framed story. Even the two characters Christopher Robin and Winnie the Pooh appear different there. In spite of important differences, both frame and interior story are alike in one way: in contrast to Hitty's wandering and longevity, they are limited in time and space. In *Winnie the Pooh*, time and space emphasize security and control, fighting against flux and change.

Complexities of point of view abound in these framing passages, however, unlike the seemingly self-created and imaginatively independent auto-biographical reminiscence of Hitty. In the beginning frame the narrative penetrates Pooh's consciousness. The bear sometimes feels, in the wavering, (perhaps Tao-ish?) way that becomes characteristic of him, that "there really is another way" of coming downstairs "if only he could stop bumping for a moment and think of it. And then he feels that perhaps there isn't" (1). Shortly thereafter, he reaches bottom, and the narrator seemingly turns to the reader, noting that he (Pooh, not Christopher Robin) is "ready to be introduced to you." Pooh's name is then explained or not explained by way of a conversation between the narrator and Christopher Robin. The reader is again addressed by the narrator who notes that "it is all the explanation you are going to get" (2). One paragraph after the requested story is begun, a parenthetical continuation of the frame occurs, an interruption in which Christopher Robin and the narrator have another conversation about naming, and presumably Pooh joins in "in a growly voice" (3).

From then on comes straightforward omniscient narration with little intervention except in the framing passages noted above. Chapter breaks are not for the most part signaled by a return to the frame. In the course of the framed story, the narrator seemingly feels free to enter the consciousness of his fantasy characters, but not that of Christopher Robin, whose needs and motivations, taken at face value by the toys and animals, must be discerned from his speech and actions.

Winnie the Pooh's limited yet complex frames, which are largely abandoned in *The House at Pooh Corner* (a change in rhetorical situation that will be examined later), emphasize the imaginative connections between the toy animals—as well as the "real" animals with which they interact, like Owl and Rabbit and his kin—and their human owners.[25] The frames set limits on the toys' coming alive. In contrast, the origins of Hitty's coming alive are not recognized within that text; her consciousness seems to have sprung full blown and unmediated from the potent wood of which she is carved. The limits imposed on the stuffed toys, at least in *Winnie the Pooh,* have much to do with the power of the storyteller, the adult narrator "I," and with the intermittent reminders throughout the text of the storytelling frame. In these frame portions, even the child is largely dependent upon the adult for the imaginative bringing alive of the toys—only with the help of "I" can Christopher Robin "remember" that he gave Eeyore a paint box for his birthday.

Yet, although the adult narrator explicitly controls the frame in a gently authoritative manner, he gives some acknowledgment not only of the child's part in inspiring imaginative storytelling but, interestingly, of Pooh's possible consciousness operating between him and the child. No wonder Winnicott identifies the juggling act going in the frames of *Winnie the Pooh* as a transitional phenomenon similar to the one he postulates for the infant, the object, and the parent (although the parent is usually the mother in his scenario). The three here are mutually dependent: Christopher Robin is dependent on Winnie the Pooh for mediating between him and the narrator and dependent on the narrator for making a story of his experiences with his toys; the narrator is dependent upon both Christopher Robin and Pooh for his inspiration; Winnie the Pooh is dependent upon both Christopher Robin and the narrator for recognizing him and giving him a name (frequently the first step toward becoming a subject), a consciousness, a personality. During the period of the first frame and the first interruption, Milne captures that paradoxical quality of me/not me in Pooh that depends on the child's need for connection and power even as it realizes its separation from the sources of power; the narrator collaborates with Christopher Robin in designating Pooh mediator between them—Pooh's "growly voice" in the interruption combines all three voices.

Moreover, I think Alison Lurie is correct when she notes the power reversal that takes place in the internal story itself: "What Milne has done is to turn the child's world upside down, creating a particularly elegant reversal of parental authority. In reality Christopher Robin is a very small boy in a world of adults; but in the Pooh books he rules over—and in the illustrations physically towers over—a society of smaller beings. . . . Surely part of the universal appeal of the Pooh books is due to the pleasure any child must feel in imagining himself or herself larger, wiser, and more powerful than the surrounding adults" (*Don't Tell* 145).[26] In what Freudians would consider an overdetermined way, Christopher Robin is the authority figure in the text within the text: overdetermined partly because he has so little power within the frame and in its parallel, life itself. The godlike nature of his comings and goings in 100 Aker Wood are enhanced by the fact that neither the toys nor the reader are admitted to his consciousness.

The world that Christopher Robin rules in 100 Aker Wood is not much like the night world of coming alive under the Christmas tree and in the toy shop—which in its secrecy and forbidden energy is always at least vaguely subversive. The lack of such an atmosphere, I think, comes from the pastoral and nostalgic quality of the story, which postulates a limited daylight land-scape that completely contents its inhabitants and from which they—unlike Mole, Ratty, and Toad in Kenneth Grahame's *Wind in the Willows,* for instance, to which the Pooh books are often compared—have no reason to wander, since they experience no longing for either "higher" or "lower" things. The threats to this basically conservative society come from nature (high water and high winds) and from new inhabitants like Kanga, Roo, and Tigger, who are all put through initiatory tests, which they pass. Natural problems are solved with some ingenuity, using everyday objects that have no magic qualities but are attractive in their versatility—balloons, umbrellas, and the like. There appear to be few psychic problems: Piglet's timidity, Owl's pretentiousness, Rabbit's obsessive need for order, Pooh's overeating, Kanga's overprotectiveness, Roo's mischief, and Tigger's hyperactivity are accepted personality or developmental traits within the realm of normality. Even Eeyore's gloom does not descend into clinical depression. This world seems to have been created by an adult who remembers his own past through a blaze of sunlight and assumes that a child longs for adventure within a very narrow, controllable range of activity, where death and disorder do not loom and where, unlike the beleaguered Alice in Wonderland, the child is a god amid the toys and animals.

Like Chesterton, Milne conceives of life among toys as a peepshow into paradise and finds toys one way of stimulating the nostalgically based imag-ination. I do not think I would be fair to Milne, however, if I did not qualify this comparison with Chesterton. My perception is that those who dislike *Winnie the Pooh* dislike the sense that no serious disturbances in the 100 Aker

Wood are *internal,* either in the psyche or the landscape. The story's denial of genuine conflict implies that childhood itself is Edenic. But children, even in the "normal" course of growing up without apparent external deprivation, experience intense emotional anguish and psychic pain, which they feel powerless to overcome. When we are young, even embarrassment is excruciating.

Explicit tension does enter the story in *The House at Pooh Corner,* however, although it generally comes from outside the 100 Aker Wood; and this tension is already implicit in *Winnie the Pooh.* In *The House at Pooh Corner* both embarrassment and eventually deeper stress come from reading, writing, and the branches of arithmetic—or as Lewis Carroll's Mock Turtle would have it, Reeling, Writhing, and Ambition, Distraction, Uglification, and Derision. This tension is still basically defined in Romantic terms and is expressed most succinctly in Wordsworth's Intimations of Immortality ode (1802–04). Wordsworth's vision of school in the lines "Shades of the prison house begin to close / Upon the growing Boy" is played out explicitly in *The House at Pooh Corner.* Yet, even early on in *Winnie the Pooh* language, written and spoken, and the need of the child, the toys, and the animals to come to grips with it, become urgent and absorbing. Ancient signs appear throughout the area and are interpreted idiosyncratically—"Trespassers Will," for instance. Whole adventures are based on misunderstandings about Heffalumps and Expotitions and the physical nature of the North Pole. The culturally determined and slippery relation between sign and signified is depicted graphically in such episodes.[27] And for the most part, Piaget would find that assimilation is favored over accommodation in the first of the Pooh books: in 100 Aker Wood, language can be made to fit into schema already formed, rather than altering these cognitive maps. The narrator fosters such assimilation from the moment he explains that his description of Winnie the Pooh as living "under the name of Sanders" means "he had the name over the door in gold letters, and lived under it" (3).

The House at Pooh Corner, however, even though it uses some of the same assimilative devices, concerns—as Milne says in its "Contradiction" (a name assumed for his introduction by a like process of assimilation)—saying good-bye to the 100 Aker Wood and learning to accommodate. The real Christopher Milne's reluctance to leave Cotchford Farm and go off to boarding school at the age of nine may be anticipated in the sadness of the ending to the second book. This ending has already been anticipated in the Romantic nostalgia that permeates both books and, again, has often been interpreted as Milne's nostalgia for his own childhood and familial attachments.

The controlled frame is assumed but explicitly missing in *The House at Pooh Corner:* the narrator is omniscient but not personified as the storyteller. Thus, Christopher Robin as character and authority over 100 Aker Wood and its inhabitants is no longer as directly contradicted by the frame where the narrator is the authority. For Christopher Robin, however, this is a mixed blessing. He thereby loses the protector of the frame too. He is on his own, soon to become a ruler in exile from Eden. What Christopher Robin does in the mornings becomes a matter of some mystery. Rabbit determines— through yet another misunderstood but assimilated misspelled message— that he goes off with some mysterious friend, "Backson" (77). At the same time, gloomy Eeyore (who resembles the antipastoral Jacques in Shakespeare's *As You Like It*) anticipates the looming presence of school in all its competitive anxiety: stamping on his own attempt at forming an "A" with sticks, he claims in his best scornful dog-in-the-manger manner: "'Education! . . . What is Learning? . . . A thing *Rabbit* knows!'" (89). When, the next morning, the sign reappears ominously spelled correctly—"GONE OUT / BACK SOON / C. R." (90)—the reader can discern that C. R. will soon go out for good. Accommodation has entered 100 Acre Wood.

Paradoxically, language is both villain and savior in this book. Pooh as a bear of little brain achieves considerable heroic stature not just by the fact that he is extremely good at making the assimilation of linguistic mysteries work, but through being the bard of 100 Aker Wood. Milne does not emphasize Pooh's status as poet, but Pooh's commemoration of events is an important power, which he shares with no one: Piglet is thrilled when Pooh writes a seven-verse "hum" about Piglet's bravery, of which Pooh notes, "'You *did* it, Piglet, because the poetry says you did. And that's how people know'" (152). Eeyore's miserable attempt to write poetry in the last chapter of *The House at Pooh Corner* cements Pooh's supremacy. The first book's metanarrative emphasis on the power of storytelling is confirmed throughout by Pooh's narrative and commemorative poetic attempts to capture the moment in language.

Constant demonstrations of the ability of art to preserve the past anticipate *The House at Pooh Corner*'s ending, a paean to the mystic eternality of its fantasy land. In the book's last sentence, the limits of time and space are dissolved: in the "enchanted place at the top of the Forest a little boy and his Bear will always be playing" (178). This metanarrative slant has been implied all along. Christopher Robin knows about the power of story (and superiority of art to life?) when he demands, ostensibly for Pooh's sake, a retelling of the Heffalump tale: "'Because then it's a real story and not just a remembering'" (*Winnie the Pooh* 19).

Tigger Bounces into the Syndicates

The sixty years between Milne's and Watterson's works are filled with wonders and horrors unanticipated by Milne (if to some extent experienced firsthand by Christopher, who returned from the Second World War to suffer economic displacement and considerable personal turmoil). Nevertheless, Milne and Watterson, although coming from different ages and countries and working in different media, share similar visions of the importance of the relationship between child and toy, visions analogous to Winnicott's. The similarities of their works are enhanced by Ernest H. Shepard's "decorations," which seem an integral part of the Pooh books, and which add a visual dimension that brings them closer to Watterson's comic strips. Through Shepard, Tigger appears a distant ancestor of Hobbes, a resemblance that is more striking in Hobbes's unanimated moments.

But, just as the pictured Tigger seems captured in a younger, more innocent stage than is the pictured animated Hobbes, Christopher Robin, in picture and language, seems ages more innocent than Calvin, whose pop-culture imagination is not only marvelous in Romantic terms but polymorphously perverse in Freudian. This effect results not just from appearance (Calvin's punk haircut and striped T-shirt versus Christopher Robin's Dutch bob and smock) but also from the difference in the two media's narrative techniques. Just as Milne labors to add to the sense of mediation, of telling rather than showing (which is already more obvious in the difference between words and pictures), so Watterson suggests through his pictures a more direct, unmediated look at what is "really" going on. Calvin, unlike Christopher Robin, seemingly has no secrets from the reader. Such intimate views tend to dispel any sentimentality about childish innocence. I would not like to suggest, however, that one has in *Calvin and Hobbes* an unmediated glimpse into the mind or manners of a six-year-old: only that Watterson's medium works to foster this illusion, while Milne's method creates obvious barriers between reader and child character.

The illusion of a reality untinged by nostalgia or pastoral longings is also created by the wider field in which Calvin and Hobbes operate. The whole domestic scene is pictured, from bathroom to supper table. Both parents interact with child and toy; babysitters confront them. Readers do not have to wonder where Calvin goes in the mornings: the schoolroom and the playground, along with their inhabitants—teacher, principal, class bully, and female schoolmate—are depicted. The outdoors is subject to seasons and seasonal activities, night and day.

Christopher Robin's life includes no "modern" devices. Calvin and Hobbes are familiar not only with little red wagons and sleds but with automobiles, airplanes, and space ships. Telephones, newspapers, television, movies, video cassettes, and rock records are instrumental in their lives. No gradual initiation into the wider contemporary world is postulated here; everything impinges upon child and toy: violence and teenage sex are tinged with orality in movie titles familiar to Calvin and Hobbes—"The Cuisinart Murders in Central High," "Vampire Sorority Babes," "Attack of the Co-Ed Cannibals," and "Killer Prom Queen." The Scrambled Debutantes provide them with an album of songs that "glorify depraved violence, mindless sex, and the deliberate abuse of dangerous drugs" (47).

In addition, while the transitional relationship between boy and toy seems similarly structured in these texts, Watterson has a different vision of how it *works* than does Milne. Part of the charm for the reader in *Calvin and Hobbes* is the often-repeated confirmation of the fact that only reader and child are ever privy to Hobbes in his animated state. No pictured adult is a conscious collaborator in this relationship, as the narrator is in the Pooh books. Calvin is indeed on his own in relating to Hobbes and, unlike Christopher Robin, is rarely in godlike control. Pooh's orality is often considered idlike. And using toys (or toy animals) as projections of the human personality certainly fits in with the common perceptions of what animals represent to humans. Hobbes's connection to id urges is more complex; unlike Calvin, Hobbes has an admitted interest in the female of the species and keeps reminding Calvin, locked into his love-hate relationship with schoolmate Susie Derkin, of the more romantic aspects of relationships between the sexes. Moreover, Hobbes frequently appears cleverer, more adult, and occasionally almost superegolike. Although he has troubles of his own—fear of being stitched and dreams of weasels—Hobbes also participates in metaphysical conversations, for instance, about the existence of a god out to get Calvin. When asked by Calvin about life after death, Hobbes imagines the two of them playing "saxophone for an all-girl cabaret in New Orleans," and continues, when Calvin queries him again about whether he believes in heaven, "Call it what you like" (28). His sophisticated frame of reference is made to support adult male fantasies. Nevertheless, transitional interdependency between toy and child exists, for even if Hobbes knows and feels what Calvin does not yet consciously know and feel, Hobbes is lifeless without Calvin, just as Calvin is friendless without Hobbes.

Calvin does have imaginative fantasies without Hobbes; these are especially evident in school, where the presence of transitional objects is usually not tolerated. In these adventurous daydreams of glory, Calvin himself appears as spaceman and monster fighter. While the transitional relationship still holds in Calvin's domestic and play life with Hobbes, in these adventures the next stage of dramatization noted by Piaget appears. Calvin moves from playing out fantasies with objects to taking on roles himself, Walter Mitty fashion. In these daydreams, rather than in his relationship with Hobbes, the balance of power between self and other shifts, and self becomes conqueror. These dreams are part of the explicit emphasis in Watterson's work on the impotence of the child to do more than fantasize about righting the balance of power in the worlds of family and institution. Although Calvin makes his presence felt negatively both at home and at school, he seldom wins out, except in his imagination—and in one other way: he makes the reader question many of the values for success that society tries to impose on little boys. Not just homework but physical education and Boy Scouting are all scorned. Paradoxically, Calvin succeeds by making the losers of dubious prizes look like winners of their own integrity. Machismo is for daydreams, not for real life.

A feminist reader of *Calvin and Hobbes* and the Pooh books, however, would have to note the general absence of women and girls, except for Kanga, who represents the mother figure as annoyingly interfering, and Susie Derkin, who exemplifies the little girl as dangerous other.[28] Perhaps more interesting, though, might be to consider how these texts illustrate the ways perceived differences between boys and girls in rate of linguistic development affect the early school years.[29] Although any individual child may violate statistical norms, both authors seem to recognize that boys are believed to have more difficulty accommodating to school. Boys seem to advance linguistically at a slower rate than girls and on the whole boys, having been generally permitted more physical freedom, are not socialized as early or as completely as girls to the confinement of the classroom. As Susie Derkin does, girls often have more initial success in school. Milne's and Watterson's rather sensitive little boys (albeit hungry for power) fit this pattern. But the boys are given something of an androgynous quality by their vulnerability, which young women are apt to feel *later* in their school lives.

Both writers also make much of the slipperiness of language. Where Milne makes linguistic difficulties thematic, Watterson shows the difference between linguistic assimilation and accommodation in Calvin's rude awakenings from daydreams. Calvin unfortunately discovers that the words of his tormenting teacher or parent cannot be assimilated into his powerful daydreams but draw him back into accommodation with his powerless reality. For example, a four-scene strip:

Scene 1: Calvin, in topee with machete, narrating: "'Safari Al' hacks his way through the jungle!"; Scene 2: Gorilla with yawning mouth towers over Calvin, who is still narrating: "Suddenly, a giant gorilla rips through the foliage; Scene 3: Calvin in gorilla's paw [shades of King Kong!], with gorilla saying: "Clean your room"; Scene 4: Mother stands in doorway with hand on hip; "What?" says Calvin. Mother replies: "You heard me. It's a jungle in here." (67)

Much of the humor in the text lies in linguistic playfulness, as well as in awkward situations. Calvin and Hobbes, after all, belong to the world of what

I used to call "the funnies" back in the days when Uncle Don read them over the radio to children from a New York Sunday paper. *Calvin and Hobbes* offers strong satire of contemporary mores, both in its words and in its images. Much of the humor in the comic strip resembles that in the Pooh books, despite their different genres. It appeals strongly to adult readers who recognize the delicate balance between what the child says and does, seemingly unselfconsciously, and what the adult consciously remembers and perceives about her or his own childhood. And such humor derives from a relatively gentle cosmic irony, against a universe in which the best-laid plans of boys, toys, and grown men are likely to go awry.

Because Watterson is not verbally sentimental or nostalgic, one is tempted to say that his work is less conservative and more subversive than Milne's. I wonder, however. Watterson, working in the comic-strip medium where characters never change or grow up, has a ready made eternity that fully balances the vision in the last sentence of *The House at Pooh Corner*. Although contemporary events and fears appear in allusion and reference, Calvin's home and school as *pictured* are basically traditional: they promise a way of life that protects him from external danger. Mom looks contemporary—she usually wears slacks (never an apron), she writes and reads—but she is also the one making and serving the supper scorned by Calvin, while Dad sits in his skirted armchair and reads his newspaper or book, subject to interruption only by Calvin's demands for a bigger allowance or more television privileges. Dad wears a suit, tie, and fedora (I haven't seen one of those since my childhood except in gangster films) and carries his briefcase to work while Calvin and Mom stay home: Calvin is clearly not a latchkey child. School is depicted with traditional desk, chair, blackboard, and pointer-wielding schoolmarm (Miss Wormwood), who strikes some terror in schoolboys, but never hits anyone. Mr. Spittle, the principal, enforces discipline that is only slightly sterner. The outdoors, relatively undisturbed and unpolluted, is still a place a guy can go with his pal.

However much Calvin complains, those who actually hold power are seen to be generally kindly if somewhat neglectful of his emotional needs. In our occasional glimpses of the adults without Calvin they appear well-meaning, frazzled, and concerned in ways that middle-class guardians of children like to think of themselves. They are not harassers and purposeful tyrants: the coach cannot help the fact that as far as Calvin is concerned he thinks "violence is aerobic," and babysitters are certainly taxed beyond their limits by the ingenuity of Calvin and Hobbes. The language of the text refers to contemporary urban horrors; the pictures belie their sting. The popularity of this comic strip in family newspapers over the United States and the sentimentality of Garry Trudeau's foreword to the book, which speaks of Watterson's use of "the original source material . . . childhood in all its unfettered and winsome glory," suggest that Watterson has achieved a carefully controlled balance between subversion in the cause of individual imaginative freedom and social conservatism.[30] And in his pictures at least, which hark back to the world of the 1940s and 1950s, Watterson is as much a Romantic nostalgic as is Milne.

Both Milne and Watterson effectively succeed in evoking the needs for power of the solitary young boy and the frustrations of those needs, as well as the ways children's psyches project fantasies, with or without objects that assimilate reality in order to meet present desires. Both the clearly middle-class child protagonists are protected from serious deprivation and abuse. And for children such as these, Milne and Watterson carefully and cautiously bring toys to life to depict solitary liminal fantasizing but not much liminal activity (although Calvin's antics with the family car come pretty close to crossing the line). Neither Milne nor Watterson seems to see the world as subject to cultural change or attempts to encourage children to imagine a world of difference or self-fulfillment by identifying with toy characters that defy cultural limitations. Christopher Robin leaves his enchanted world behind in Pooh's hands and trots off to school. Calvin and Hobbes will probably play together, skirting the rim of chaos, as long as Watterson can keep up their syndicate rating.[31] Like stuffed toys for the young and not so young available in abundance in Western countries, the toy characters in these charming texts are frozen into their roles as consolers, which may, adults hope, also stimulate the individual imagination. The anxieties of adult readers, in turn, may be assuaged by the thought that such toys (and the texts in which they appear as characters) perform the job designated for them by accommodating their children to the world offered by society. This is the violent world that was experienced by Christopher Milne—if by not Christopher Robin and his toy buddies—and dreamed of, if not experienced by, Calvin and his toy buddy Hobbes.

4 Coming out in Flesh and Blood

*The strange rabbit stopped dancing and came quite close
. . . and then he wrinkled his nose suddenly and flattened
his ears and jumped backwards.*
*"He doesn't smell right!" he exclaimed. "He isn't a
rabbit at all! He isn't real!"*
*"I am Real!" said the little Rabbit. "I am Real! The Boy
said so!" And he nearly began to cry.*
—Margery Williams Bianco, *The Velveteen Rabbit*

The rules of the game have suddenly changed. The Velveteen Rabbit had
previously been instructed by his mentor, the Skin Horse, about "nursery
magic" (16) and how toys become real. "'When a child loves you for a long,
long time, not just to play with, but REALLY loves you, then you become Real'"
(17). Yet now the Velveteen Rabbit fails a smell test that none of Christopher
Robin's nursery animals needs to pass and to which no real feline ever subjects Hobbes. Although seemingly close to Milne's and Watterson's texts in
providing consolation, Margery Williams Bianco's first tale, published in
1922, harks back to an older tradition.

Toys in *The Velveteen Rabbit* finally become "real" in a way that has to do
less with the needy child's wishes for a companion or the intervention of a
parent or storyteller than with myths like the ones found in Ovid's *Metamorphosis* or the shape-changing enchantments of fairy tales. Christian fun-
damentalists, who have recently urged censorship of the *Velveteen Rabbit,*
have perhaps rightly detected (if certainly unrightly banned) the whiff of
paganism that such metamorphosis brings with it. As Leonard Barkan persuasively argues in *The Gods Made Flesh,* "The history of metamorphosis . . .
is the history of a two-thousand-year counterreligion of paganism" (18). At

any rate, *magic* of the sort associated first with pagan stories plays a role equal to love in such works. The two other toy texts examined in this chapter, Carlo Collodi's *Pinocchio* (1883) and E. T. A. Hoffmann's "Nutcracker and Mouse King" (1816), also fall in this magic metamorphic tradition. Yet all three still retain a human psychological dimension: each pictures a young male at a level of human development where physical and emotional instability test his sense of being or becoming "real"; together they can constitute a survey of key points in the process called growing up.[1]

Where the Wild Rabbits Grow

Popular as it has remained since its first publication a few years before *Winnie the Pooh, The Velveteen Rabbit* has recently not only wrinkled the censor's nose but lost critical esteem. Some of the trouble seems to arise from its change in midstream from the notion of a toy becoming animated through child love— but remaining a toy—to that of one undergoing magical metamorphosis into a flesh-and-blood animal.[2] Even to a nonfundamentalist, the text seems to obfuscate the difference.

At the nadir of his experience, the Velveteen Rabbit is thrown into the trash while the Boy, recuperating from a fever through which Rabbit was his constant companion, goes off to the seashore with a new bedmate. The forgotten Rabbit despairs, and "a tear, a real tear, trickle[s] down his little shabby velvet nose and [falls] to the ground" (37). From this tear a "mysterious flower" grows, and the Nursery Magic Fairy emerges from its petals and tells him that she takes care of once loved but now discarded toys, making them "real" not only to the children but "'to everyone'" (40). Holding him "close in her arms," she summons a group of wild rabbits to gather in a ring around her and introduces to them the "'new playfellow'" who is going to live with them "'for ever and ever!'" In his earlier encounter with these same wild rabbits, the fabric Rabbit had been able to communicate, but he had not been one of them. Not only had he failed the smell test, but he had noticed that he had no hind legs when the other rabbits rejected him. Now, set down on the ground, he experiences the fleshly metamorphosis denied him earlier: "He found that he actually had hind legs! Instead of dingy velveteen he had brown fur, soft and shiny, his ears twitched by themselves, and his whiskers were so long that they brushed the grass" (41).

Critics have objected to this scene on the grounds that the fairy's magical intervention exalts self-pity and helplessness. But Pinocchio is rescued through fairy magic more than once; scenes of worthy protagonists needing help from their friends are common in fairy tales. Clear lack of conformity to genre expectations lies elsewhere. The two stages of Rabbit's becoming real have different explanations: at first human love alone seems responsible, but then magic intervention is required. These divergent explanations no longer seem inconsistent when the fairy notes that only loved toys reach the second stage. But Rabbit acquires, along with his naturalistic body, *immortality*—the ability to live "for ever and ever" in the midst of mortal rabbits—which is a violation of the mythic metamorphic tradition.

In a later Bianco story, Rabbit's first toy mentor, the Skin Horse, finds himself in a hospital comforting a boy who dies; Skin Horse apparently ascends to heaven with the child. Skin Horse's metamorphosis from material to spiritual toy depicts transformation in a credible, if necessarily numinous, way. But in the mythic tradition, those who are granted immortality without first making special arrangements about their flesh-and-blood bodies usually suffer for it.[3] A toy like Hitty survives her first hundred years primarily because she is made of "stout mountain-ash wood" rather than flesh and blood like her mortal owners.

The Velveteen Rabbit not only evades the issue of the imminent death of wild rabbits but shows the Boy playing a rather unfaithful and cavalier role, which reflects badly on the concept of a child's love animating his toys. Even before his final desertion of Rabbit, the Boy has left the toy behind several times, and in bed the Boy used to hug him "very tight, and sometimes . . . rolled over on him, and sometimes . . . pushed him so far under the pillow that the Rabbit could hardly breathe" (21). But this rough treatment too is typical—even Edward Bear gets bumped down the stairs. The race of literary toys, like that of dogs, can be forgiving and seemingly more faithful than the race of boys (although, when toys get a chance to turn tables, their revenge can be used for humorous, didactic, or menacing effect, as I show in Chapter 6).

These are some of the surface difficulties with this metamorphic text. Its popular appeal probably lies at a deeper level, in its exploration of child development, although here the reader is asked to identify with a toy rather than with a human protagonist. As I have noted, one seductive motif of toy narratives reflects the struggle of both children and adults to feel "real"—to become a conscious, powerful subject rather than an object dependent upon others. In many transitional stages of human development that sense of being real and powerful is challenged and made vulnerable. According to a thoughtful recent study, *The Velveteen Rabbit* may also fall short in its attempt to show Rabbit's metamorphosis as a mirror of early human development.

In "*The Velveteen Rabbit*: A Kleinian Perspective," Steven Daniels carefully works through Melanie Klein's findings—which influenced Winnicott's theories of transitional phenomena—concerning the child's ambivalence about the process of differentiation and achieving independence from the primary parent. If Rabbit rather than the Boy is supposed to be undergoing important psychological development, then he fails, for Rabbit, who longs both to remain with the Boy and to go with the wild rabbits, does not resolve these ambivalent feelings in the course of the story. He feels guilty, and therefore defensively chooses to feel abandoned and persecuted by the Boy, punishing himself for his own wishes for independence. The crying scene, therefore, which as we saw has been criticized for being full of self-pity and cruel, in that it offers no way out but heartbreak, is also pivotal to Daniels's critique: it does not adequately deal with what Klein calls "the process of displacing love," which enables a child to "find other objects of interest and pleasure" (quoted by Daniels 27). Daniels finds that Rabbit experiences a depressive anxiety, which he centers on the line "Of what use was it to be loved and lose one's beauty and become Real if it all ended like this?" (37). Rabbit's anxiety is not "repaired" adequately in psychological terms by the final metamorphosis through the fairy. Although Daniels does not say so, I speculate that Rabbit himself needs a transitional object to carry out such reparation.[4]

The problems of *The Velveteen Rabbit* arise partly through its tight compression, which is driven by the need of a young reader whose anxiety level may be elevated through identification with both the faithless Boy and the abandoned Rabbit for a quick, happy, unexamined ending. Not so strangely, the powerful attraction of this toy narrative may actually lie in its apparent weaknesses. Readers of all ages have been known to adore resolutions that are "bad for them" or only "wishful thinking" in psychological terms. But longer texts like Hoffmann's "Nutcracker and Mouse King" and Collodi's *Pinocchio* perhaps do better both with the issues that metamorphosis raises and developmental questions centered on the notion of becoming "real."[5]

The Nutcracker Sweets

When Maurice Sendak was asked by the Pacific Northwest Ballet to design the stage sets and costumes for a new production of Tchaikovsky's *Nutcracker,* his immediate reaction was negative: he "didn't *want* to be suited to the confectionery goings-on of this . . . most bland and banal of ballet productions." This sated, vaguely nauseated feeling, which Sendak describes in the introduction to Ralph Manheim's lavishly illustrated 1984 translation of Hoffmann's "Nutcracker and Mouse King" (which I shall hereafter call, as Manheim does, simply *Nutcracker*), persisted until Sendak and Kent Stowell, the director of the ballet company, decided to revive the "weird, dark qualities" of Hoffmann's tale, which, they thought, Tchaikovsky's music already suggested in "overtone and erotic suggestion" (xi).[6] As it happens, Sendak and Stowell were not the first to search for Hoffmann's original intention. In 1976, Mikhail Baryshnikov choreographed an "adult" *Nutcracker* that goes as far or farther into Hoffmann's erotic possibilities than the Pacific Northwest's version. For me, what drove Baryshnikov and what Sendak describes is their dawning recognition of the power of this toy narrative, using many of the holiday, coming-alive-at-night scenes that later become commonplace in such works, to evoke a sense of the secrets of the night, both sensual and sexual.

Hoffmann's text is multilayered. Differences between the familial daytime and alien nighttime life of the child Marie (traditionally called Clara in the ballet) are heightened by a story told by the Stahlbaums' enigmatic family friend and toy maker, Judge Drosselmeier.[7] Hoffmann's tales usually develop a protagonist or protagonists who experience a new level of reality—unfamiliar to and misunderstood by a philistine bourgeois society—that puts them in some danger in ordinary life. Other ambiguous characters, who may or may not be antagonistic to the protagonist(s), guide them to the better new world. At some point what critics call a "myth" emerges that not only gives ontological credence to the alternative reality but suggests a double life for the characters, first as figures in "reality," then as figures within the myth. Together Marie and Nutcracker experience the protagonists' adventure and danger; Drosselmeier and the Mouse King act as guides; "The Story of the Hard Nut" that Drosselmeier tells constitutes the "myth."

One biographical detail seems important: Drosselmeier stands in the same storyteller/mentor relationship to the two youngest Stahlbaums, Fritz and Marie, that Hoffmann did to the two children of his friend, publisher, and biographer, Julius Eduard Hitzig. So when Mrs. Stahlbaum asks Drosselmeier not to tell "as gruesome" a story as he usually does and he promises instead a fairy story, Hoffmann demonstrates his own awareness of the restrictions on children's stories.[8] Yet, as Kenneth Negus points out, "Hoffmann himself claimed that there were features of [his fairy tales] that only a grownup could understand" (120). Many critics have found such grownup features present in this tale.

The mythic "Story of the Hard Nut" told by Judge Drosselmeier, restored in abbreviated form in the Sendak-Stowell and Baryshnikov ballets (and comprising the whole of act 2 of Mark Morris's 1992 "The Hard Nut"), is essential to understanding as an adult what lies behind the framing Christmas revels, as well as what is the nature of Marie and Nutcracker's relationship and their victory over the Mouse King. For Marie's Nutcracker

turns out to be Drosselmeier's nephew, and the events in which he participated in another time and place involve traditional fairy-tale elements of
revenge, quest, combat, and rescue.

Once upon a time, a king set traps for the Mouse Queen's family as punishment for their eating the fat intended for his special sausages; the Mouse
Queen therefore cursed the king's daughter, Princess Pirlipat, with extreme
ugliness, setting up elaborate requirements for lifting the curse that involve a
lengthy quest undertaken by the older Drosselmeier and the court astronomer for an especially hard nut (Krakatuk) and for a beardless and bootless
young man to crack it. This special young man—Drosselmeier's nephew as it
turns out—is in turn cursed with both woodenness and ugliness by the
revengeful Mouse Queen when he succeeds in rescuing Princess Pirlipat.
Thus, as Nutcracker, he must battle the Mouse Queen's monstrous son and
win the love of a young woman who will lift his curse after Pirlipat rejects
him. The fabulous nighttime adventure that makes up the familiar ballet
story is the working out of the combat portion of Nutcracker's curse and the
beginning of his courtship. His metamorphosis back to flesh and blood must
wait, however, until Marie, the little girl with whom he has shared this secret
nighttime life, grows into the faithful, loving adolescent who can remove the
curse through her love. Eventually, Marie and Nutcracker, now returned to
human form, are permitted to marry and go off to rule in the Land of the
Dolls.

Marie and Nutcracker thus develop into sexual beings—a later stage of
becoming "real" from the one explored in *The Velveteen Rabbit*. The Mouse
Queen's curse has psychic resonance.[9] Following rejection by the newly
beautiful Princess Pirlipat, Nutcracker's wooden paralysis into ugliness embodies adolescent despair over the volatile, desiring, but perhaps still virgin
(beardless and bootless?) self.[10] Moreover, at a generic level this first wooden
metamorphosis can be linked with all those punishing enchantments meted
out to mortals in both myth and fairy tale for gross, earthy desires. Like most
eligible males in such stories, frog princes and Beauty's Beast included, Drosselmeier's nephew must prove himself worthy of love, yet he would feel most
securely loved in all his ugliness. Like the good females in these stories, Marie
has to undergo physical pain, sacrifice, and generally passive suffering.[11] She
must also be perceptive enough to discern Nutcracker's real self and to love
him before he is returned to his former beauty. Princess Pirlipat, who is
clearly Marie's bad double in the inserted tale, disqualifies herself immediately.

Gourmet and gourmand details constitute a layer of disguise in many
children's books, standing in for all id impulses, and sometimes, as Sendak
and others discerned, substituting oral for genital desires. This oral layer of

desire in *Nutcracker* is not so simply subsumed under seemingly innocent confections. It points, I think, to matters more subversive than adolescent sexual/affectional need. Sugarplums aside, not all the orality is sweet here. Browned fat and hard nuts form part of the food motif as well. The Mouse Queen and Pirlipat's father the king quarrel over food, leading him to destroy all her relatives in his excessive greed for fatty sausages; she in turn bites his daughter and so begins the "ugliness" that is eventually transferred to the Nutcracker. Fat, an earthy substance, becomes the subject of a conflict of power between the human king and the Mouse Queen. In trying to control the fat, Pirlipat's royal father exerts tyranny over the mice—as well as over his own queen, who must herself make the sausages from the fat, and over all his subjects, including the exiled astronomer and the elder Drosselmeier, who cannot return until they achieve their quest.

Although I too have found the Krakatuk a hard nut to crack, I speculate that such nuts, with their hard shells and liberating meat, can stand for human puzzlement over the difference between appearance and reality as well as for human hopes that a hard exterior will be prove to be only defensive, concealing inner treasures from all but the most worthy. As such, Krakatuk certainly can stand for Marie's and Nutcracker's mutually positive discoveries. I am also struck, however, by how much, unlike the eating of sweetmeats, the nutcracking business that permeates the story requires sharp teeth and biting (even the infant Pirlipat has preternatural teeth)—a vision of voracious human hunger and need that can both injure and consume the desired object. This brings me back to a taboo subject that I, like the story itself, might like to evade; it concerns that family friend and toy maker Judge Drosselmeier himself.

In discussing Hoffmann's "mythology," Kenneth Negus wonders why Judge Drosselmeier, the presumed family friend, need be such a ugly, menacing figure with his black patch over one eye and bewigged bald head. Why does he not protect Marie either from nocturnal attacks or from the familial teasing that her belief in her encounters earns her? Judge Drosselmeier even appears as a menacing owl in her first nocturnal adventure. Indeed, like powerful figures manipulating automata in other Hoffmann stories (such as "The Automata" and "The Sandman," discussed in Chapter 10), he displays all the outer signs of evil that are confirmed in these stories but smoothed over and unpursued here.[12] Disguised in various ways, Drosselmeier's still-evident menace lies, I think, in his connection to the secrets of the night at a level deeper than that of the adolescent attraction between Marie and Nutcracker.

Present knowledge of the vagaries of human sexuality would not dismiss even seven-year-old girls as objects of older men's desire.[13] Running through the text is a special intimacy between Marie and Drosselmeier that manifests itself in her comments on Nutcracker's resemblance to him, comments that annoy her parents. By biographical extension, even Hoffmann's feelings toward young girls might be considered.[14] Whether this story is overdetermined by Hoffmann's doubts about and sublimation of his own feelings, I think that it depicts not only adolescent sexuality but repressed "inappropriate" adult desire as well. Of course, not the clever ugly old Judge Drosselmeier but Drosselmeier's young gentle handsome nephew must be rewarded with the innocent girl's love; Godfather Drosselmeier must not get too close—a sugary layer must be dusted over the whole cake. Yet, suggestively, in Rudolf Nureyev's 1968 production of the ballet, Drosselmeier, the Mouse King, and the Nutcracker Prince are all danced by the same dancer. A sublimating way around the impasse is to divide acceptable and unacceptable desires up among various characters—a process colloquially known as having your cake and eating it too!

Unfortunately, repression also has the odd habit of forcing the repressed emotions into other clearly destructive, even violent forms; neither comedy nor sugar can entirely mask the tyranny of powerful male and female figures who cast shadows over the story. I will deal more fully below with female power in all these metamorphic narratives. In *Nutcracker,* male power threatens less obviously but compellingly as an aspect of repressed desire. Fritz's "man-handling" of the Nutcracker introduces this idea at the familiar level of boyish roughness—after all, Nutcracker will replace him too as his sister Marie's ideal. The exercise of brute power and revenge by adult males is, however, more telling. The sausage-eating king holds the power of life and death and exercises it in accord with his appetites and anger. The Nutcracker is endangered by the mutant seven-headed Mouse King, a figure of frightening phallic abundance with the golden sign of power, a crown, on every head. In Candy Town, the capital of the Land of the Dolls, lurks a Giant SweetTooth (ancestor of the Cookie Monster?) who threatens to gobble up the city and can be bought off only with the offer of "a whole precinct of a city and a considerable part of Marmalade Grove" (91–92); also present is the shadowy, menacing figure of the Pastry Cook, "an unknown but cruel spirit, which is thought to have total power over the people" (90). His terrible name alone can quell all disorder among the inhabitants.

In contrast, Drosselmeier's nephew (who lacks a name of his own other than Nutcracker or Drosselmeier) is a gentle man, like the somewhat more authoritative Dr. Stahlbaum, Marie's father, who is shown in the bosom of the bourgeois family to which Judge Drosselmeier is admitted as valued family friend. Small, dainty, and still beardless, the youth can only take his bride, Marie, back to the Land of the Dolls. His effete nature and the need of the couple to inhabit a fairy land seem also overdetermined: as the "appropriate" suitor (who had to borrow a sword from Fritz and give it back later) he is made somehow less sexually exciting than the ugly older man. The older, larger, or more powerful male characters suggest that Drosselmeier (and Hoffmann) could, if he unambivalently wished, involve Marie in a story more violent and less sweet than this tale of adolescent testing, where a gentle (and, I'm afraid, rather foppish) young man is turned into an ugly wooden nut-cracker and back again into a flesh-and-blood princely suitor. But as Dros-selmeier promises Marie's mother, and, by implication, Hoffmann promises Mrs. Hitzig, this story is not as gruesome as his stories usually are.

Puppets Will Be Boys and Vice-Versa

Between 1881 and 1883, Carlo Lorenzini (1826–90)—Tuscan journalist, theater and opera critic, free-lance writer and playwright, and former Italian Republican army volunteer—assumed the now famous pen name of Carlo Collodi to write for the *Giornale per i bambini* a serial story that became *The Adventures of Pinocchio,* first translated into English in 1892.[15]

The German Hoffmann's and the Italian Collodi's personal struggles to make their livings as writers and critics were not all that different; the cul-tures that produced them, however, and their own sense of place in those cultures make their children's stories quite different from each other, even if both writers focus on metamorphosis into flesh and blood and feature fairy-tale motifs. Hoffmann, psychologically subversive and satiric toward author-ity but not, like Collodi, associated with revolutionary movements, does not abandon the Romantic attempt to create an alternative reality that is equally luxurious if at odds with the style of the German Philistine; like a Romantic Bohemian, instead of preaching to the child, he hints at what might *épater les bourgeois.* Moreover, the human poor are not present and hunger seems mainly a metaphor in *Nutcracker.*[16] Not so in *Pinocchio,* explicitly grounded in the reality of the plight of the poor in the newly united Italian nation, a reality with which Collodi actively associated himself in his endeavors to create a didactic as well as imaginative literature for Italian children. Shortly before and throughout the time that he was writing *Pinocchio,* Collodi was also producing what translator Nicholas Perella calls "school books" with "child protagonists who ask questions for the purpose of being instructed" (9), that is, like the instructional books being written in the late eighteenth and early nineteenth centuries in England and America in order to spread literacy over a broader base.[17]

Atmosphere and setting seem emblematic of the contrast in the immediate concerns of Hoffmann and Collodi. This scene greets Marie and Fritz on Christmas Eve:

The big Christmas tree in the middle of the room was decorated with any number of gold and silver apples, and sugared almonds, bright-colored candles, and goodies of all kinds shaped like buds and blossoms hung from every branch. But the most startling thing about this wonderful tree was that hundreds of tapers glittered like stars in its dark branches, and the tree itself, shining with an inner light, invited the children to pick its blossoms and fruits. Round about the tree everything glittered splendidly—no one could even have described all those wonderful things. (6)

Every wish would seem to be fulfilled by this tree, and the gifts themselves, also described in delicious detail, are still to come.[18]

But what does Geppetto come home to, carrying the lively block of wood that will become Pinocchio? A cold, dark, room with sham comforts:

Geppetto's home was a small room on the ground floor that got its light from the areaway under a staircase. The furnishings couldn't have been more modest: a rickety chair, a broken-down bed and a battered table. At the back wall you could see a fireplace with a fire burning; but it was a painted fire, and along with the fire there was painted a kettle that boiled merrily and sent up a cloud of steam that really looked like steam. (97)

Hoffmann begins his description of Christmas with a mere bow toward the idea that children must earn their holiday treats: "The children must have been especially well behaved that year, for they had never before received so many splendid presents" (6). In contrast, only after many trials and tribulations can Pinocchio himself bring about a transition in setting that accompanies his own transformation into flesh and blood: "Now just imagine his amazement when, upon awakening, he found that he was no longer a wooden puppet, but that he had turned into a boy like all other boys. He gave a look around him, and instead of the usual straw walls of the cottage, he saw a beautiful, cozy room, furnished and decorated with tasteful simplicity" (457–59). Simplicity over conspicuous consumption is exalted; hard work over play. Pampered children who spend their time as the Stahlbaum children do throughout Hoffmann's tale turn into donkeys in Collodi's.

These are not just surface considerations. Hoffmann's tale, which pinpoints one area of adolescent development in Nutcracker's metamorphosis, wraps it in a sensually stimulating fairy tale. Collodi, didactic and cautionary, begins his tale by disappointing fairy-tale expectations: "Once upon a time, there was . . . 'A king!' my little readers will say right away. No, children, you are wrong. Once upon a time there was a piece of wood" (83). Collodi thus fashions, in contrast to Hoffmann, a bildungsroman with fairy-tale elements, one of which is metamorphosis. Pinocchio's psychological changes have

At the word
« Three!. » the
two boys pulled
off their caps ---

"At the word Three! the two boys pulled off their caps—." From *The Adventures of Pinocchio.*

moral and ethical implications. Everyday, long-term behavior is tested. To be a puppet or a toy is shown to have developmental potential but also to be only marginally real—equipped with uncontrollable id urges over which no so-cially determined superego stands guard. Thus no ego can develop to medi-ate between the two.

There are, of course, many ways to read *Pinocchio,* but in line with my interests in this chapter and with Collodi's own didacticism, I shall concen-trate on the developmental. Freudians and Jungians have found much to interest them in the sexual implications and the archetypal elements of which the story is full.[19] But I should like to look at the book from a new perspective: that of the theories of child development discussed by the neo-

Freudian Erik Erikson, in "Eight Ages of Man," a chapter in *Childhood and Society*.

Viewed as an unintentional yet telling depiction of Erikson's fourth stage of development—the stage of "industry," when the child between the ages of seven or eight and eleven or twelve receives "some *systematic instruction*" in order to develop the *"fundamentals of technology,"* so that it "becomes ready to handle the utensils, the tools, and the weapons used by the big people" (259)—*Pinocchio* presents a perceptive picture of the developmental problems and challenges in meeting societal demands and the changes that Collodi himself as writer of "school books" consciously espoused.[20] These demands arouse conflicts and tensions in Collodi and in many another—Christopher Robin and Calvin among them—in the process of conforming to them.

But Collodi, unlike Milne, for instance, is not a product of Anglo-Saxon Romanticism, and shows little nostalgia for the golden age of carefree childhood; nor does *Pinocchio* advocate cultivating the imagination of the child, as many twentieth-century theorists do. If Pinocchio wishes to become flesh and blood, he also must acquire practical experience. Springing immediately from a block of wood into a conscious puppet of the size and apparent age of a schoolboy, Pinocchio must catch up on the earlier developmental stages described by Erikson—in which the child develops trust, autonomy, and initiative—at the same time he enters a severely testing, poverty-stricken environment with only one parent figure. Yet, while Pinocchio does not come into the human world trailing clouds of glory, he is not an example of Locke's tabula rasa either. Collodi endows him, almost from the moment of appearance, with two attributes that will clearly stand him in good stead: "a good heart," which responds to love, and a wooden body that will both withstand hard knocks and keep him afloat in the water until he is ready to become flesh and blood.

This good heart shows itself fairly early. In chapter 4 Pinocchio kills the talking cricket in a fit of pique, but by chapter 8, recognizing that Geppetto has sold his coat for a schoolbook, Pinocchio is unable to "restrain his heart's true impulse" (135) and embraces his father; in chapter 10 Pinocchio offers to sacrifice himself for his brother puppet. This attribute, though one of impulsiveness, identifies Pinocchio, even in his puppet state, as a child not immediately damned by original sin in Calvinist terms. It also links him to a literary type of considerable importance in late nineteenth-century English and American literature for children: the Good Bad Boy, as critic Leslie Fiedler calls it, prefigured in Henry Fielding's Tom Jones, who is contrasted with his hypocritically pious half-brother. The Good Bad Boy is a "scamp but not a reprobate," as Nicholas Perella points out in his introduction to *Pinoc-*

chio. There is a tendency among critics like Perella to compare Pinocchio as a Good Bad Boy to Huckleberry Finn, but I think that in his final development Pinocchio more closely resembles Tom Sawyer, who arrives at maturity by his own mischievous path, is loved the better for his misdemeanors, and eventually accedes to society's demands.[21]

In British and American children's literature, the Good Bad Boy develops on the eighteenth-century model of Tom Jones, evolving in direct contrast to the didactic characterization of the good child hurrying to heaven that was prevalent in children's literature of the late eighteenth and early nineteenth centuries. These good children recur especially in tract literature like Elizabeth Turner's *Ministering Children* (1007–10).[22] Beneath the Good Bad Boy image lurks the sense that those who have never been tempted to do wrong can never really do good, as well as a more sexist sentiment that, particularly in boys, too fine a tuning of the superego will result in an unnatural prig and a sissy.[23] Combined with an ability to love, the aggressive energy potent in the Good Bad Boy is part of Pinocchio's charm as well as Tom Sawyer's; this energy is also implied in the smiling resignation of the phrase "boys will be boys" and suggests what society thinks constitutes "a *real* boy." The Good Bad Boy in Erikson's age of industry is still the American ideal—Calvin with Hobbes has some of this quality. Collodi's apparent recognition of this type even within his didactic framework accounts for much of the continuing popularity of *Pinocchio*.

In life, boyish adventure is often physically, even violently, dangerous (Tom Sawyer skirts the edge of death in the confrontation with Injun Joe in the cave), so that for someone who has to learn the hard lessons of Italian poverty confronting Pinocchio, having a reparable and unsinkable wooden body is certainly a help. Pinocchio's being a puppet helps assure the survival of his good heart until his metamorphosis, but it also suggests existential concerns intrinsic to puppets and to their relationships with their puppeteers, who not only create them but pull their strings.[24] In the scenes where Pinocchio first meets the puppets who are Fire Eater's virtual slaves his relationship to them is emphasized: they recognize him as one of their own immediately. His differences from them also emerge, however. His relative freedom belongs to the potentially human father-son relationship that, by contrast, he has with Geppetto, his creator father.

Who made us and who pulls our strings? are questions especially associated with puppetry. Those who write about puppet theater note how the debate on free will versus determinism creeps into observations about puppets. These existential concerns are also common to toy narratives in general. Although they are not as fully articulated here as they will be in Hoban's *Mouse and His Child*—with the quest of a mechanical toy to become "self-winding" (see Chapter 9)—the process of Pinocchio's development from puppet to boy does suggest some of the choice making that dominates the notion of free will, which operates in the face of both biological limitations and socioeconomic restraints: the determined strings that seem to manipulate humans in their everyday lives. Pinocchio's development illustrates also a tension between dependence on the good and bad influence of others and a seemingly independent sense of obedience to an inner conviction of right and wrong that implies, like the image of the Good Bad Boy, more than just conforming to the demands of society.

In *Pinocchio,* this sense of the importance of free will is enhanced, as it is in both *Tom Sawyer* and *Huckleberry Finn,* by the concomitant and ultimately subversive social satire. The criminal-justice system is especially subject to such satire in Collodi's text, first when a gendarme arrests Geppetto for child abuse and next when a gorilla judge in gold-rimmed spectacles and white beard sentences Pinocchio to prison for *being robbed,* and he is allowed to participate in a general amnesty only when he claims to be a rogue. Still other incidents indicate that the arrival of the gendarmes never signals rescue for the innocent. Forces of law and order cannot be trusted to distinguish properly between good and evil—fate, not the legal system, may eventually punish the wicked Cat and Fox. Collodi also shows little pity for victims of the system; all his admiration goes to its survivors. Pinocchio must develop an ethical system of his own.[25] This he strengthens through harsh experiences that wipe out his gullibility but intensify his love and loyalty to those who love him.[26]

Much of this material, including its ambiguities, makes Collodi's text vital today. Completely familiar in late twentieth-century American nostalgic, reactionary pleas to return to "good, old-fashioned values" is the text's emphases on the work ethic and filial piety. Indeed, as Perella points out, for all Collodi's interest in literacy and emphasis on Pinocchio's schooling in the early part of the text, the fact that Pinocchio works to support Geppetto after he rescues him from the Shark—which prevents any more formal schooling for the time being—is necessary to his earning his metamorphosis. Begging is scorned almost as much as thieving; in the characters of the Cat and the Fox the two vices go hand in hand with the confidence game. The notion of there being a worthy versus an unworthy poor is incompatible with those theories of welfare, "safety nets," or subsidized education that also are under attack today. At one level, Pinocchio must pull himself and his father up by his own proverbial bootstraps. Patriarchy and patriarchal society in both their benign and malignant aspects are finally accepted and adopted.[27]

Another idea is at work here as well, a notion that further complicates the messages about filial piety, the work ethic, and the absence of justice in the forces of law and order. For some reason, perhaps lack of inspiration, Collodi briefly stopped writing his serialized version of *Pinocchio* at a point in the narrative where the Blue-Haired Fairy has appeared as child who dies because of Pinocchio's neglect. When Collodi decided to take up his pen again with chapter 25 (the muse taking pity on him, perhaps?), he added an element that can be discerned in all three of the tales considered here: the power of the female to effect "magic" changes in the realm of flesh and blood that symbolize more than physical development. In considering this element, the ages of protagonists become crucial.

Cherchez la femme

In the classical history of metamorphosis and in fairy-tale enchantments female and male transformations occur at the whim of gods, witches, or magicians; both male and female beings experience metamorphosis. But while the texts in this chapter may seem to deal with magic changes in being and psychological development common to both males and females, all three texts show only *male* characters going through these metamorphoses at particular stages of their development. Therefore, I view them as possibly conforming to concepts of gender formation that are determined, at least in part, by differing social demands made of males and females at these points of development.[28]

Common notions of gender formation require boys to separate from their mothers more completely than girls are usually asked to. This separation and early movement out from the domestic, relational world anticipates a life where individuation and independence in a wider world of men are continually cultivated. As Robert J. Stoller notes, "The first order of being a man is, don't be a woman" (183). Yet, refusal of familiarity with the female after early childhood can breed a sense of female mystery—power of a sort quite different from that of men, bewitching and seductive.[29] When males are urged to go out into the world, the men they meet may become good or bad role models, but the females may seem—paradoxically since they have rarely held political or economic power in recorded Western history—to control good or evil fates. Lady Luck is a volatile mistress![30] (In early pagan religion, female powers, associated with fertility, were often worshiped as earth and nature goddesses, whose power to deal in death as well as life made them formidable, fateful protectors and destroyers. Traces of these ideas remain in classical mythology, Celtic myth, and, most pervasively, fairy tales. Females in these narratives can experience female power, although usually passively. But for the male hero who quests or journeys, female power becomes a particularly formidable force: he sometimes must tame or destroy it; if he is lucky, it becomes his to enjoy.)

In *The Velveteen Rabbit,* our little male Rabbit is deprived from the very start of primary parenting. He receives some from the Boy, before he is again harshly deprived. The fairy who emerges from the flower carries the resonance—here slightly denatured by sentimentality—of both lost mother and goddess. Her nurturing and power are necessary for the little Rabbit to become a part of the natural world into which he is sent off. Of course, the Velveteen Rabbit need not have a gender at all. Certainly, whether he acquires genitalia along with his hind legs is a moot point. But Bianco makes him male and, given little choice in pronouns except dichotomizing gender-based ones and a sense of the difficulties of the male differentiation process, I too might have called Rabbit "he" while letting him enjoy female power in his momentous change into flesh and blood and his traumatic separation from the domestic that accompanies his journey into the wild.

Pinocchio, like the Velveteen Rabbit, is a lucky boy (equipped with a phallic nose if not other male signifiers). His paternal lineage may be poor and working class, but he acquires a powerful patroness to supplement this lack, the Blue-Haired Fairy. After chapter 25, Collodi, who had adopted the name of his mother's village as pen name, endows this female figure with none of the sentimental, slightly laughable, "there are fairies at the bottom of our garden" aspects of the Nursery Magic Fairy. The Blue-Haired Fairy represents a mercy that qualifies the harsh and too-frequently corrupt system of justice that prevails in Pinocchio's world. As an image of female power, she operates as something between a pagan goddess and a semi-Christianized Virgin Mary (which in the unofficial Catholic cult of Mary, takes female power into account without awarding it deity), as well as fills the role of Pinocchio's lost or missing mother.[31]

Following pagan tradition, the Blue-Haired Fairy's helpers include nearly all the animal world—except for the renegade Cat and Fox—even insects, such as crickets. The sky-blue color that characterizes her gives her an ethereal rather than earthy character, however, more in keeping with the tradition of the Virgin, which emphasized purity over fertility. Pinocchio's rebirth in the sea when he saves both himself and his father and emerges from the belly of the Shark, partakes of both pagan and Christian traditions as well. The watery (amniotic) fluids of the setting subliminally evoke the female powers of life and death while overtly alluding to the biblical Jonah.

This combination of earthiness and spirituality in the Blue-Haired Fairy, as well as her original appearance as child who dies when Pinocchio betrays her and is then resurrected in adult form, permits a satisfying interpretation of her in Jungian terms. As anima she eventually presides over Pinocchio's becoming human in a way that emphasizes his taking the previously rejected female element into himself. Unlike its Anglo-Saxon analogues (Twain's books, for instance), this narrative seems to posit a tender, mutually nurturing relationship between father and son, which includes Pinocchio's ministering to his sick father's needs in a domestic setting that his personal efforts make "cozy." Such domestic testing is usually the lot of the heroine rather than the hero in either Good Bad Boy or quest literature.[32] Contempt for the female sometimes cultivated in latency is not demonstrated here, but rather the incorporation of domestic as well as worldly virtue in the puppet who would be a boy.

In *The Velveteen Rabbit* and *Pinocchio*, the female power associated with becoming flesh and blood is shown as basically benign; mercy, rather than justice or revenge, characterizes it. Not so in *Nutcracker*, where part of the weird, dark quality comes from the menace of powerful male figures and the revengeful and rejecting female figures in the world that is the source of the nighttime adventures. The Mouse Queen first intimidates Pirlipat's mother to get the brown fat from her, then bites Pirlipat in revenge for the slaughter of her relatives, and finally transfers the ugly enchantment to the young hero, only then turning her revenge over to her mutant son. Princess Pirlipat's inability to love the ugly Nutcracker shows destructive female power as well. The gentle Marie is left to undo the wrong that these females have perpetrated in the myth and to complete the metamorphosis back to flesh and blood.

Marie's role is the compensatory one common to theories of male psychological development where the boy who has successfully negotiated his separation from his mother is granted a "suitable" female in her place; Marie's motherly cradling of the initially injured Nutcracker suggests the nurturing role such females are asked to take in place of the long-lost mother.[33] In fairy-tale terms, Marie's human love is able to reverse the bad magic wrought by the females who have come before her. Hoffmann depicts in this tale a period of male development where the male must confront the female as a sexual partner and compete with other males to do so. He manages, however, to suggest below the confectionery surface the life-long ambivalence toward females that can arise in the process of male gender formation.

Magic metamorphoses into flesh and blood for toy or toylike characters obviously take more than a wave of a wand, particularly when, as in the case of Pinocchio, social and economic factors are not particularly favorable. It can hurt, as the Skin Horse, "always truthful," tells the Velveteen Rabbit (17). So these narratives resonate with the suffering, confusion, and release of psychic energy that dominate the process of coming to feel independently real, a subject rather than an object.

5 Where Have All the Young Men Gone?

"For [toy soldiers] to be successful they have to be seen through the rosy glasses of time," Mr. Lobeck said. "The awful questions can no longer be asked or answered."
—Chris Hedges, "Tin Armies and Fond Thoughts of the Past"

In Hans Christian Andersen's "Steadfast Tin Soldier" (1837), Pauline Clarke's *Return of the Twelves* (1962), and Lynne Reid Banks's *Indian in the Cupboard* (1980) and *Return of the Indian* (1986) toy soldiers and other warriors are rarely involved in direct combat; like other toy characters they participate in a whole range of activities, involving both domestic and romantic relationships. And particularly in the twentieth-century texts, these miniature figures are very involved with their young owners. In their lives as inanimate objects, however, these playthings are indeed war toys as well as collectors' items. The status of toy soldiers—as stimuli for the reenactment of historic scenes of hostility, death, bravery, treachery, honor, and patriotism, or as nostalgic memorabilia of such violent (or gallant?) moments—helps us consider their roles in fiction and the sublimated or silenced associations behind these roles. And in my analysis of the three modern narratives involving these toy combatants the political and social struggles for power implicit in these memorable moments will be brought very much to the fore.

War Games

In 1913, H. G. Wells published *Little Wars*, patronizingly subtitled *A Game for Boys from Twelve Years of Age to 150 and for That More Intelligent Sort of Girl*

Who Likes Boys' Games and Books. Little Wars is a curious, ruminative, "how to" book with a wry rhetorical stance—perfect, in fact, for my consideration of toy soldiers as artifacts and war toys. Like Wells's earlier *Floor Games* (1912), this text was probably intended to unite adults and children, particularly fathers and sons, in the contemplation of an activity seductive to both: building elaborate battle sets in which tiny soldiers can be moved around in tune with the whims and narrative impulses, historical or imaginative, of the beings who set them up.

In *Floor Games,* Wells bemoans the lack of civilian miniatures for imaginative activities, but in *Little Wars* he gives himself, his children, his visiting friends, and his readers over to the delights of an ever-popular pastime.[1] A self-proclaimed pacifist, Wells imagines that war games can be useful sublimations of the real thing; he fantasizes putting "this prancing monarch and that silly scaremonger, and these excitable 'patriots' and those adventurers, and all the practitioners of *Welt Politik,* into one vast Temple of War, with cork carpets everywhere and plenty of little trees and houses to knock down, and cities and fortresses, and unlimited soldiers," to "let them lead their own lives there away from us" (98–99). Eighty years after Wells and with the benefit of hindsight, I picture this vast Temple of War as five-sided, inordinately expensive, and hardly self-contained; Wells, however, considers that in it "war, done down to rational proportions, and yet out of the way of mankind," might be "played" (99). And he assumes that his warmongers would all discover—having played Little Wars, and been subject to "difficulties and confusions among even the elementary rules of the Battle"—what a "blundering thing Great War must be. . . . not only the most expensive game in the universe, but . . . a game out of all proportion" (100). Then they would study war no more.

In his introduction to the facsimile reprint of *Little Wars,* Christopher Ellis points out that Wells was not alone among his contemporaries in being interested in toy soldiers and war games; Robert Louis Stevenson, for instance, published a magazine article about *his* war games in 1898. Indeed, the evocative possibilities of toys of all kinds permeate several of Stevenson's essays and poems, two of which deal with toy soldiers. Stevenson's poems emphasize an insurmountable distance between these figures and their owners. In "A Martial Elegy for Some Lead Soldiers," the narrator notes that "Death grimly sided with the foe, / And smote each leaden hero low." In the end, his sympathies lie elsewhere:

> But while unmoved their sleep they take,
> We mourn for their dear Captain's sake,
> For their dear Captain, who shall smart
> Both in his pocket and his heart,
> Who saw his heroes shed their gore,
> And lacked a shilling to buy more." (426)

A second poem, "The Dumb Soldier," imagines the experience of a toy soldier whose narrator-owner has buried it in the new-mown lawn and hopes to resurrect it after the next mowing. The boy does not expect to have any inkling of the soldier's experience:

> Not a word will he disclose,
> Not a word of all he knows.
> I must lay him on the shelf
> And make up the tale myself. (403)

A boyish longing for communication emerges from this somewhat bathetic poem, but Stevenson, unlike other authors with whom I deal in this chapter, is unable to imagine these figures that fascinate him as subjective beings: the fantasy realm in which toys come alive is not one he enters in his fiction, although he shares his contemporaries' nostalgic engagement with war toys and games.

Fascination with toy soldiers is, of course, not limited to Wells and Stevenson's era. Isaac Asimov introduces the facsimile edition of *Little Wars* with these words of longing: "Ah, for the innocence of 1913, when men could still, in all honesty, think of war as an exercise for tin soldiers." Asimov describes the nostalgia for war's "dangers and the daring and the gallant defeats and the clever stratagems, and the final triumph" that prevailed among Wells's generation in England, which had enjoyed peace of unprecedented duration. Asimov continues: "But the year after 1913 was 1914 and it was then that man's innocence vanished forever." Like Wells, Asimov nevertheless yearns for play war: "Why can we not innocently play at it once again in the fashion of an older day, and kill our plastic soldiers with wooden pellets, maneuvering them through a countryside of cardboard and harmlessly expend the aggressive passions we must somehow control?"

To understate the case, the twentieth century has indeed not proved itself peaceful and in control of aggressive passions, even after the end of the war to end all wars. Yet Wells's and Asimov's sublimation theory of war games continues to attract proponents, who debate those who would see children socialized without war toys. These pacifists were particularly strong in the wake of World War I, when, Chris Hedges notes, "British companies that had done a brisk business before and even during the war found the public less receptive to toy soldiers. . . . Firms expanded their output to include toy farmers, complete with village idiot." As the "village idiot" reference suggests, proponents of peace toys have not only had to fight arguments based on what is assumed to be human nature but frequent ridicule as well.

Ridicule wins out in Saki's story "The Toys of Peace," in which boys given a set of "peace" toys (including municipal buildings and lead figures of a sanitary inspector, a district councillor, an official of the Local Government Board, and the like) rename the characters and turn them into war toys: "'[Madame de Maintenon] begs Louis not to go on this expedition, but he turns a deaf ear. He takes Marshal Saxe with him, and he must pretend that they have thousands of men with them . . . ' " (445).[2] "So it goes," as Kurt Vonnegut's narrator has frequent cause to remark in *Slaughterhouse-Five.*

Post–World War II war toys from GI Joe to the latest state-of-the-art paraphernalia of the Gulf War continue to enrich the military toy establishment, while video display terminals replace tabletops and floors as the settings for war games. As Stephen Balkin, proprietor of a Madison Avenue store catering to toy-soldier collectors, told Chris Hedges, reporting for the *New York Times,* "I do not promote war. . . . I sell toy soldiers. I sell imagination."

So do writers about toy soldiers, of course, and my prime interest here is what imaginary goods Andersen, Clarke, and Banks are offering. As a matter of fact, when I contemplate toy narratives in which the toy combatants themselves are protagonists or interact with preadolescent boys, I am struck by the way these tales emphasize not so much the power as the vulnerability of toy warriors. Frozen into drill or battle stance, the toy soldier, equipped— as many are—with undetachable weapons, would seem the ultimate war toy, brewed up in some Celtic cauldron or grown from dragon's teeth with no other purpose than fighting. And yet paradoxically, these miniature beings (in contrast to toy weapons alone) may move the beholder by their apparent weakness and the bravery with which they endure it.

I am not alone in my sympathy nor is it only women writers like Clarke and Banks who consider that our attraction to toy combatants goes beyond interest in battle maneuvers and war games; G. K. Chesterton, as nostalgic as Wells and Stevenson, remarks about Andersen's "The Steadfast Tin Soldier": "[Andersen] suggested, in the true tradition of the folk tales, that the dignity of the fighter is not in his largeness but rather in his smallness, in his still loyalty and heroic helplessness in the hands of larger and lower things" (quoted in Bredsdorff 325). I do not think, however, that empathy with the helplessness of the tiny soldier need be an example of the "romantic militarism" Chesterton explicitly endorses in this same statement; rather, it is a natural reaction to an intricate anthropomorphized miniature living being. Chesterton's use of the hands image in this passage is important.

When an adult or child picks up a toy soldier, which is typically two to four inches tall, and holds it in the palm of his or her hand, gazing at its little face and the details of its uniform, I suspect that a near-universal urge manifests itself to project upon it hopes, fears, joys, bad dreams, indigestion, and guilty desires. Above all, the holder imagines its feelings of powerlessness, its dependence even as a combatant not only upon its imagined commander but upon the god that holds it and creates its character and story. Miniature soldiers thus arouse feelings of affinity, as well as of power and control, especially when the models are of creatures that in real life are proportionately bigger, sometimes *much* bigger and more powerful than the person holding them. Jonathan Swift explores relative size in both its political and emotional dimensions by depicting Gulliver as both "holder" and "held" in the first two countries of *Gulliver's Travels,* Lilliput and Brobdingnag. Children, like young Alice in her Wonderland adventures, surely sense the politics of size even more than adults do.

Moreover, in addition to empathizing with the vulnerability of these objects, the beholder may also sense that they have an elusive life of their own. In *On Longing: Narratives of the Miniature, the Gigantic, the Souvenir, the Collection,* Susan Stewart uses *The Return of the Twelves* to delineate the role that miniature size itself plays in stimulating dramatic imagination: "The miniature becomes a stage on which we project, by means of association or intertextuality, a deliberately framed series of *actions.* That the world of things can open itself to reveal a secret life—indeed to reveal a set of actions and hence a narrativity and history outside the given field of perception—is a constant daydream that the miniature presents" (54).[3]

Andersen Hears Voices

Hans Christian Andersen's tales bristle with a consciousness of secret lives that remain hidden from human beings not only in objects modeled on human beings, like tin soldiers and China shepherdesses, but in shirt collars, teapots, scraps of pigskin, tops, and balls. Getting to know the entire range of Andersen's tales is to plunge oneself into a near-schizophrenic awareness of multiple tiny voices competing for attention—animism run riot, but lacking pagan divinity. States H. Joseph Schwarcz:

Andersen's animated man-made objects inhabit a strange land. They are alive, so it seems; they are personified and equipped with human attributes; they are conscious of their existence; they contemplate their experiences and become wiser for doing so; they are very sensitive creatures. On the other hand, though, they are wrong in assuming that they are important to man; they are alive, but they are so much wrapped up in their narcissistic memories that they never realize that they are not free to act; they strive for independence but fail to attain it. . . . They are alive enough to lead their illusory existence. (79)

Schwarcz goes on to speculate about Andersen's "existentialist" attitude toward objects without taking what would seem the next logical step—to consider how his scenarios reflect upon *human* existence and perhaps humans' false sense of significance.

"The Steadfast Tin Soldier" (the epithet is sometimes translated *dauntless* or *staunch*) is a good case in point, since unlike the object-protagonists of many of Andersen's other stories—the self-important shirt collar, for instance—the soldier is made in human form and sympathetically portrayed. But the one-legged soldier who falls in love with a paper ballerina pirouetting on one leg is at the mercy of a jack-in-the-box troll and various little boys, who force him to fall from his home and go sailing through the gutters (where he is eaten by a fish) and who finally throw him into the stove, where he melts into the shape of a heart. In this regard, the children who "own" him are apparently no more responsible than the street children who set him afloat: all act to reduce the toy soldier to yet another symbolic object; however, it is at least an object that his own loving subjectivity seems to have determined. The heart shape is the one transcendence that Andersen allows in a world of gratuitous acts in which no creature seems to make contact with any other. Boy and tin soldier seem irrevocably and mutually other—socially if not actually incapable of communicating. The soldier, for example, does not feel that it would be "proper" to call out when he falls from the window. Finally, the more powerful creatures, natural or supernatural, behave like wanton gods. Distance between animated man-made objects and human subjects thus tends to prevail in Andersen's tales. This detachment may reflect Andersen's view of human relationships to God or to powerful worldly beings.

As in many of Andersen's other stories concerning animated beings, romantic love, seen through male eyes, is important here. Biographical explanations are frequent in discussions of this element of Andersen's work, although many of his motifs may be traced to folk sources. Andersen's fictional toy soldier, for whom there is no known source, was probably created in the mid-1830s when Andersen was about thirty years old and reputedly recovering from a romantic disappointment. But rejection by the love object is not explicit here, as it is in another of Andersen's toy narratives, "The Top and the Ball," where the snobbish Ball, made of Moroccan leather, refuses the advances of the shabby Top, who gradually becomes more elegant as he is refurbished by various owners. Nor is the Tin Soldier anything but faithful to his first love object, unlike the Top, who enjoys his retribution against his former love when she is old and shabby and lying in the gutter. Rather, Andersen's reputed propensity to unsuitable and unrequited love is given its most attractive, regenerative form in the Tin Soldier's romantic stoicism. Andersen does not even make much of the ballerina's possible indifference or even falseness, which is only suggested by the fact that she, unlike the soldier, leaves not a heart behind in her fiery grave, but rather a tawdry spangle. The suitability of the love object and the insignificance of the toy soldier in the face of the menacing forces that control him do not necessarily make the tin soldier any less heroic; but they do permit ironic readings.

Some ten years later, a possibly more mellow Andersen wrote "The Old House," in which a toy soldier is portrayed much less sympathetically. He is as self-absorbed as many of Andersen's other object protagonists are. This tale is reputedly based on Andersen's own experience of receiving a toy soldier from a young fan; it features a neighborly little boy giving a toy soldier to an elderly man. The human world is more positive, the object less attractive here than in "The Steadfast Tin Soldier": the boy appears sympathetic, the tin soldier a narcissistic solipsist. The toy's vulnerability is clear, but it is neither the center of the story's interest nor a catalyst for the development of the boy's sensitivity to others. The caring relationship lies between the boy and the old man.

Although the character of the protagonist in the "The Steadfast Tin Soldier" is closer to that of the toy soldiers in twentieth-century toy fantasies than is that of the egocentric toy of "The Old House," Andersen does not generally distinguish toy characters from other man-made objects or take advantage of opportunities for depicting either human development through relationships with toys or toy development. With the exception of the hero of "The Steadfast Tin Soldier," Andersen gives consciousness and voice to powerless objects without making them particularly attractive. And although he animates them, he never permits toys to tell their own stories in the lengthy and apparently unmediated fashion of the Kilners' protagonists or Hitty. In other words, animistic as Andersen's tales appear, and wide-ranging as they are, they operate in a relatively narrow range with regard to toy narratives. Had the steadfast tin soldier in his uncomplaining vulnerability been able to interact with the caring boy of "The Old House," their story might have prefigured the toy-soldier tales of the mid-twentieth century.

The Return of the Genius Children

In order properly to introduce one of these twentieth-century tales, Pauline Clarke's *The Return of the Twelves,* I must go back to 1817, the year that the Danish Hans Christian Andersen was twelve years old, when in northern England Charlotte Brontë was born. In rapid succession her mother, Maria Branwell Brontë, then bore Patrick Branwell, Emily Jane, and Anne before she died in 1821 at the age of thirty-six, leaving the care of the four toddlers (as well as two older sisters, who died in adolescence) to her clergyman husband, the Reverend Patrick Brontë, a maternal aunt, and a servant.

Hardly the hovering parent, Patrick Brontë rarely interfered or even concerned himself with the creative, communal life his younger children early established for themselves, based at first on imaginative "plays" involving a set of wooden soldiers given to Branwell by his father in June 1826, several weeks before his ninth birthday. In play, these figures, known as "The Twelves," were shared with his sisters, as earlier sets had not been. In 1941 Fannie Ratchford, in *The Brontë's Web of Childhood,* related how communal play with these toy soldiers had inspired a massive juvenilia, recorded in minute handwriting in small books, some of which are now on view in the Brontë Museum at their old home, Haworth, and in rare book libraries.[4]

The original wooden soldiers have long since disappeared. For my purposes, they are of even greater interest than the manuscripts because of the light they throw on how toys may inspire narrative dramatization and then become unnecessary to it.[5] In the case of the Brontë children, the wooden toys themselves seemed to be in use for over a year. Each of the children pretended to control his or her own island inhabited by people ten feet high, ruled by his or her favorite soldier in one guise or another; by December 1827 these islands were identified as "real" places: the Isle of Wight for Charlotte, Arran for Emily, Guernsey for Anne, and the Isle of Man for Branwell. Activities on the islands became more involved and their inhabitants were drawn from the children's eclectic reading: historical, political, military, and travel, as well as fictional.

In 1031, Branwell wrote that he still had the original Twelves and some other toy figures, including some ninepins from a miniature bowling game that apparently doubled as Ashanti warriors; Barbara and Gareth Lloyd Evans note, however, that as early as 1828: "the reality of the toy figures probably mattered less. . . . Instead of, or more likely, as well as actively playing games with the figures, the two eldest children began not only writing about them but, what is perhaps more important, writing as though they were the characters themselves" (158). The Brontës also wrote stories for their characters to read, reputedly written by the characters themselves. Two of the more widely known and more informative of the juvenile volumes are Charlotte's "History of the Year 1829" and Branwell's "History of the Young Men Volume I in Six Chapters."[6] The children, probably inspired by the *Arabian Nights,* imagine themselves appearing to their fictive inhabitants of "Angria" in the form of powerful Genii—Branii (Branwell), Tallii (Charlotte), Emmii (Emily) and Annii (Anne)—who can control weather and fates and bring dead soldiers to life.[7] All the children took their creations seriously; they have trouble pulling themselves mentally and emotionally away from these imaginary countries to live in the "real" world.

This large body of juvenilia in both prose and poetry—strange, wonderful, and convoluted as it becomes, with a cast of characters far exceeding the original Twelves—forms a backdrop for a modern toy narrative based upon it: Pauline Clarke's *The Twelves and the Genii* (1962), called in the United States *The Return of the Twelves* (1963).[8] The paths of inspiration are somewhat circular: inspired by actual play with toy soldiers, the Brontë juvenilia depict characters who are neither miniature nor toys; the juvenilia in turn inspire a later writer to write a fantasy about the Brontës' original toy soldiers, which come alive in the mid-twentieth century in the attic of a house near Haworth in the hands of an eight-year-old boy named Max Morley. Clarke's book, unlike the juvenilia, thus deals with toys who are or come alive. So rather than featuring stories about fantastic people that were originally inspired by toys, as in the juvenilia, this narrative highlights toys that come alive as flesh and blood, although one of the rules of their coming alive, as Max quickly discovers, is not to treat them as toys.

Max is the same age Branwell Brontë was when he received the Twelves from his father, and *The Return of the Twelves* uses the meeting of the boy and the toy soldiers as the occasion for Max's gaining power over others—previously denied him as the youngest child in the family—and for developing his creativity, as well as his concern for other beings. During the course of the story, Max learns enough about the Brontës to identify with Branwell and to wish to help the Twelves return to Haworth, now a museum. The sometimes contradictory feelings of power and empathy that I discussed as being aroused by miniature soldiers are given full play here, while the text exploits existential ramifications, which, in Clarke's text, are at first implicitly associated with institutionalized Anglicanism, but which appear to widen almost pantheistically to include "all God's creatures great and small."

Branwell's original story, "History of the Young Men," which interests Clarke more than Charlotte's "History," does not govern Clarke's plot, but it is embedded in the fantasy premise and becomes a virtual ontological myth in the same way that "The Story of the Hard Nut" operated in Hoffmann's *Nutcracker*.[9] The modern-day plot is itself complex; the narrative consciousness changes toward the end, when the soldiers go off on their own and the reader no longer perceives them through Max's consciousness.

After Max discovers the soldiers he learns that they not only unfreeze into flesh and blood but that they already have names, personalities, an adventurous history, and a well-established hierarchy, with a Patriarch, Butter Crashey, and four kings, all of which come from their original roles in the

Brontës' plays. Max decides to keep their coming alive his secret and maneuvers to stay home alone with them in order to take them on an expedition to explore the house.

This first adventure, which is cut short by the early return of the family, establishes several basic ideas with regard to the Twelves. One is that they prefer to go places and do things on their own, although they will make use of physical aids that Max ingeniously provides for them, such as a string tied along the rungs of the banister that they can shinny up or down. They are also enthusiastic eaters and drinkers and makers of mirth when they can find the food and alcoholic beverages (the family sherry on this occasion). Most significant, Max can use a type of mind control on them—he imagines scenarios for the soldiers to follow in order to get out of scrapes, which they perceive as part of their own subjectivities: Stumps, a soldier who is trapped in the kitchen by the unexpected return of the older Morleys, makes his way back to Max's room by the means that Max imagines for him. After further discussions with the Patriarch, Max realizes that he is taking the same role as the Brontë Genii, who had the power of "making alive"—that is, the power to bring supposedly dead soldiers back to life—in imagining similar activities.

Pressures within and without the family threaten Max's secret; after an American professor, Seneca Brewer, offers five hundred pounds for the Brontës' toy soldiers, Max and his sister, Jane—who has now seen them as well—decide that if these are indeed the Brontë soldiers they belong in Haworth.[10] The soldiers, hearing Max and Jane discuss this, decide to return to Haworth on their own, and here the narrative switches point of view; the consciousness is now that of the soldiers, who, after several perilous episodes, try to signal Max, through reciprocal mind control, to help them on their way and to find Stumps, who has managed to become separated once again. Max receives their message, and he discovers that his dreams tell him how the soldiers left and where they are. He and Jane are thus able to find them and to rescue Stumps, who has encountered a talking Water Rat, after which they all plan a night march to Haworth.

To complicate matters further, or perhaps to complete the pattern of the four Brontës, Max and Jane are not destined to remain the only Genii. Their older brother, Philip, who had precipitated the crisis by writing Seneca Brewer that he knew where the soldiers were, follows his siblings and sees the toys alive. Overwhelmed and intrigued as well as guilt ridden, Philip offers to help get them back into Haworth. In the last hours of the toys' and children's march the local clergyman, Mr. Howson, a Brontë fan (or as Max first hears it, a Brontyfan, some kind of prehistoric creature) joins them. Several possible sightings along the route both by other, delighted children and by bemused adults add to the excitement and danger (and confirm the "reality" of the

"The Feast at Sandwich." From *The Return of the Twelves*.

fantasy). The Genii's scheme works: Philip, who has secreted himself in the closed museum, opens a window to admit them, Jane drums them in on the Ashanti drum brought back from Africa by their missionary ancestors, Max watches proudly, and Mr. Howson stands guard in religious awe. The Twelves have returned, or have been returned, depending on one's point of view, to Haworth, where they continue to come alive in off-hours of the museum (a topos in toy narratives) or for special audiences, like Max.

Critics have on occasion compared *The Return of the Twelves* to Mary Norton's Borrowers series, which involves a race of people about six inches high who live in the walls of houses and similar hiding places, dependent on the debris of human beings for their livings. The texts are alike particularly in their rural English country-house settings and in the effort to imagine what might be the experience of life at a small scale relative to human beings, animals, and natural or human-made objects. Power relationships between human beings and the Borrowers are of similar concern, and a young boy also functions as the chief human being in *The Borrowers* (1952). But the Borrowers as characters are realized in quite a different way from the Twelves, and they function in a fantasy that observes the logical rules of what fantasy theorist William Robert Irwin calls "the game of the impossible," where the reader has only to suspend disbelief for one premise—in this case that the Borrowers exist and are descendants of a race of small people that has gradually mutated to its present size—from which all else follows.[11] The Borrowers never existed as human-made objects, and the idea of their being put on view in a museumlike setting is made specifically repugnant in *The Borrowers Aloft* (1961). The fantasy situation with regard to the toy soldiers in Clarke's text is much more complex. Reversible metamorphoses from wood to flesh and blood, as well as the role of the human mind and imagination in their coming alive and functioning in an active way, contribute to this complexity.

Clarke really stretches the fantasy boundaries, opening up the text in an intriguing way, so that just when I have become convinced that the Twelves' existence depends upon human imagination I perceive that the fantasy has moved in the direction of religious allegory. Through Max's experience and Mr. Howson's comments, Clarke appears to be claiming that as human beings are to a Judeo-Christian God so are the Twelves to imaginative human beings. Howson exclaims in astonishment: "I cannot believe it, and yet here they are before my eyes. Such is the power of genius to make things alive. So do creative genii echo their Creator" (241). But if Clarke intends this story to be an allegory, it is a complex one. The teleological, or at least theological, picture is complicated by the fact that not only have the Twelves been able to turn the power of mind control onto Max but that at one point one of them, a soldier named Parry, accuses another, named Sneaky, of conceptualizing the Genii in his own ingenious image (212). This suggestion, which has some of the existentially upsetting potential of Tweedledee's statement that Alice in Looking-Glass Land is herself being dreamed by the Red King rather than dreaming of him, could be taken as an allegorical joke on the human condition of doubt (a joke more accessible to adult than child readers). Something weird happens to Stumps, as well, something only the reader witnesses, which is never known to any of the Genii. Stumps is rescued from drowning by a water rat, who speaks to him in Yorkshire dialect. This talking animal, who seems to have wandered into an allegorical fantasy about toys coming alive through the human imagination, operates on a different level of reality from that established earlier, in which animals and toys do not communicate.

The Brontës, who quickly moved from toy soldiers to humans in their plays, concerned themselves not at all with talking animals. I suggest, therefore, that Clarke here invokes not the Brontës' characters but the water rat who was hostile to Andersen's tin soldier, reversing that water rat's role, however, to posit, unlike Andersen, a benign rather than threatening universe.[12]

Perhaps Clarke envisions a god in nature *not* concerned with human beings as first priority—as conventional Western religions stipulate in their most androcentric moments—a god truly, not just metaphorically, concerned with the fall of the sparrow and other cosmic life beyond human needs, desires, and control.[13] Similar feelings seem to stimulate Max, early in *The Return of the Twelves,* to extend his concern beyond himself and his fellow humans: "Max wondered whether it felt terrifying to be so little in such a huge world, under such an enormous moon-washed sky! He thought of all the other small creatures, mice, toads, beetles . . . ants, spiders and furry caterpillars. No doubt to God, he, Max, seemed quite as small and needing help. He felt that he would like to protect all the creatures, and wondered who did" (66).

Indeed, animal imagery pervades the text. Watching the Twelves move, Max wonders whether their tiny sounds might not be mistaken for a rat, or "a thrush breaking a snail shell; or a woodpecker at a tree's bark" (15). Max himself becomes "stealthy as an animal" in spying on them. As he tries to approach them, "It felt to him as if they were keeping cautious eyes on him. It was like two cats casually looking away from each other, but really each wondering if the other were going to pounce. . . . They stopped. Froze, like a toad which freezes when you meet him coming along the lawn" (20–23). This posits a desire for alliance among all creatures, one that operates largely at a sensual level. The longing may govern the text's emphasis on the fleshliness of the toy soldiers in their animated state (which brings it into the complex realm of metamorphosis discussed in Chapter 4).

The reader becomes very aware that coming alive in this text means more than it does for Hitty, for instance, who never loses her physical woodenness; the transition is materially more than the awakening of consciousness for the toy soldiers. This coming alive may tie in with the Christian allegory: the Word made Flesh. But the explicit fleshliness that appears here seems more pagan than Christian. Jane, for instance, having "put her finger and thumb round [Butter Crashey's] body" and "felt the taut, thrilling wriggle of life," exclaims, "'Max, the *feel* of him'" (104). But there are still problems with a specifically allegorical reading. For not only do phallic possibilities intrude in this particular passage, but I find problems with regard to the Twelves' corporeality in the text as a whole.[14] Unlike characters developed in the Brontës' late juvenilia, who are eventually permitted access to love, sex, and indeed violence, Clarke's spunky little men (whose given ages vary between 5 and 104) are locked into only those carnal pleasures that are imagined, or more accurately, acknowledged, by Branwell and Max, two boys in latency. The soldiers are thus limited to oral delights and adventuresome gymnastics, so that this text seems unduly to honor developmental arrest. More generally, the complex, regressive, reflexive implications of constant metamorphoses back and forth from wood to flesh challenge the aspirations of this text to be allegorical in a specifically Christian rather than pagan setting.

But the inconsistencies in the text represent departures, more pleasurable than not, from what otherwise seems a too-pat evocation of a conservatively controlled world, where the distinctions between groups of human beings seem both more stereotyped and more noticeable than those between humans and toys or between toys and animals. There are still things undreamed in either Max's or Howson's philosophy—Stumps and the water rat have a kind of experience beyond the scope of an eight-year-old or a clerical mind.

As if to emphasize further possible ambiguities, Clarke employs a complex imagery in this book; in addition, she recognizes that language is rather comically slippery, as when Max hears "Brontyfan" for "Brontë fan." Language is often used as well to disguise motivation, as when both Philip and Max use big words as ploys to impress and persuade their mother. Elsewhere, letters to the editor and reports from the local paper suggest alternative and conflicting ways of perceiving an intertextual reality.[15]

The Return of the Twelves emphasizes the individual toy soldiers' vulnerability and thus suggests relinquishing the use of power that comes with relatively greater size and strength. Nevertheless, admirable messages given by attractively pacific interaction can be undercut by texts that, at the same time, continually set up groups of human beings as "other" to the sympathetic protagonists. Although in *The Return of the Twelves* the toy soldiers are not other to the human beings, nor the animals other to the toys, Americans are other to the British, and gender, race, and class distinctions among human beings subtly multiply throughout the text. I myself am used to being placed in the category of other by certain British texts, but I am forced to consider problematic a text that honors the subjectivity of wooden soldiers and admires their imperialist adventures in Africa, yet still offhandedly echoes self-righteous nineteenth-century missionary generalizations about the bloodthirsty nature of the religion of the defeated Ashantis.[16]

Clarke recognizes and works with the individual power relationship to be negotiated between Max and the toy soldiers. Unlike the Brontë characters (or the characters in Banks's books for that matter), neither the returned Twelves nor Max engage in warlike deeds, although Clarke perpetuates the memory of the soldiers' former exploits in Africa. In doing so, she opens the peacekeeping text up to broader power questions that can be raised about the soldiers' acknowledged and approved combative history in the Brontës' own literary exaltation of British imperialism and about how subsequent missionary efforts—like those Clarke assigns to Max's grandparents—aided this imperialism. Clarke plays on the present-day vulnerability of the miniaturized soldiers to elicit protective feelings toward them from the readers, as well as from the child characters. She does not acknowledge what I perceive to be the paradoxical aspects of this protective attitude by recognizing the bloody past that their uniformed figures may represent to others, who saw real ships that resembled the Twelves' *Invincible* land on their real shores.

Indians, Cowboys, and Patriarchs

More recent toy narratives by Lynne Reid Banks, *The Indian in the Cupboard* and its sequel, *The Return of the Indian*, are imaginatively and interestingly written, if not as complexly puzzling as *The Return of the Twelves*. But they raise difficult questions about narratives involving toy combatants: May a text that shows attractively sensitive relationships between boys and individual toy soldiers, thus presenting alternatives to warlike play, nevertheless undercut its pacific messages by presenting various groups of humans as other to the protagonist, especially through stereotyping? And—remembering how boys behave toward toys in Andersen's "Steadfast Tin Soldier"—Does such a text operate within the rules of patriarchal dominance, leaving vital questions about war and imperialistic ambitions unanswered? My answer is yes, on both counts.

Banks clearly employs different fantasy conventions from Clarke, avoiding both religious implications and certain complexities of bodily metamorphosis. In Banks's books, the child protagonists, preadolescent boys of Max's age or slightly older, are not Genii, and they do not engage in imagining or in creating the subjectivity of toy characters, or in employing mind control in a godlike way. Rather, in these works, the more conventional fantasy use of magic objects helps bring to life miniature beings—an Indian, his bride, a cowboy, a British soldier from World War I, and a nurse—who supposedly existed originally in another time and place. (Toys are brought to life by putting them into a wooden cupboard and locking and unlocking it with an ornate key—a family heirloom—or conversely, they are returned to their original form by the same method.) These characters from other times now interact as miniatures, in the present, with the boy characters. As such, they are snatched out of their original lives and involved in time travel at the whims of two preadolescent boys. In addition, in *The Return of the Indian*, the children themselves travel back to the time of the toys. Interaction with the toys who come alive helps resolve some personal problems in the life of the principal child protagonist as well, and he becomes artistically creative as a result of his contact with these miniature beings.

The fantasy premise of Banks's two novels is one that by its very nature brings to the fore questions of power that often operate in toy stories, and her narrative takes these issues seriously. As much as any owners of plastic or wooden toys, Omri, the main protagonist, and his friend Patrick are given absolute control over the present-day existence of miniaturized adults who had been engaged in real lives of their own, which are interrupted by these circumstances that they cannot control. What a desirable but scary proposition for any child! (Some of the books' attraction obviously comes from the dangerous subversion of parental roles implicit in these role reversals— reversals already present in having adult soldiers at a child's command.)

Added to this heady stuff is the volatile combination of cowboy and Indian, which also emphasizes, in postcolonial times, conflicts that are associated (like the battles with the Ashantis depicted in the Brontë juvenilia) with the armed subjugation and near extermination of indigenous peoples. Banks depicts a process in which newly empowered children—in particular the more sensitive Omri—are to be educated in the appropriate use of power over other beings. But in the background of this education of an individual lie historical global political and social issues that are rather superficially considered here but which any concerned reader may wish to explore.

Although initially prizewinners, for instance, the toy narratives have brought British writer Banks criticism about her insensitivity to issues in the depiction of Native Americans. Opal Moore and Donnarae MacCann quote Mary Gloyne Byler, a Cherokee Indian, who comments upon recent works about Amerinds in general: "There are too many books featuring painted, whooping, befeathered Indians closing in on too many forts, maliciously attacking 'peaceful' settlers . . . ; too many books in which white benevolence is the only thing that saves the day for the incompetent, childlike Indians" (26). Both troublesome elements, stereotypical depiction of race and patronizing attitudes toward Indians and "others"—the second more subtle than the first and, unfortunately, perhaps endemic to these toy narratives— seem present in Banks's books.[17]

Fatal perhaps to the cause of taking seriously the adulthood of the Iroquois Indian, Little Bear, and his desperate fight for the survival of his tribe against the French and their ally Algonquins in his "real" life, is the guttural movie-Indian English given him to speak. His speech infantilizes him, along with the fiercely combative and impulsively "savage" attitude he maintains throughout both volumes. The depiction of Little Bear is more stereotyped than that of the Cowboy, who has an unmanly tendency to weep in sad moments. But the latter's alcoholism seems troublesomely, obviously "adult," involving the child protagonist, Omri, in stealing from the family liquor cabinet to feed the Cowboy's thirst—an act treated as nurturing but questionable in terms of the educative process.[18] The developing friendship between the two traditional enemies seems to break down some barriers and give the appearance of more pacific possibilities, even though the volatile Indian, in his impulsive reaction to a film of cowboys and Indians on television, almost fatally wounds the Cowboy.

An antiwar stance might also be sensed from the fact that the British medical-corps soldier whom Omri and his friend Patrick bring to life to help heal the injured Indian is killed by a shell in his "real" World War I world. Omri's terrifying experience of watching helplessly a battle in the French and Indian War between the Iroquois, "his" Indian's tribe, and the Algonquin might also support an antiwar stance. But it is undercut by the portrait of the Iroquois in this battle, who, inexperienced in estimating the range of the guns that Omri and Patrick have provided them, encircle the Algonquins (the French invaders of native America are mysteriously missing) and not only destroy them but shoot and kill each other. Of course, damage from "friendly fire" is not limited to inexperienced Indians. The deaths of the Iroquois at their own hands are used here, however, to emphasize the wrongness of the boys' interference in a past battle largely because the Indians themselves cannot be trusted to get it right.[19] This again infantilizes the Indians.

Banks makes obvious attempts to have Omri and Patrick treat their miniature friends with respect and adopt responsibilities appropriate to dealing with live beings; food gathering, shelter, and health problems play a more realistic part in these texts than in *The Return of the Twelves*. Efforts to move toward a concept of blood brotherhood are partly obviated, however, by the savage, childish, or inept characteristics imposed upon the miniature figures. In addition, during crises, the boys clearly bring to life the plastic adult toys according to the needs of their more powerful selves, thus exercising a power at least as conscious—and even more direct—than that of Max and the other Genii.[20] Patriarchal patterns appear, as in this scene in the first book when the Indian and the Cowboy come to blows:

The next moment each of the men found himself pinned down by a giant finger.
    "All right, boys. That's enough," said Omri, *in his father's firm end-of-the-fight voice.* "It's a draw. Now you must get cleaned up for school." (emphasis mine, 103)

If in the attitude toward the Indians a philosophy of the White Man's Burden seems finally to prevail, a more generalized patriarchal stance appears as well, made to seem both natural and irresistible in a situation where size differences operate, where Indians mess up battles, where cowboys drink and weep, and where plenty of models of benevolent dictatorship are available in real life. The Cowboy is likely to die in an alcoholic stupor. And those who know what happened to Little Bear's descendants when they trusted the Great White Fathers—those patriarchs who sometimes turned a benevolent face toward them—cannot avoid a grimace at the end of *The Return of the Indian,* when Little Bear holds his recently born son "high in both hands, as if offering him to the future" (189).

Alert as they may be to problems in Banks's texts with regard to the Amerind, Moore and MacCann seem not to notice hostilities toward "others" of the same race as the protagonists, but of a different sex or class. In the present of *The Return of the Indians,* Omri and Patrick "borrow" a toy nurse from Patrick's nasty female cousin, battling her physically in the process. Later Omri, newly returned from the hideous Indian conflict, uses the toy combatants to fight with some "skinhead" adolescents whose resemblance to the Algonquins is easily discerned. The "lower-class" local boys have been bullying Omri as he returns every day in uniform from his public school; when they attempt to rob his house, they "naturally" must be met by force. "Others" begin to multiply, and violence rather than conflict resolution prevails. The division into "us" and "them" happens so easily. Little wars sprout up all over.

Clarke and Banks clearly see the possibilities toy narratives have of helping young boys become nurturers, as well as find satisfying means of individuation. These authors understand family dynamics: the important boy protagonists are the youngest children of three. Their ability to keep the secrets of their toys' coming alive and to deal with those toys in relatively responsible ways is not only somewhat subversive of family hierarchies based on age and size, but also helps the boys to become imaginatively creative. Max finds unusual ways to solve problems, Omri writes a prizewinning story about his experiences.

I begin to think it not enough to reject arguments based on human nature, like Saki's in "The Toys of Peace," or on the sublimation of hostile instincts through nostalgic little wars, like the ones postulated by Wells. It is not even enough to substitute for these depictions of boys acting relatively nonaggressively with toy combatants, to the extent that Clarke and Banks have managed to do. For they too conform to patriarchal assumptions, and their use of toy figures who come alive supports these assumptions on a communal level while subverting them somewhat on the familial. Notions of male hierarchy permeate the texts—Omri is named after an ancient king; Butter Crashey is the Patriarch. In addition, Clarke deliberately invokes the Judeo-Christian tradition of the omnipotent male god. Finally, the might of the godlike toy "owner" is curbed solely by goodwill toward little creatures, a phallacy of power politics that supports every "benevolent" dictatorship.

The family hierarchy is, indeed, not the only one at stake. Omri and Max, the principal male white middle-class British protagonists are—like Pinocchio at a very different class level—depicted at Erikson's preadolescent stage of industry.[21] They are thus learning to take their appointed places in the hierarchical world outside their families. In modern wars they, in contrast to young men of color or of the working class, are not likely to become cannon fodder. Born to a class of powerful patriarchs, they may, however, have many future opportunities to display toward "others" less fortunate than themselves the behavior they practice in dealing with their vulnerable toy combatants. Perhaps fortunately for boys like these, they can take for granted the benevolence of their system. Moreover, they can often write off its oppression as "testing" and imagine that everyone has an equal opportunity to pass these tests. Here the protagonists are not encouraged to examine these underlying assumptions or how such constructs govern their own behavior toward the less powerful "others."

An outsider like Andersen, poor himself in his early life, may have been desperate to join this system, but had reason to know and portray ambivalently the behavior of powerful boys, men (and women), or spirits of the universe in "The Steadfast Tin Soldier." In spite of their probable experiences as women within the patriarchy, neither Clarke nor Banks seems to have Andersen's consciousness of how difficult it is to join the system and how arbitrary if not malevolent can be its testing. So, in the last decade of a singularly bloody century in which men and boys have played war games with both flesh-and-blood soldiers and civilians without regard to sex and age, I must ask: Can texts like *The Return of the Twelves, The Indian in the Cupboard,* and *The Return of the Indian*—which embody so many patriarchal constructions—even ask the right awful questions that lie behind peace as well as war, much less answer them?

6 The Doll Connection

She crept out from under the table on hands and knees, made sure once more that nobody was watching her, then darted quickly to the doll, and seized it. An instant afterwards she was at her place, seated, motionless, only turned in such a way as to keep the doll that she held in her arms in the shadow. The happiness of playing with a doll was so rare to her that it had all the violence of rapture.
—Victor Hugo, Les Misérables

This attic was Maggie's favourite retreat . . . and here she kept a Fetish which she punished for all her misfortunes. This was the trunk of a large wooden doll, which once stared with the roundest eyes above the reddest of cheeks, but was now defaced by a long career of vicarious suffering. Three nails driven into its head commemorated as many crises in Maggie's nine years of struggle . . . [now she] soothed herself by alternately grinding and beating the wooden head against the rough brick of the chimney.
—George Eliot, The Mill on the Floss

If we are to believe numerous autobiographical and fictional accounts of childhood, the doll, created in the unsexed image of the human yet by custom and imagination usually considered female, is, beyond all other play-things—teddy bears, toy tigers, or toy soldiers not excepted—the most capable of arousing a child's violent longing or loathing. Accounts like the two quoted above often depict not only intense absorption in the doll but abusive acting out of negative emotions on its body. Modern empirical studies of larger groups of children, particularly but not exclusively boys, confirm the tendency to turn physically violent toward dolls.[1]

Narratives in which dolls come alive demonstrate too the intense complexity of this relationship between child and doll by presenting a range of negative as well as positive directions it might take when the dolls themselves are permitted to respond to the love, hate, or ambivalence that children have directed toward them. Some of the texts examined in this chapter, Richard Hughes's *Gertrude's Child* (1966) and Rumer Godden's *The Dolls' House* (1947) and *Impunity Jane* (1954), were chosen for their imaginative concern with the doll-child relationships, as well as for the way they show the conflicts that often arise in these relationships' being resolved. Three texts (even combined with a number of other doll stories that are briefly analyzed throughout this study) cannot adequately represent the range of emotional territory explored by the many doll narratives or the psychological, social, or literary contexts from which such narratives arise, but they do offer insight into the kinds of issues that appear in doll literature.

The Doll as Transitional Object

The assumption that little girls will be socialized by being provided with the dolls denied their little brothers unduly focuses attention on the relationship between child and doll as a proto-maternal one, ideally characterized by nurturance and care.[2] Such a limited point of view both tempts the reader to assume that abandoned, abused, and needy Cosette in *Les Misérables* will be a "natural" mother and warns her or him that the abusive antics of Eliot's Maggie bode ill for her future children. Indeed, some often-quoted lines from *Les Misérables* seem to argue for the primacy of the maternal in the relationship between doll and girl: "A doll is one of the most imperious wants, and at the same time one of the most delicious instincts, of the feminine child. . . . The first child is a continuation of the last doll" (390).

Closer examination points to the oversimplification embodied in the girl as mother, doll as child formula. In her introduction to *The Silent Playmate,* Naomi Lewis states the antimaternal case emphatically: "Make no mistake— unless this happens to be the play of the moment. . . . the child is not the parent of the doll, nor the doll the child of the child." Lewis goes on to discuss the doll as "the first really private and personal friend and ally," as "both playmate and confidant in a problematic world" (8). Further understanding of the girl-doll relationship emerges from reading Frances Hodgson Burnett's autobiography, which depicts her doll as playing heroine to Burnett's hero in the scenarios little Frances created for her. Rather than accepting the female roles, many of them passive, suffering, or martyred like Mary, Queen of Scots, Burnett shoved them off on her doll while she herself played powerful male rescuers. Burnett's contemporary E. Nesbit, a fellow writer of superb children's stories, claimed never to have been able to love a doll in her life, but there was one doll of whom she writes, "I made her play the part of heroine in all my favourite stories" (quoted in Doris Langley-Levy Moore 25).

Responding to the dictum about girls and dolls laid down by Hugo's narrator, Valerie Lastinger demonstrates that *Les Misérables* illuminates a relationship between doll and girl of far greater complexity than Hugo's narrator acknowledges. Indeed, Lastinger notes, Hugo's Cosette is depicted as treating the doll given her by Jean Valjean as a grown-up mentor and guide; Cosette names it Catherine but also calls it "*the Lady*." She does not treat the doll as an object to cuddle as she had previously cuddled a small sword (sharp enough to cut fruit) or the doll that she briefly kidnapped from her more privileged foster sisters.[3] Hugo (as Lastinger reads him) and Lewis thus see the relationship between girl and doll as positive even when it is not maternal. Hugo even implies that the child-doll relationship reverses conventional interpretations: the doll becomes the lost, idealized mother to the motherless Cosette.

This case of doll taking the part of mother is hardly unique; the baby doll arrived late in doll history (early nineteenth century), and dolls frequently represent the noninfant female in any of her socially constructed (or literary) roles. Extending the examination to accounts of child-doll relationships that involve boys makes the doll's adult role particularly clear. Autobiographical and fictional accounts of child-doll relationships are not limited to those between girls and dolls. And these accounts of boys and dolls suggest the need I find in other toy narratives to return to the preoedipal period of object relationships in order to estimate the strength of children's feelings toward dolls. In the process of examining the doll as transitional object, it seems to me, we can also get a sense of the oedipal origins of the sexual differences in relationships to dolls carried into the period of latency.

I have already discussed Winnicott's theories with regard to transitional objects: here I would like to add some telling information about his own childhood relationship to dolls, taken from Clare Winnicott's "D. W. W.: A Reflection." She quotes a love letter her husband wrote her in 1950 describing a dream revelation about his own transitional object:

"Suddenly you joined up with the nearest thing I can get to my transition object. . . . There was a very early doll called Lily belonging to my younger sister and I was fond of it, and very distressed when it fell and broke. After Lily I hated *all* dolls. But I always knew that before Lily was a quelquechose of my own. *I knew retrospectively that it must have been a doll. But it had never occurred to me that it wasn't just like myself, a person, that is to say it was a kind of other me, and a not-me female, and part of me and yet not, and absolutely inseparable from me. I don't know what happened to it. If I love you as I loved this (must I say?) doll, I love you all out. And I believe I do.*" (emphasis mine, 31)

Clare Winnicott also quotes from Winnicott's description of the time he took his croquet mallet and "bashed flat the nose of the wax doll," Rosie, that belonged to his sisters. As Winnicott describes this doll abuse, he attributes it to his resentment of his father's teasing, and he recognizes that he was really angry not at Rosie but at his father, and violently so.

Who could resist here an oedipal reconstruction of the child-doll relationship? Winnicott's early transitional object is a doll who, like the mother, is female—"part of me and yet not." His father seems to be taunting him by singing a ditty about a relationship with another doll (mother?) who may not love him, making the boy feel so angry that he takes a scaled-down phallic weapon, "my own private croquet mallet (handle about a foot long because I was only 3 years old)" and smashes Rosie since he, of course, cannot smash his father (who must have had a full-sized croquet mallet). Then too, after Lily fell (or was she pushed?) and broke, Winnicott forever hated all dolls.

The sadness of the violent rejection of the female, not just the mother, and perhaps sisters as well, but the female as part of the self, a rejection supposedly required of young boys in accepting their inability to fight their fathers for the favors of the mother, goes unremarked in these reminiscences. Rather, Winnicott's "all out" love of Clare, which he equates in part with his early love of the first, transitional doll (the one that Lily approximated but the only one that satisfactorily negotiated the growing separation between Donald and his mother) marks the healing reacquisition of the female in the form of the "other," as projected by the Freudian oedipal paradigm. Like the Nutcracker with Marie, Winnicott has been lucky.

Other male reminiscences add resonance to the concept of preoedipal experiences of dolls that are subsequently buried. In a strange essay that meditates upon wax dolls, Austrian poet Rainer Maria Rilke (1875–1926) relates his own hostility to them in terms more metaphysical than psychological. He suggests, nonetheless, the depth and frustration of what seems like a transitional relationship with a doll in which it, unlike other play objects, made no response to his needs but instead made undue demands on him—forcing him to do all the work in the relationship in his endeavor to bring it to life: "With the doll we were forced to assert ourselves. . . . It made no response whatever, so that we were put in the position of having to take over the part it should have played, of having to split our gradually enlarging personality into part and counterpart; in a sense, through it to keep the world, which was entering into us on all sides, at a distance" (45). This marred transitional experience is rejected by the grown man in words that sound like Winnicott's "hatred of *all* dolls": "If we were to bring all this to mind again and at the same moment to find one of these dolls . . . it would almost anger us with its frightful obese forgetfulness, the hatred, which undoubtedly has always been a part of our relationship to it unconsciously, would break out, it would lie before us unmasked as the horrible foreign body on which we had wasted our purest ardour" (45). The silence of the doll is compared to the silence of God.

Toward the end of Rilke's ruminations, he describes the dolls of childhood as sexless, with "no decrease in their stagnant ecstasy, which has neither inflow nor outflow" (50). Yet all the anger of the rejected lover (or son?) seems to emerge from these pages, which take a directly gender-linked point of view at only one point: "Are we not strange creatures to let ourselves go and to be induced to place our earliest affections where they remain hopeless? . . . Who knows if such memories have not caused many a man afterwards, out there in life, to suspect that he is not lovable? If the influence of their doll does not continue to work disastrously in this and that person, so that they pursue vague satisfactions, simply in opposition to the state of unsatisfied desire by which it ruined their lives?" (46–47). I cannot escape the sense that Rilke—who, after a brief marriage led a markedly reclusive life—is, indeed, as he writes, "confronted and overwhelmed in the end by [the dolls'] waxen nature" (50), which brings back memories of a failed transitional experience.

My own sense of the importance of the buried memory of relationships with dolls in the psyches of grown men and its probable symbolic significance was further enhanced by the discovery that a doll apparently haunted adventure writer H. Rider Haggard, whose misogynistic tale *She* hit the bookstands in 1887 and became an immediate best-seller. In *Sexchanges*, Sandra M. Gilbert and Susan Gubar analyze this work as "a definitive embodiment of fantasies that preoccupied countless male writers who had come of age during a literary period in which, as Mario Praz remarked . . . 'sex'—and specifically the female sex—had been 'obviously the mainspring of works of imagination'" (6). Gilbert and Gubar see *She* as not only the product of a prevailing zeitgeist but as one based on Haggard's early experiences, "a complex of early private humiliations [that] might well lead to later fantasies about power and powerlessness" at the hands of a female. They note: "For instance, he had actually owned a fierce-looking rag doll that was used by 'an unscrupulous nurse' to frighten and bully the terrified boy, who therefore called it 'She-who-must-be-obeyed'" (25). Only many years later, in the conquest and ruin of the fictional She-who-must-be-obeyed, can Haggard get back at the rag doll and all the subsequent humiliators for whom she stands.[4]

Still another turn-of-the-century writer, D. H. Lawrence, in his autobiographical novel *Sons and Lovers* (1913)—a text that clearly depicts oedipal issues—includes a scene of hostility displaced onto a doll. Here the protagonist, Paul Morel, accidentally jumps on the face of Arabella, a doll of which his sister Annie is "fearfully proud if not so fond." Remorseful at the sight of his sister's initial grief, Paul persuades his sister to "make a sacrifice of Arabella" by burning her, which he "watched with a wicked satisfaction." The narrator continues: "He seemed to hate the doll so intensely, because he had broken it" (74). Grover Smith suggests that Arabella is a substitute for Paul's mother and that Paul's lover Miriam will be sacrificed for the same reasons (32).[5]

The weight of the anecdotal evidence suggests that dolls can be as significant in the early lives of boys as in the early lives of girls, but that dolls' later significance, after a boy's "successful" passage through the straits of Oedipus, is barely recognized. During latency boys may be permitted only an aggressively hostile relationship to the doll, which has become the epitome not only of the dangerous female "other" but of the even more dangerous internal female as well. Children's books about doll play are likely to show boys who will be boys as destructive. These children tend to resemble Sam, in Mrs. Ewing's "Land of the Lost Toys," who scalps his twin sister's new doll, fastening "the glossy black curls to a wigwam improvised with the curtains of the four-post bed in the best bedroom" and reenacts the Lisbon earthquake: "the whole toy-stock of the nursery sank together in ruins" (151, 155). Boys like Sam roam the nurseries of nineteenth-century doll stories. Their occasional reformation in the course of the story is, like Sam's, sufficiently detached to take away the onus of "playing with dolls." Sam, for instance, sets himself up as "Mr Sam, Dolls' Doctor and Toymender to Her Majesty the Queen, and other Potentates" with his sister Dot as assistant to do the dirty work, and receives "a fine box of joiner's tools as a reward for his services, Papa kindly acting as spokesman on the occasion" (182–183). Need I say more about the worldly rewards of a successful male oedipal passage?

The female oedipal passage, however, was believed by Freud to be abbreviated and incomplete, since the girl was required to internalize the female image, as well as compete with the mother for the father's love. As subsequent feminist revisionists have noted (if they accept the notion of an oedipal stage at all), this process is not necessarily a "natural" one and may be as complex and ambivalent for the female as it is for the male. Such ambivalence may be displaced in hostility upon the doll as transitional object that later represents the mother as well as herself to the girl.

Leslie Adrienne Miller, in a poem entitled "My Mother's Doll" (1990), suggests all the complexity of the primal relationship between girl and mother. The narrator's mother allows the child to lie in her bed and play with "Lilly / with her white china hands" only when the child is sick, "as if, in my weakened state / I could not hurt her." This trust proves misplaced: "But once I tipped poor Lilly / too far over on her head / and her blue glass eyes rolled back, / lost in her china skull." Although Lilly seems to be blinded by this act, the mother promises: "Someday when you learn / not to be rough with things / you will have my doll for keeps" (31). As the little girl caresses the doll's real hair, she imagines the sacrificial price of such a gift:

> I imagined [the hair] had come
> from a sick child like me
> who lay in her mother's bed
> holding just such a doll, gently,
> dying not to hurt her mother. (32)

Even as I typed these words, I shivered.

Still, unlike boys, girls have clearly been permitted to act out a whole range of emotions upon the doll over a much longer period of development. They can imitate the mother in their relationship to it, and they may consider it a projection of their own potential in all its guises, conventional and unconventional. They may also consider it nonfemale by fiat not phallus, declaring its gender (at least temporarily) to be male, especially when, as is the case with most dolls, only "the clothes make the man."

A girl's resistance to conventionally feminine identity begins during latency, when the social disadvantages of being a girl become clear. Tomboys do not play with dolls for many of the same reasons that boys in latency do not play with dolls—or with girls, for that matter. Boys, however, are rarely asked to play with dolls. Nesbit's and Burnett's gambits of requiring their dolls to take on all the undesired traits of their gender as powerless heroines is a neat, subversive way of gaining what may be perceived as masculine power within the confines of accepted play for young middle-class females.

Texts in which dolls come alive may give mixed messages about female power in a patriarchal world. In Julia Charlotte Maitland's *The Doll and Her Friends: or Memoirs of Lady Seraphina* (1852), the doll narrator claims: "I belong to a race the sole end of whose existence is to give pleasure to others." She further emphasizes the socializing functions of dolls: "Some will even go so far as to attribute to our influence many a habit of housewifery, neatness, and industry" (1). She delineates her "negative merits" as a role model: "never out of humour, never impatient, never mischievous, noisy or intrusive" (2). Clearly, here little girls should be more like dolls, whose histories should wipe all trace of pride and aspiration to power from their minds. One might cite a number of doll books, particularly the doll memoirs of the nineteenth century, that expect from the female an angel-in-the-house role and sometimes complete self-sacrifice.

Yet, even in the nineteenth century a rare literary fairy tale like Mary De Morgan's "The Toy Princess" (1877) overturned the image of the doll-like girl; in this case first by magical intervention of a concerned guardian fairy who whisks the princess away from the land in which no one is to show personal preference or emotion, substituting an obliging doll in her place, and then by permitting the real princess, grown to womanhood in relative poverty, to choose obscurity, work, and love over resumption of her royal doll-like servitude (see Zipes, *Victorian Fairy Tales*).[6] In the hands of a twentieth-century writer like Rachel Field a doll memoir may be used also to show that a wooden doll like Hitty can survive a hundred years as an unmarried woman and still be going strong. A similar message about potential female independence is given in Margery Williams Bianco's *Poor Cecco*—and denied in Carolyn Sherwin Bailey's *Miss Hickory* (see Chapter 8). Doll stories may support or subvert contemporary society's construction of female identity, just as little girls may use their dolls in conformist or subversive ways when playing out the scripts of everyday life.

The Doll as Other

A powerful literary rejection of socially acceptable femaleness—which reminds us that both racial and class strictures have an impact upon the function of the doll as well—appears in Toni Morrison's first novel, *The Bluest Eye* (1970). Her shocking story forces the reader to recognize that constructions of self and other are not based on gender alone: in the United States, race is a potent factor in identity formation. Morrison's story of a little girl's fall into madness brings to mind the studies made by Kenneth Clarke (used in 1952 to argue *Brown v. Board of Education*) that show that many black children considered black dolls ugly and chose white dolls as more desirable.

Morrison's exploration of constructed self-hatred begins early in the novel with a magnificent coda detailing the aversion of the narrator, Claudia, for the supreme Christmas gift of "a big, blue-eyed Baby Doll," which her loving parents assume is their little girl's deepest desire.[7] Claudia, however, recognizes the enemy when she sees her, in contrast to her friend Pecola, who by the end of the novel internalizes maternal neglect, paternal rape, and general societal rejection into a mad obsession for blue eyes and the sad conviction that she has magically acquired them.

Claudia's complaint against these dolls is multiple. First, she is not very interested in playing with dolls: "What was I supposed to do with it? Pretend I was its mother? I had no interest in babies or the concept of motherhood. I was interested only in humans my own age and size, and could not generate any enthusiasm at the prospect of being a mother." Then too she finds it "a most uncomfortable, patently aggressive sleeping companion. To hold it was no more rewarding." In fact, she has "only one desire: to dismember it." In this act she hopes to find the secret of its desirability, which everyone seems to see but herself:

I could not love it. But I could examine it to see what it was that all the world said was lovable. Break off the tiny fingers, bend the flat feet, loosen the hair, twist the head around, and the thing made one sound—a sound they said was the sweet and plaintive cry "Mama," but which sounded to me like the bleat of a dying lamb, or more precisely, our icebox door opening on rusty hinges in July. Remove the cold and stupid eyeball, it would bleat still. "Ahhhhhh," take off the head, shake out the sawdust, crack the back against the brass bed rail, it would bleat still. The gauze back would split, and I could see the disk with six holes, the secret of the sound the mere metal roundness. (20–21)

Such an orgy, of course, brings down parental outrage. But Claudia does not allow memories of her parents' anger to interrupt her complaints about their neglect.[8] Instead she describes other disappointing play experiences with the gifts of Christmas Day before returning to her argument: "I destroyed white baby dolls."[9] Like Winnicott, however, she recognizes her displacement of violence onto the doll, here "the transference of the same impulses to little white girls." She suffers mightily from the white girls' "magic": "What made people look at them and say, 'Awwwww,' but not for me? The eye slide of black women as they approached them on the street, and possessive gentleness of their touch as they handled them" (22). Claudia recognizes that later in life she took refuge from "the disinterested violence" of her hostility toward little white girls by adopting that exaggerated love for them that she noticed in the black women who neglected her in their favor.[10]

More remains to be said about the literary doll's appearance as other in terms of race and class, as well as gender. Class distinctions—often based on the origin of the doll and the material from which it was made—have always been exploited in doll books.[11] Like many other children's books of that period, doll memoirs of the nineteenth century were bent on inculcating middle-class values. Plain, sturdy dolls knew their places and criticized the pretensions of aristocratic but more flimsy elaborate dolls, as well as those of their aristocratic owners, with their weak morals. Charity was praised: dolls no longer in their first freshness and vigor were happy to comfort needy children in poorer homes rather than be relegated to the junk heap (a comedown similar to the one undergone by governesses past their prime). Says the sturdier of two dolls in seeing the fate of another: "We had entered the world together, her beauty and her fine dress had been the cause of her misfortunes" (Constable, *The Two Dolls,* 1846). The doll in Mary Mister's *Adventures of a Doll* (1816) is disappointed when she is bought by a young heiress rather than by a plainly dressed Quaker girl: "Although I slept in a bed of damask, and was dressed so splendidly, I was weary of belonging to so disagreeable a mistress" (9). In an 1879 story by Mrs. Castle Smith, Victoria-Bess, a doll from a Regent Street shop window, looks down at the ragged children who gaze adoringly at her, but having been mutilated by her first rich owner she is happy to end up in the arms of one of these street waifs, who loves her despite her appearance (in Avery, *Victoria-Bess and Others*). A sensational downward career leaves the doll in *Lady Arabella: or the Adventures of a Doll* by "Miss Pardoe" (1856) on a junk heap, from which she tells her clearly satiric story. She was bought by the the Honourable Miss Tantrum, whose mother, Lady Breezeby, in the course of the story runs away with another man, leaving husband, daughter, and vast debts behind. The doll ends in the arms of a poor crazed man whose wife has just died in childbirth and who thinks she is his dead baby; from the wife's deathbed she is thrown onto the rubbish heap. The wages of pride are inevitable.

In the twentieth century, class lines become somewhat blurred while race and gender lines remain. Even after black dolls began to be marketed, the toy fantasy tradition persisted in certain invidious distinctions. Many of these fantasized dolls are clearly of the "Aunt Jemima" type and as such play roles marked by society for black women—cooks and child tenders in particular. Dinah is such a doll in Josephine Scribner Gates's *Story of the Live Dolls* (1901). She cooks the picnic for the dolls and their owners and then is almost left at home. Fortunately, she is of the type often described as enduring, and she consoles herself by singing, "Der's a good time comin' by and by." Another such figure appears in Johnny Gruelle's 1920s Raggedy Ann series as "Beloved Belindy, a nice soft cuddly 'mammy doll' with lovely shiny pearl-button eyes and a wide smiling mouth" (*Marcella Stories* 17). Marcella, the dolls' owner, instructs her at one point: "'Now, . . . you are the mammy doll, so if any of the children need anything in the night, you must hop out of the bed and take care of them. Will you do that for me?'" Since, in Gruelle's fantasy, children do not know that their dolls can talk, Marcella answers for her: "'Oh yes, indeedy'" (39). In Anne Parrish's *The Floating Island* (1930), another cook doll, named, as usual, Dinah (after "Someone's in the kitchen with"?), rebels against her domestic servitude and seizes her chance to become queen of the monkeys (revealing other common racist associations) when her bourgeois doll "family" are shipwrecked.

Here, as in the society that spawned both texts and dolls, black female dolls are generally placed in roles convenient to those in power. After all, as young Joan points out to young Peggy in Mrs. Craddock's *Peggy and Joan* (c. 1922), "But Peggy, we can't have all the dolls for children; some must be the cook and maids" (59). (Without black dolls, other dolls may play these menial roles in doll books; they occasionally rebel also.)

Meanwhile, dolls representing the male other, either black or (occasionally) Asian, play familiar roles of another variety: would-be seducers of "fair" ladies. E. L. Shute's *Jappie-Chappie and How He Loved a Dollie* (1890), a charmingly illustrated book in verse, has "a moon faced little man / In garments loose and flappy," falling in love with "a lovely English Dollie!" He pursues his suit with a poem that she scorns: "'How could I e'er be seen with you, / Slit-eyed, moon-faced, and fat?'" But one day he rescues her from monsters, and she decides he is "'the best of men'" and promises to marry him. In contrast, Kenneth Grahame depicts a scene in "Sawdust and Sin," one of his *Golden Age* stories (1895), that permits no such misalliance. Grahame, not known for his racial tolerance, has a Japanese male doll dragged off by the family dog after a youthful onlooker imagines it to be engaged in sexual hanky-panky with an English doll (this scene is discussed further in Chapter 8).

A famous children's series of Grahame's period, however, successfully stretches conventional racial roles to the point of virtual biracial romance. This is the Dutch Doll and Golliwog series (1895–1910) by the daughter and mother team of Florence (illustrator) and Bertha (author) Upton. In five-line stanzas the Uptons tell in the initial book, *The Adventures of Two Dutch Dolls—and a Golliwog*, about two dolls that come to life at midnight on Christmas Eve and meet what they at first perceive as "the blackest gnome." After he reassures them with "kindly smile," telling Sarah Jane that he is "the 'Golliwog' my dear," he becomes their friend and constant companion:

> Their fears allayed—each takes an arm
> While up and down they walk
>   With sidelong glance
>   Each takes her chance,
> And charms him with "small talk." (24)

Their unconventional adventures last through some twelve further books where the two Dutch Dolls defy color lines in their flirtatious friendship with the Golliwog—who, despite his outlandish name, black skin, and unruly hair, is clearly a gentleman in both manners and somewhat dandified attire. The dolls cross gender lines as well, engaging in adventures that would hardly be considered ladylike. Peggy and Sarah Jane are indeed iconoclastic—naked when they came alive, they cut up an American flag for dresses: Peggy gets the stripes and Sarah Jane the stars. And Golliwog is

"Their fears allayed—each takes an arm." From *The Adventures of Two Dutch Dolls—And a Golliwog*.

neither an Uncle Tom nor a "sissy." When the toys gang up on him, he knocks them all down with snowballs, "for Five to one's not fair":

> "Vengeance," he cries, "I'll pay them out!"
> If girls will play with boys.
>   There's got to be
>   Equality,
> So he's for equipoise. (55)

I like the Uptons' stories but am sorry to say that the gentlemanly Golliwog—based on one of Florence's old dolls—appears even in these texts as an exception to the idea that the "other" is dangerous, as if he, following another proto-racist construction, is really "white inside." To confirm his position as an anomaly, later adventures like *The Golliwog's Desert Island* (1906) portray black "natives" in stereotyped ways, as Marilyn Olsen points

out. Moreover, the comic incongruity of his gentlemanly demeanor, combined with his minstrel-show features, could only, in a basically racist society,
lead to a degeneration of both his situation and his name—Golliwog—
which Florence apparently made up (a degeneration that possibly sank as far
as the derogatory epithet "wog"),[12] while commercial spin-offs made money
for others besides the Uptons. So, in an anonymous book of the period,
Dainty Dolly's Day, we have appearing the scene that lies in silence behind the
Dutch dolls' first meeting with the Golliwog: "Our dolly cried aloud in
grief / Her screams rang far and wide, / When the Golliwoggies' ugly
Chief / Did claim her as his bride." The message is clearly not that of *Jappie-
Chappie,* which, for all of its racist descriptions, has the "other" as good
rescuer. The Golliwog in *Dainty Dolly's Day* is the dark, monster other from
which a crew of British sailors must save the dainty dolly. And the Society for
Promoting Christian Knowledge published Mrs. Craddock's *Where the Dolls
Lived* (1920), in which a Golliwog is banished from the Smith family of dolls
as "dirty, vulgar, and ugly" (62).[13]

Perhaps the most effective if oblique way doll stories challenge racism has
been to emphasize the role that dolls themselves play as objectified other,
subject to the whims of the powerful. Such a concept appears didactically in
the anonymous English *A Doll's Story* (c. 1852). Two dolls, one of whom has
just been bought, are talking to each other:

"It is not pleasant to be sold, is it?" said little Minna; "so like slaves, of whom Emilie
often tells me tales as I sit in her lap."

"I never heard much about slaves. To be sure you don't mean *blacks?*" said Fanny. "I
hope you don't mean to compare pretty wax dolls to negroes! There was a doll or two
of that sort in the Exhibition, but we never took any notion of them."

"Did you not? Why, they were made of wax, I suppose, just like ourselves, and
Emilie says black slaves are made of flesh and blood just like herself, and that no one
has a right to buy or sell a fellow creature.

"You have some very odd notions," said the Exhibition doll. (8)

The wrongs more subtle than slavery, yet deeply affecting all children in this
society, have for the most part been ignored, however, or even perpetuated, in
narratives of dolls coming alive. When the child-toy relationship is central,
these narratives tend to depict white children relating to toys in plots and
settings that embody the traditional values and aspirations of middle-class
white families.[14]

The Battered Doll

Abuse is recognized and widespread in doll stories. In a horror story written
by Algernon Blackwood and included in Seon Manley and GoGo Lewis's

collection *The Haunted Dolls,* a child has a frightening relationship with a doll sent to kill her father. Her governess makes an observation about the maternal instinct and dolls that seems a perverse expansion of the dictum about dolls and the female propounded by the narrator of *Les Misérables:* "The maternity instinct defies, even denies, death. The doll, whether left upside down on the floor with broken teeth and ruined eyes, or lovingly arranged to be overlaid in the night, squashed, tortured, mutilated, survives all cruelties and disasters, and asserts its immortal qualities" (84).

Not just horror stories, but autobiographical or fictional accounts of intense child-doll relationships, as I have claimed, frequently depict these relationships degenerating into severe mistreatment of the doll. This abusive relationship is the concern of Richard Hughes's stark tale *Gertrude's Child* (1966). The tradition of the toy's revenge in which Hughes's tale falls is a strong one. In traditional stories of dolls coming alive the motif is usually more a matter of threat than actuality, unlike the mutilation and burning of dolls themselves in realistic fiction. Revenge may appear, as in Ewing's "Land of the Lost Toys," inside of a nightmare, for instance, from which the former abuser, now grown up and reformed, awakes at the crucial moment. I have found no story willing, as *Gertrude's Child* is, to carry to grotesque lengths a role reversal that reflects so clearly the phenomenon of actual child abuse, often implicit in the mistreatment of the doll—the opposite side of the idealization of the maternal in the child-doll relationship.[15] Nineteenth-century novelists revealed and reviled the child abuse permeating society at all levels—both on the streets and in the family. Yet at the end of the twentieth century parents and other adults can still treat children as badly as children treat dolls. Hughes's manipulation of the revenge motif in his fantasy offers an unusually explicit depiction of abuse as well as a sensitive reconciliation of the conflicting needs of nurturer and dependent played out in abusive relationships.[16]

Such a reconciliation might not seem characteristic of a writer whose best-known book is *A High Wind in Jamaica* (1928), in which a ten-year-old girl kills a man and then manipulates the justice system to convict an innocent one. Hughes shows little belief in the Romantic notion of childish innocence or in the capacity of society to recognize the truths behind its sentimental yet often corrupt view of reality. Nevertheless, his three collections of children's stories, *The Spider's Palace* (1931), *Don't Blame Me* (1940), and *The Wonder-Dog* (1977), show traits similar to ones in Andersen's tales: an interest in animated objects, a willingness to depict the grotesque, and an unsentimentalized compassion for children's bewilderment in an adult world.[17] Moreover, Hughes had a strong belief in the power of fiction to make the reader "apprehend . . . the fact that other people are not 'things' but 'persons'" (quoted in Thomas 1). In *Gertrude's Child* he chose paradoxically to have a "thing" recognize a "person" and vice versa.

The tale begins with Gertrude running away from an abusive owner, rejoicing in the fact that she is "made of wood and not easily hurt," unlike the little girl, whom she "*couldn't* be sorry for" (n.p.). But she becomes lonely, and fantasizes about acquiring a friend, "not a soft one of course, but a sensible hard one like herself." On the second lonely night she comes across an old man who asks if she would like a little girl of her own: "'*You* wouldn't belong to *her,* she would belong to *you.*'" He invites her to come pick one out at his shop the next day, and she chooses a little girl "with a happy look in her eye." Remembering her own experiences, Gertrude reasons that if "she's naughty . . . , I'll smack her and smack her and smack her!" although the old man warns her to be kind since children are not hard like dolls.

But once she gets the child home Gertrude treats her like an object, undressing her outdoors in the snow, impulsively cutting her hair ineptly, and insisting that Annie go dinnerless because she looks so unattractive. After neglecting Annie, she finally brings her to bed, where Gertrude exhibits the emotional turnaround familiar to dolls (and abused children), calling her "'Darling Annie,'" to which the child responds pathetically, "'Darling Doll! . . . How kind you are to me.'"

This familiar, alternately abusive and adoring relationship continues. When Gertrude gives a party for other toys and their children to celebrate Annie's supposed birthday, the now shabby child is not allowed to attend. But when a lion tries to eat Annie, Gertrude rushes to rescue her. The lion grabs Gertrude by the arm, at which Annie refuses to leave her, pelting the lion with snowballs; he retreats, after biting off Gertrude's arm and finding wood not good to eat.

Rescued and obviously aroused to a new level of understanding, Gertrude finds herself vulnerable to the pain of the missing arm: "Never in her life had she felt so *unwooden* as now! Indeed her gone arm was hurting her horribly—almost as if she wasn't a doll, but a person." A little boy belonging to the rocking horse is able to mend her with his carpentry tools (oh, those handy little boys!), after which she proposes a new idea to Annie: "'Listen. I think it's a stupid idea, dolls *having* to belong to children or children to dolls. Why can't they just be friends?'" Annie catches on quickly: "'And both look after each other?'" They go off, arms around each other's waists, traveling "that hard black road together. And the curious thing was this: Annie thought Gertrude's arm now felt soft, and warm—almost like the arm of another child: while Gertrude found Annie's arm comforting and *strong*—almost as if it too were a wooden one."

These grim details of parental neglect and abuse take place in a fantasy world that has its hellish aspects for Gertrude as well as for Annie: Hughes depicts in Gertrude a consciousness that recognizes both her own loneliness and the arbitrary, revengeful aspects of her treatment of Annie, so that the rescue of Annie from the lion and subsequent "softening" are part of a psychologically realistic process. Similarly, Annie's forgiveness of Gertrude despite Gertrude's neglect and abuse seems not just the usual self-sacrifice displayed by doll characters but also a familial loyalty familiar to those who know child survivors of such brutality. The healing solution achieved in Gertrude and Annie's friendship is not one that many parents and children involved in abusive relationships can reach without therapy, good fortune, and time. Yet in its fantastic way, this little tale suggests that the recognition by the parent figure of the source of her need for revenge and the depth of her own vulnerability may fruitfully combine with the neediness of the child and its willingness to forgive: that in their troubled relationship may still lie the psychic materials of a mutually strengthening reconciliation that has always been deeply desired by both. Hughes implies that survivors of child abuse may through denial become "wooden" and that this very woodenness may make it impossible for them to respond to their own children. The ameliorative ending proposes, however, that if children and parents travel together down a long dark road they can break the cycle of abuse, partly through recognition of the vulnerability of the parents and of the strength of children.[18]

Wish-Mates

Sentimentality about dolls and children is still so pervasive in contemporary culture that I wanted to detail the dark side of their relationships before attending to the positive aspects, also well-recognized in doll literature. In "Old Gutty," for instance, the first story of Arthur and Eleanor O'Shaughnessy's *Toyland* (1875), a cheap but sensitive gutta-percha doll shares the dying days of her loyal young mistress, who comforts herself by comforting the gradually disintegrating Gutty. Enys Tregarthen's *The Doll Who Came Alive* (1942) shows a neglected foster child, Jyd Trewerry, transformed by her experience in caring for a Dutch doll that she loves "into life." In turn, the doll—for mutuality appears in this relationship—rescues Jyd from her unhappy familial situation. The narrative is saved from sentimentality by the realistic depiction of the child's situation. But the aspects of fantasy wish fulfillment are obvious.

Much more subtle in their fantasy premises, but similarly positive about the power of loving and wishing, are the many popular doll stories written by Anglo-Indian author (Margaret) Rumer Godden (1907–), whose novels for

adults are also well known. I have chosen two of her doll texts, *The Dolls'
House* (1947) and *Impunity Jane* (1954), as representative.[19] Unlike the characters of some other doll stories examined in this book, who have adventures
and journeys independent of children, the "live" dolls in Rumer Godden's
works, with a few significant exceptions, are generally confined to the domestic, familial scene and integrally involved in the play of the child.

The toys' communication with the children on whom they know they are
dependent for mobility and the satisfaction of their material needs remains,
however, what might be dubbed telepathic rather than direct; as Godden puts
it in *The Dolls' House*: "It is an anxious, sometimes a dangerous thing to be a
doll. Dolls cannot choose, they can only be chosen; they cannot 'do'; they can
only be done by; children who do not understand this often do wrong things,
and then the dolls are hurt and abused and lost; and when this happens the
dolls cannot speak, nor do anything except be hurt and abused and lost" (13).
But dolls also have the power of wishing, which in Godden's work proves
itself a subtle yet potent force. These tenuous communications from the dolls
may be perceived as either pure imagination or psychological projection on
the children's part, although the weight of the fantasy leans toward volition
and consciousness on the part of the dolls, if not the actual power to act
independently found in Tregarthen's *The Doll Who Came Alive*.

As Margaret and Michael Rustin recognize in a thoughtful analysis of *The
Dolls' House*, issues that concern the development of young children are
usually woven into Godden's doll stories; these problems cross with the
differently patterned lives of the dolls. Such issues are more elusively drawn
in Godden's works than they are, for instance, in the works of Sylvia Cassedy
(examined in the next chapter). Godden's texts focus attention rather on the
solution to the dolls' problems, brought about with the help of the children;
somehow solutions to the children's needs and conflicts come in tandem with
the resolution of doll problems.

The Dolls' House introduces a doll "family" brought together in the nursery
of Elizabeth and Charlotte Dane, who have determined that Tottie, an old-
fashioned wooden "farthing" doll, be the daughter of Mr. and Mrs. Plantaganet and sister to Little Apple. As the designated older child, Tottie is the
mainstay of the family in a way dependent not entirely on the human fiat but
on her own clearly defined character as well. Mr. Plantaganet, her so-called
father, who has a china head and real hair, had been abused by his former
owners and is still timid; his "wife," known as Birdie, is a celluloid doll who
came as a party favor. Charming and flighty, she has something that rattles in
her head under her fluffy yellow hair. Apple, a tiny boy doll, is made of pink-
brown plush and is "irresistible," if often naughty. Darner, their dog, was
created from a darning needle backbone covered with wool pipe-cleaner legs;

he has a well-defined personality and warns of danger by growling "Prick." These dolls constitute a motley crew, brought together almost by chance (as doll families tend to be), but full of affection for each other in their appointed roles. As the story opens, they are hoping for a home of their own that will be larger than their temporary shoebox.

Tottie describes a home for them to wish for that she inhabited years before when she belonged to the Dane girls' grandmother and great-aunt. Unfortunately, it also contained an unpleasant doll named Marchpane, after "a heavy, sweet, sticky stuff like almond icing. . . . You very quickly got enough of it," as Tottie noted (27). As if in response to the family's wishes, the dollhouse, much in need of repair, arrives as the Dane girls' inheritance. Marchpane, who has been sent to be cleaned and renovated, will eventually join them as well.

At first the dollhouse does seem the answer to the dolls' prayers. And the younger human sister, Charlotte, shows some newfound leadership qualities in overseeing its cleaning, while the girls consider together grownup problems in its renovation and furnishing. As the children act and plan, the dolls watch eagerly, speaking to each other in counterpoint to the children's dialogue. Godden is extremely skillful in using this stylistic device suggestive of the silent, subterranean communication going on between children and dolls, but never made directly available to any of them:

"We shall do what other people do when they want things," said Emily. "We must make money."
"But how?" asked Charlotte.
"How?" asked all the Plantaganets.
"Somehow," said Emily. (47)

In order to obtain money for further renovation of the house, the sisters finally contribute Tottie to an antique doll exhibition, where she catches not only the attention of the queen but also meets up again with the haughty Marchpane, who is jealously determined to return to "her" dollhouse.

On her return home, Tottie joins the others in joyful preparation for Christmas. But the Dane sisters receive a package containing Marchpane (in addition to a toy post office for Mr. Plantaganet, who needs an outside occupation). Her beauty captures Emily's fancy, and Marchpane's invasion of the dollhouse begins, with Emily's forceful personality overcoming Charlotte's protests. The desperate conflict that ensues between Marchpane and the gradually dispossessed Plantaganet family is to some extent reflected in the children's disagreement and ensuing hostility over Marchpane's hegemony.

Yet the family of dolls does not lose faith in the hope of reform. Tottie, despite the fact she had previously misunderstood the girls' lending her to the exhibition as a rejection, states this faith explicitly: "We must be patient and go on wishing. One day Emily will find out she is wrong" (115). And Mr. Plantaganet, even though the girls seem to be betraying his family, defends them against Marchpane's disdain of children's play—play that, according to Godden, is the very stuff of the relationship in which children respond to the wishes of dolls and therefore make them come alive.

Nevertheless, the circumstances become more and more trying. The Plantaganets are relegated to the attic of the dollhouse while Birdie and Tottie are forced to play maid and cook and Mr. Plantaganet, butler. Only naughty Apple, with the manipulative power of the three-year-old, manages to carry on a relationship with Marchpane, who in her dog-in-the-manger way attempts to win his favor by spoiling him when she sees that Birdie and the others are concerned. Finally, Emily, still responding to Marchpane's wishes—which to some extent reflect her own needs for power over her younger sister—declares Apple to be Marchpane's child.

Charlotte, who was never under Marchpane's spell but is still under Emily's thumb, cannot right the situation in time to avoid the tragedy that occurs when Birdie rescues Apple (whom Marchpane had been neglecting) from the flames of the birthday candle that lights the dollhouse lamp. Birdie herself goes up "in a flash, a bright light, a white flame," her celluloid body consumed. Charlotte insists that this rescue is not accidental, persuading Emily that Marchpane deliberately took no part in it. Taking the initiative, Charlotte helps her older sister to recognize that the Plantaganet family, with their happy memories of Birdie's gaiety and warmth must be restored to the dollhouse proper and Marchpane donated to a museum, where a glass case would be entirely appropriate housing for her. The dollhouse is thus cleansed not only of dirt but of its hostile invader. And perhaps Charlotte has grown more bold and Emily more thoughtful through the experience.

The Rustins, psychotherapist and sociologist, interpret the activities in the dollhouse as very much controlled by the subconscious wishes of the children rather than by the wishes of the dolls, and the text certainly lends itself to this interpretation. The Rustins astutely observe how the contrasting settings of dollhouse and museum illuminate conflicting desires to relate to others and to dominate them. Such a conflict is played out in Emily's infatuation with Marchpane, whom they interpret as a projection of Emily's aggrandizing desires. The timidity of the doll parents is seen by the Rustins as not only a projection of Charlotte's timidity but a way of accommodating natural disillusionment with parents as they diminish in perfection in the developing child's eyes.

But Frank Eyre's perception of *The Dolls' House* as succeeding "brilliantly

. . . in depicting *adult* situations and conflicts" (emphasis mine, quoted in *Oxford Companion to Children's Literature* 209) seems equally astute. Godden balances child consciousness and doll consciousness in her depiction of doll play while manipulating the doll characters in a fantasy situation, making them play roles on her own creative agenda. As a consequence, her texts resonate with conflicts beyond the projections or perceptions of the child characters. Remembering the early dramatic doll play of Burnett, who also later wrote a socially satirical doll story, *Racketty-Packetty House* (see Chapter 7), we can see Godden too taking the next step in that creative play known as art: using doll characters to illuminate human roles—female roles in particular.

Like earlier writers of doll stories, Godden relies to some extent on the material substance of the individual dolls as a metaphor for their basic characters. For instance, to support the depiction of Tottie as a reliable, helpful older daughter, Godden builds on accepted ideas about the sturdiness and durability of wooden dolls. Like Field's Hitty, Tottie is a familiar doll type, who finds her emotional strength in her origins: "She liked to think sometimes of the tree of whose wood she was made, of its strength and of the sap that ran through it and made it bud and put out leaves every spring and summer, that kept it standing through the winter storms and wind" (12). Marchpane, the stereotype of the cold, vain, aggrandizing woman, finds all of her inflated self-esteem in the beauty of her materials—china, kid, and real hair—as well as in the fine clothes with which elegant and expensive dolls of her type were usually adorned so as to make them suitable playthings for well-to-do children. Her dislike of children could come from her fragility: she was not created for play but for contemplation. Godden does not make her pay the price of her pride at children's hands paid by similar proud nineteenth-century doll characters but lets her become instead an object in a museum—a fate that responsive and responsible Tottie could never endure.

In addition to being familiar contrasting doll types, Tottie and Marchpane are familiar contrasting female characters. With doll mother Birdie, however, made of cheap celluloid and of dubious origins—the kind of doll that is frequently described as working class in toy narratives—Godden departs from custom and stereotype. Her touching portrait shows a simple young woman, not quite right in the head, whose worth cannot be measured in terms of the usual material or practical values. Birdie's name suggests her bright, responsive spirit, and she is linked throughout with both feathers (Emily recognizes that she needs a feathered hat; Birdie adores her feather duster) and music (she hears the dollhouse bird singing; she responds with delight to the tinkly music box). She is further characterized by a full acceptance of the here and now and an intuitive perception of danger to her loved ones. Her self-sacrificing immolation in the candle that threatens her son Apple is celebrated in this text: she is given an immortality of spirit reminiscent of the fate of Andersen's Tin Soldier. A female character like Birdie is often marginal in real life, and her flighty "feminine" personality may present a problem for the feminist, but Godden's recognition of the doll's value should teach readers something about her worth.

Also important to recognize about these doll characters is that like other females (and many males) they are trapped in a world they have not made and over which they have little power—except, apparently, in the communication of their wishes. The sympathetic characters fight with Marchpane for a way of life that has its traditional aspects, but it is also one that values relationship and accepts differences in needs and abilities as well as in experience.[20] So these dolls do not play center stage simply to advance Emily and Charlotte's inner development and to reconcile their sibling struggles. They are characters in a drama of even greater implications and potential, of concern to adults as well as children.

Godden's fantasy premise—"Dolls, of course, cannot talk [to people]. They can only make wishes that some people feel" (12)—is applied in *Impunity Jane* as well, although the later book is much more untraditional than *The Dolls' House*. The break with tradition is announced in the first paragraph: "Once there was a little doll who belonged in a pocket. That was what *she* thought. Everyone else thought she belonged in a doll's house. They put her in one but, as you will see, she ended up in a pocket" (7). And although the development of a child protagonist is an issue here, Impunity Jane is still another doll whose needs are not a mere second to those of the child. She waits more than fifty years to make contact with a child who will meet her longings—not for domestic security but for worldly adventure: *he* turns out to be a rather sensitive, imaginative boy named Gideon. Their relationship and what it does for both him and her is charmingly unconventional, breaking gender roles to some extent.

By impulsive theft, Gideon rescues adventurous Jane from a dull life in a dollhouse with an indifferent owner. Her small eyes can see through the weave in the cloth of his pocket, and she loves his active play and all the mess of intriguing items that also inhabit his pocket, including a little snail whom Gideon has named Ann Rushout. Both Jane and Gideon are aware, however, of the unconventionality of their liaison: "Gideon was a boy, and boys do not have dolls, not even in their pockets" (27). He is particularly concerned that other boys will call him "sissy," especially the gang of boys that meet in his neighborhood, led by nine-year-old Joe McCallaghan, who "wore a green wolf cub jersey and a belt bristling with knives" (28). Gideon's worst fears seem realized when he is surrounded by the boys as he is mailing a letter and they search him; on finding Jane they react as expected until Gideon insists: "'She isn't a doll, she's a model. I use her in my model train'" (34). Joe, who has already shown signs of liking Gideon, is intrigued, and asks to take her down to the pond to sail her on a model boat: "Now began such a life for Impunity Jane. She, the little pocket doll, was one of a gang of boys! Because of her, Gideon, her Gideon, was allowed to be in the gang too" (36). Every adventure that Jane ever wanted comes true.

This bliss is briefly interrupted when Gideon makes a belatedly conscience-stricken attempt to return Jane to the inactive Ellen, from whom he had stolen her, but fate (or Jane's wishes) intervene when Ellen, before he can confess, offers him a choice of her toys, which she wants to give away. So Gideon and Jane's companionable adventures resume.

Jane's dependence on Gideon and the boys for adventure, as well as the inactive or conventional imaginations of the girl characters in the story, raises some feminist questions. However, as a text for young boys, the clear acknowledgment of Jane's femaleness, combined with her sense of adventure, makes her connection with Gideon a positive one: it opens those doors that have been closed to boys during latency as a result of their being asked to purge themselves of affiliation with the female. That Gideon has tried to do so is fully acknowledged by his worries about being a sissy. Jane's female presence—in his pocket, as it were—becomes a source of power for Gideon, opening up new possibilities not just for himself but for the entire gang of boys (whose leader has previously been well hung with phallic symbols: "he had every kind of knife, and he had bows and arrows, an air gun, a space helmet, and a bicycle with a dual brake control, a lamp, and a bell" [28]). Of course, the boys feel obliged to disguise their interest in and affiliation with Jane by calling her a model rather than a doll, but *model* has many meanings. Some may emphasize status as an object, but others refer to a standard of excellence worthy of imitation. Indeed, I see vital, free-spirited Jane—who declares early in the story, "A bugle, a horse, a bell, a shuttlecock—oh, I want to be everything!" (12)—as a good approximation of the Jungian anima, which Gideon, lucky boy, has not lost in the oedipal shuffle.

I suspect more girls are likely to read this book than boys. For them, Jane—clearly established as a strong protagonist in the first half of the text before Gideon appears—is not a bad model either. Her sense of adventure, impunity, and undomestic connection are worth emulating. Like Birdie, she is a blithe spirit, but unlike her she is a survivor.

Although in a few of her doll stories Godden depicts needy and/or angry and destructive children, on the whole the dolls themselves represent a range of human characteristics and possibilities. In spite of their prevailing middle-class domesticity, her doll narratives seem also to recognize on the one hand the desirable, yet perilous, security that domestic coziness affords (especially to unconventional females) and on the other, its customary stifling conformity. In this context, the dolls appear to be the embodiment of what Lynne Rosenthal, in an unpublished manuscript, considers Godden's prevailing theme: "Permeating Godden's writing is a faith that deeply felt wishes (which seem to serve as a form of prayer in her work), when allied with determination (devotion to one's integrity and goal) and will-power, will be rewarded by the universe and that, in many cases, the reward will extend beyond the individual to serve as a form of social Grace in which others are mysteriously helped as well." Clearly, Godden sees overt doll-doll connections (despite outer differences), as well as intuitive child-doll connections (despite their differences in "reality") as mutually rewarding, symbolic of the power to transcend the abyss between self and other and between the individual and the prevailing forces in the universe. For some of the writers considered here, connection with dolls serves troubled needs and exploits the weakest elements in human nature. For Godden, relationships with dolls can bring to the fore positive strengths and humans' most attractive, creative aspirations.

7 Magic Settings, Transitional Space

[The dollhouse] is the home, the evoked dream. . . . It is the old human dream of being small enough, Thumbelina on the lily leaf, Alice outside the passage leading to the garden. Now we are standing in the room in half-light; it is furnished strangely and enormously, the door handle is set very low down and does not turn, the stairs are steep and narrow, fierce red foil glitters in the back grate and the vast cups and dishes are painted with roses.
—Vivien Greene, *English Dolls' Houses*

There you were, gazing at one and the same moment into the drawing-room and dining room, the kitchen and two bedrooms. That is the way for a house to open! Why don't all houses open like that? How much more exciting than peering through the slit of a door into a mean little hall, with a hat stand and two umbrellas! That is—isn't it?— what you long to know about a house when you put your hand on the knocker. Perhaps it is the way God opens houses at the dead of night when He is taking a quiet turn with an angel.
—Katherine Mansfield, "The Doll's House"

In this chapter, I depart somewhat from the exploration of toy characters to consider narratives in which the setting itself seems to determine the nature of the experience, providing the appropriate space and time for magical adventures—not all of them pleasant. Such magic seems to be woven especially into dollhouses and appears occasionally in more elaborate, "found" constructions—to which I arbitrarily give the name *Spielstädte*, toy cities—

like the one that E. Nesbit actually built with her children and brings to life in *The Magic City* (1910). Although many dollhouse stories can be shown to illustrate this magic, as well as the capacity for dollhouse society to mimic society at large, *The Magic City* and Sylvia Cassedy's *Lucie Babbidge's House* (1989) merit closer reading, for in addition to offering magic settings, they seem even more clearly than Godden's doll stories to offer what Winnicott calls transitional space to a child protagonist in need of a link between inner and outer reality. Furthermore, participation in the making, furnishing, and demolition of the magic structures in both books—*The Magic City* in particular—helps the child solve its problems, which is a function Erikson assigns to toy play

"The Home, The Evoked Dream"

The lure of the dollhouse is one I know well. In Freudian terms, it may betray a longing to be small enough to return to the womb, as Vivien Greene implies in the passage quoted as epigraph. Katherine Mansfield suggests further that a powerful voyeurism is present in this lure (the same kind of voyeurism I enjoy when looking into lighted windows on nocturnal walks). Moreover, beneath the fascination of gazing upon other people's domestic arrangements lies a narrative impulse: to construct stories from these settings about the secret lives of their mysterious inhabitants.[1]

Since I have never owned or managed to talk myself into buying for my daughters the type of elaborate dollhouse that lends itself most easily to such fantasies, I began to indulge my adult self in museums, like the Thorne Rooms in the Art Institute of Chicago: a set of sixty-eight miniature rooms, viewed at eye level and constructed to suggest that each exists in its own larger indoor and outdoor miniature setting.[2]

The collection brochure states that their creator, Mrs. James Ward Thorne, was "attracted to the educational value of the period room—a room furnished in a style typical of a specific period and country." But the effect of these miniature rooms is much different from that of the typical life-size model. Beyond the educational or even the physical and aesthetic attractions of fine materials—crafted with exquisite and delicate fidelity to scale—lie the evocative qualities of these tiny spaces. They seem to be waiting for beings of a similar scale to enter from the doors through which one glimpses gardens and cityscapes, or from which one intuits hallways to other, unseen but imagined, rooms belonging to dollhouses of the mind. Or, from another perspective, the miniature rooms provide the "felicitous space" that Gaston Bachelard, in *The Poetics of Space,* requires to facilitate the imaginative faculty.

No matter how much museum literature might like to emphasize the educational "facts" about dollhouses, it often slips into anthropomorphism. I was particularly taken with this tendency in London's Bethnal Green Museum of Childhood, where I jotted down such exhibit descriptions as these: Of Mrs. Higg's House, "One Edwardian fireplace . . . is to be seen in the top-floor bedroom; the others must *have been modernized by the house's inhabitants*"; in Dudley Hall, "There are rather a lot of soldiers . . . *living in the house* and the domestic chapel on the top floor seems to be a Roman Catholic one"; in Mrs. Neave's House, "The rooms are badly proportioned. . . . Yet the dolls and furniture are good and harmonious, and *they have settled comfortably* into every available inch of space"; Mrs. Hibberd's house has an attic bedroom *"occupied by a deplorable young man who probably smokes and certainly drinks;* he plays the piano, guitar and accordion, and also has a fruit machine (from Las Vegas) and a superbly made Scrabble set (in the red box)" (emphasis mine). The introduction to the catalog, in keeping with this tendency, ends on a speculative note: "What remains the same . . . is the collections of exhibits, so the rest of this book is about them. Do they always remain silent and motionless behind glass? Or, when the front door has closed in the evening behind the last visitor, do the showcases fly open and toys scramble out to play? Visitors, unfortunately, will never know" (5).[3]

The child visitor is solicited by this catalog, but neither catalog nor exhibit description is addressed to children alone. Both partake of the same narrative urge that Dickens indulges in describing the dollhouses in Caleb's workroom in *The Cricket on the Hearth*: "There were houses in it, furnished and unfurnished for the Dolls of all stations in life. . . . Some of these were already furnished, according to estimate, with a view to the convenience of Dolls of limited income" (61). This passage suggests, in addition, the social structures that dollhouses reflect and the way income and class are mimicked in domestic arrangements in doll or human houses.[4]

Beatrix Potter's *Tale of Two Bad Mice* (1904), which uses the dollhouse to reflect socioeconomic distinctions, shows a rather remarkable resistance to the urge to bring dollhouse inhabitants alive. Supposedly written to celebrate the redbrick dollhouse constructed by her fiancé, Norman Warne, for a mutual child friend, Potter's text and illustrations seem, in fact, to do the opposite, subversively backing the *bad*, home-wrecking mice. Potter's dollhouse and the stiff dollhouse creatures, Jane and her cook Lucinda, "who" inhabit it, represent, with their beautiful but fake food that will not come off the plates, all that is bourgeois, repressive, and (to use a contemporary term) plastic in society.[5]

Tom Thumb and Hunca Munca, the mouse couple who try to make a home in the dollhouse, are frustrated by its fakery, yet they and their children triumphantly evade both the toy policeman and the more dangerous mouse-trap set for them; the restitution that they make at the end of the book seems less real than the glorious sacking of the house at the center of the story. As the illustrations make amply clear, Potter is willing to dress her natural creatures in human clothes, but she refuses to bring the dolls to life. The gift of speech enhances the vitality of the mice; nothing, Potter suggests, is real about human-made toys. (Curiously, the dolls look in the illustrations exactly like the intriguing dolls that come to life in so many other nineteenth- and twentieth-century stories.) So children are encouraged here to identify with the hearty, if naughty, animals, not with the overcivilized toys.

Potter's own experience of thwarted early life, which she sublimated into art and scientific research, would make the Victorian dollhouse seem as much a prison for her as it is for Henrik Ibsen's Nora.[6] Other writers, for whom the domestic past is still nostalgically attractive, exploit those anthropomorphic narrative urges when creating a dollhouse setting. In *Racketty-Packetty House* (1906), Frances Hodgson Burnett, whose better-known books include the romantically realistic novels *Little Lord Fauntleroy* (1885) and *The Secret Garden* (1911), shows no scruples about bringing dolls to life. As the novel's putative author, Crosspatch, queen of fairies, says: "If you think dolls never do anything you don't see them do, you are very much mistaken. . . . They can dance and sing and play the piano and have all sorts of fun. But they can only move about and talk when people turn their backs and are not looking" (5). Moreover, she maintains that agreeable dolls are assisted and visited by fairies while those that are "proud or badtempered" are dolls on whom the fairies "never call."

Burnett's two contrasted dollhouses, Racketty-Packetty House—old and shabby and now discarded to a corner of Cynthia's crowded nursery—and Tidy Castle—Cynthia's newly acquired, swanky dollhouse—are only as good as their inhabitants. In the former we find the old, unfashionable Dutch dolls: "You never saw a family have such fun. They could make up stories and pretend things and invent games out of nothing," so that "everything was as shabby and disrespectable and as gay and happy as it could be" (19, 24). In Tidy Castle dwells a stiff and elegant doll family not unlike the stiff beings in Potter's dollhouse, and fully as representative of correct, upper-class stuffiness. They are nevertheless "alive" enough to have a daughter, Lady Patsy, who falls in love with Peter Piper of Racketty-Packetty House. After all, as Peter himself notes, "'Ladies of high degree always marry the goodlooking ones in rags and tatters'" (61). His agreeable if eccentric family comes to the rescue of the Tidy Castle family after Cynthia decides to give the latter household scarlet fever and then abandons them in their delirium.

Although Harrison Cady's illustrations to the 1961 edition of this story enhance the elements of social satire, Burnett as usual romantically shows that although the upper classes may need to be educated by the lower, they can be reformed into enjoying fun and games. Unlike Potter (but like the fantasists explored in Chapter 8), she sees no objection to postulating close relationships between animals and dolls: two cock sparrows and a gentleman mouse keep wanting to marry several of the dolls of the Racketty-Packetty clan, who refuse to leave their happy family.

Rose Fyleman's *The Dolls' House* (1930) follows the same line of dollhouse adventures, with much the same initial fantasy assumptions (minus the fairies): "You see, most people who live in dolls' houses have a rather dull time. No lives of their own so to speak; or at any rate, only at night. All day long they have to stay where they are put and do just what they are made to do, and they hardly ever get a chance to do any of the things they really enjoy, because they never know when they may be disturbed" (2). Interesting social commentary appears when the daughter of the dollhouse family meets and then marries a Canadian Mountie doll, who will not take off his hat because there is "a price on [his] head" (40)—the type of pun that occurs frequently among the dolls. Pansy, his bride, states that "'where people come from'" does not matter as long as "'they are brave and good'" (41). But the story's democratic leanings do not apply to a family of black beetles who want to rent the dollhouse. They become that undesirable element, squatters, when they are refused admission to the nursery: "The news about the impudence of the black beetles soon spread over the whole nursery. Everybody was indignant about it. What made the nursery people even more annoyed was the fact, which they soon discovered, that there was not just one small family living there. The Jim Jettys appeared to have brought with them all their cousins, uncles, aunts, grandmothers, grandfathers, sons-in-law, and daughters-in-law. There must have been at least fifty of them" (76). The racial antagonism prevalent in human housing codes underlies the mystique of the bourgeois dollhouse.

Human beings feature only marginally in Potter's, Burnett's, and Fyleman's dollhouse tales, which also do not try to maintain that delicate balance between child play and dolls' coming alive that Rumer Godden establishes in her doll books. Of some considerable but different interest are those works that open up the dollhouses to human habitation (as Vivien Greene seems to wish they could be); these texts begin appearing in the mid-twentieth century. Among the earliest of these fantasies I have come across are the Five Doll series (1953–56), by Helen Clare, which is the pseudonym of Pauline Clarke, author of *The Return of the Twelves*.

In *Five Dolls in a House* (1953), the narrator notes, echoing Burnett and Fyleman, that when the child owner, Elizabeth, opened the front of the dollhouse, "nothing happened except what she made happen herself. But when the dolls were shut in and nobody stared, they did all kinds of things" (7). Elizabeth, however, suddenly finds herself able to enter the dollhouse, where she identifies herself as the dolls' "landlady," to whom they complain about the accommodations and the inedible food. She returns often, and she and the dolls have unremarkable domestic adventures, invigorated by playful use of language and the presence of a mischievous monkey who lives on the roof with his "invisible" friend, Hugo. Explaining Hugo's presence, the monkey tells Elizabeth, "'You have to make people up for when you're lonely'" (*Five Dolls and Their Friends*, 1957, 258). A fictional monkey thus explains his fictional friend to an equally fictional human being.[7] The author, who in *The Return of the Twelves* also speculates on the nature of reality, records the following metafictional conversation among the dolls involved in a theatrical performance of *Cinderella*:

"Oh, I wish I were in a play, Vanessa, I wish I could be," Lupin sighed as they arrived.

"Why perhaps we're all in a play, Lupin, who knows? I often wonder why I'm Vanessa. Perhaps people like it."

"They do," said Elizabeth at once, without having to think. "They like you all being you." (*Five Dolls and Their Friends*, 271)

Only minor crises occur in this domestic narrative, but this is not always the case in dollhouse stories, where the domestic can change quickly into the gothic, or as Freud would call it, the *unheimlich*—translated into English as "the uncanny," but also rooted in *heim*, that is, "home." About the most terrifying of such stories is William Sleator's *Among the Dolls* (1975). Sleator—a science-fiction author, pianist with the Boston ballet, and nonfiction writer about behavior modification—depicts his child protagonist, Vicki, playing roughly with an unwanted dollhouse. As she plays, the general atmosphere of her own house deteriorates, and nasty things happen to her family. She suddenly finds herself inside the dollhouse, where she discovers that the papier-mâché mother-and-daughter dolls who came with the house feel that they have been mistreated and plan to make her their slave. She further finds that her *own* house is a dollhouse in the dollhouse's attic. The dolls have been playing with *her* family. Eventually she manages to get back inside her own house and disassemble the dollhouse (in order to remove her house from its attic). Fortunately, her parents immediately return to normal and decide to sell the dollhouse. On a somewhat falsely didactic note, Vicki hopes that perhaps the next child to receive the dollhouse will play more gently with the toys and not have her experience.

Sleator plays on familiar motifs of role- and power reversal and doll revenge, like those found in Hughes's *Gertrude's Child*.[8] In doing so, he brings up existential anxieties about who plays with humans the way humans play with toys, but he contents himself with a superficial investigation of the psyches of his characters. The dollhouse itself becomes a potent object with magic powers to crystallize and magnify otherwise trivial domestic hostilities. The physical rather than psychic threats to the child protagonist caught in the dollhouse are the main disturbing element.

Other fantastic stories about dollhouses play on the theme of haunting— dollhouses modeled on houses in which unsolved murders have taken place become sites for replaying these murders. M. R. James's "The Haunted Doll's House" (published in Manley and Lewis) finds a none-too-ethical antiques dealer, Mr. Dillet, mesmerized and terrified by the murder that takes place in his bedroom when the gothic house that he has picked up cheaply comes to life with all its bygone inhabitants, as if "a real house, but seen . . . through the wrong end of a telescope." He discovers that the dollhouse comes from Ilbridge Hall, where suspicious deaths occurred that might be the originals of these scenes.

James is a writer of horror stories for an adult rather than a child audience, but writers for children also use the dollhouse for gothic effect. In *The Dollhouse Murders* (1983), Betty Ren Wright depicts a similarly haunted dollhouse whose nocturnal reenactments are witnessed by a child, Amy, in the attic of her Aunt Clare's house, which the dollhouse replicates. The scenes in the dollhouse replay and thus solve an old murder and free Aunt Clare from her guilt over a psychically disabling event of her adolescence.[9] Martha Bacon's *Moth Manor: A Gothic Tale* (1978) evokes like echoes of past hostilities surrounding a dollhouse and the dolls themselves. The gothic elements are somewhat toned down in this case and are not really scary, although they feature a vaguely menacing antiques dealer. The antics of the dolls are of the charmingly eccentric variety earlier embodied in Burnett's Racketty-Packetty House inhabitants and Clare's five dolls, which also takes away from the uncanny effect.

Marjorie Tilley Stover's *When the Dolls Woke* (1985), like *Moth Manor* and *The Dollhouse Murders,* makes much of familial inheritance and relationships between original past owners and present child inheritors of dollhouses. The modern child in this work receives a dollhouse made by an ancestor. It becomes apparent that she will not only be able to bring the doll inhabitants to life again but to solve an old mystery involving a treasure in the dollhouse itself.[10] The child, Gail, is a sturdy and determined child and, refreshingly in doll literature, does not recognize the class hierarchies among the dolls, putting the upper-class doll, Lady Alice (but not her husband!), to work in the kitchen. In keeping with this democratic attitude (if still patronizing), Gail also feels sorry for a black West Indian doll, Martinique, whom the other dolls ostracize. Through helping Martinique and making her feel part of the family, Gail brings about the desired denouement to the mystery as well.[11] The treasure-hunt plot at the center of Stover's dollhouse fantasy, unlike the stories of most such romantic fantasies, does not sanction the hierarchies and racism of the past.

Transitional Space

The narratives described above are evocative and interesting from general psychic and social angles. They do not tend, however, to use the dollhouse story to examine developmental needs and problems in the child protagonists, even when the relationship between the child and dolls evokes strong powers of imagination in the child.[12] In contrast, *Lucie Babbidge's House*, by Sylvia Cassedy, and *The Magic City*, by E. Nesbit, while quite different from each other, suggest deep desires beyond an immediate loneliness, played out in the magic spaces that dollhouses, or in the latter book *Spielstädte*, provide. When those structures seem to be designed or altered by the child to meet inner needs, I suggest they may also provide transitional space. In addition, these texts about older children seem to allow problem solving in this transitional space.[13]

After publishing a number of volumes of poetry for children and teaching creative writing in the New York schools, Cassedy (1930–1989) began writing novels for children in the sadly foreshortened fifth decade of her life. Her first novel, *Behind the Attic Wall* (1983), won great critical acclaim; her third, *Lucie Babbidge's House* (1989), was published posthumously. In *Behind the Attic Wall* an orphaned and much damaged child, Maggie, uses dolls found in an attic, and in *Lucie Babbidge's House*, a similarly circumstanced little girl, Lucie, uses dolls and a dollhouse discovered in a boarding-school storage room as transitional objects in transitional space. The child protagonists in both these novels seem in deeper and more desperate need than the misunderstood protagonist of *M. E. and Morton* (1987), the work that came between the two. M. E. finds relief not in playing with objects but in role-playing, a stage that Piaget considers more developmentally advanced in symbolic thinking. The protagonists' loss of their parents in the first and third novels seems to have demanded from them more psychically regressive tactics, but their ages permit them to move past this space when the time comes to abandon it.

Orphaned Maggie in *Behind the Attic Wall* is a desperately rebellious child, but her experience with the dolls in their houselike attic surroundings is not postulated as pure psychological fantasy. The dolls she finds in the attic appear to be virtual ghosts of two former residents of her great aunts' mansion (and their dog). Although her play with the dolls seems meant to compensate for the inability of her great aunts to deal with the vulnerability that Maggie hides behind the dirt, kleptomania, and insubordination that have previously taken her from boarding school to boarding school, she eventually finds nurturing refuge with a foster family, of which she is now able to take advantage.

Lucie Babbidge's plight as a seemingly passive sufferer with no family ties appears even more desperate than recalcitrant Maggie's. The strength of Lucie's defenses in this text become a plot device as well. The first part of the novel is largely confined to exploring her consciousness; the reader may suspect but will not know until the beginning of part 2 that the warm and loving family to which Lucie retreats after her excruciating school experiences at the hands of her smarmy teacher, Miss Pimm, and her fellow classmates is one she has created with dolls in an antique dollhouse she discovered in a storage room. She has maintained this imaginary after-school life for two years while to all outer appearances her "real" life has come to a standstill. Once readers recognize this fact, they must determine what is real in Lucie's sad life and what is imaginary or limited to Lucie's conscious and perhaps unconscious desires.

Lucie "really" lives at Norwood Hall—a barren, atmospherically Victorian yet apparently modern American establishment—among fifty other girls, who are probably also orphans, although the word is one, the reader is told, that is no longer used. The chapter that produces the bald revelation of Lucie's real surroundings bluntly describes the psychic evolution of the members of Lucie's doll family—Mumma and Dada ("which is what some children called their parents in a book she knew," 83), young brother Emmet (from a song), and sister Lucie (whose identification with the protagonist is obvious). Equally part of Lucie's inner as well as outer reality are the dolls Lucie makes from found materials—the maid Olive ("Once long ago, she had *eaten* an olive," 12), and Mr. Broome, the music teacher, both originally wooden clothespins. The bean that Lucie was supposed to plant in one of Miss Pimm's "miracle" botany projects (Cassedy is deadly on teachers), instead becomes a new dollhouse baby whom Lucie names Maud, after Tennyson's "Come into the Garden, Maud." (In the scene preceding Maud's naming, Lucie suffers an excruciating verbal paralysis; she cannot recite in front of her class even the first verse of this eleven-verse poem, but is later able to sing it in its totality to her "family.") The narrator also makes clear that the doll conversations, including the loving and accepting things that both Mumma and Dada say to Lucie, as well as Emmet's silly puns, take place only in Lucie's head. Moreover, the reader can discern that the dolls' activities are frequently based on the "adventures" of the four Pendletons in a stuffy British family story that Miss Pimm insists on reading to her class each year.

In counterpoint to Lucie's grim reality and her compensatory dollhouse fantasy, her intermittent daydream of a day at the seashore with a loving mother and father exists clearly as a memory of real but happier times some six years before, probably when she was about five years old. This enchanted day, preserved in Lucie's memory in all its initial glory, also includes a fantasy developed by her father, who describes for her a mermaid club in the middle of the sea and writes letters in the sand to be delivered by the waves to mermaids. Her father's mermaid story too provides material for Lucie's dollhouse play. But Lucie must eventually face the reality of the train ride that came at the end of that day—she must also reexperience the agonizing train crash that she survived but her parents did not.

Besides grim present reality, "make believe" dollhouse play, and warm as well as agonizing memories, this complex text also provides a layer of fantasy, where a blurring of inner and external reality takes place. The fantasy offers Lucie a magical, transitional space that resembles but does not replicate the fantasy space of *Behind the Attic Wall*. As the result of a letter-writing scheme set up by Miss Pimm, Lucie has begun receiving letters (which she enjoys but does not answer) from the charming and friendly twelve-year-old Delia Hornsby Booth, whose ancestor brought the dollhouse (a replica of her house in England) to America. The letters describe a setting and a family situation peculiarly similar to the one that prevails in Lucie's dollhouse. When Lucie tests that possibility by twisting Olive's arm, she is not surprised to hear from Delia that the Booths' maid has injured her arm. Parallels begin to build up beyond coincidence, so that the discovery of the dollhouse and the confiscation of the "real" dolls by Lucie's classmates puts Delia's real family in desperate peril. Lucie, in order to rescue them, has to abandon her passivity and "steal" the dolls back from a fellow classmate's desk, thus restoring order in her dollhouse. To protect Delia's family, she closes up the dollhouse that so magically seems to have come alive transatlantically. At the end of the story, Lucie not only comes to grips with her traumatic memories but actually replies to Delia's letters. She further abandons passivity when she decides to speak up in class, using the kind of punning language that will connect her to her classmates (who, though cruel, are in many ways as needy as she). She has previously reserved her wit for the voice of the doll brother, Emmet.

The text closes on an allegorical note: the beans that were planted by Miss Pimm's class in the first chapter have, by the last, gone through all the "miracles" that Miss Pimm promised and now have provided seeds for another planting. Miss Pimm's pompous lecture on this natural phenomenon concludes, "From death there is birth. . . . Always remember that class. From death there is birth" (242). Subversively inattentive, Lucie is busy secretly writing a letter to Delia, but the reader is clearly supposed to pay attention and connect this botanical miracle with Lucie's psychic rebirth, which has come about in part through the problem solving that the dollhouse life provided.

Cassedy's doll books insist on some space in which external and inner reality are blurred; like other dollhouse narratives in which toys come alive, they express this space in terms of the literary conventions of fantasy. In order to do so they not only use dollhouse settings but place their protagonists in larger surroundings that evoke familiar nineteenth-century British novels like *Jane Eyre*—virtually deserted mansions with something mysterious in the attic, or boarding schools for orphans—rather than the urban apartments and streets in which Cassedy's realistic middle novel takes place. Nevertheless, like her *M. E. and Morton*, Cassedy's doll fantasies share many aspects of what is known in children's literature circles as "the new realism" or "the problem novel"—in which a preadolescent with little help from the adults around her or him is forced to deal with a life crisis. The novels of Judy Blume are often used as examples of such texts. (In spite of their popularity, however, Blume's books tend to be condemned by educators and literary arbitrators alike as "biblio-therapeutic" at best and simplistic, unliterary ephemera at worst.)

Not only the fantasy element but the complexity of Cassedy's texts— particularly *Lucie Babbidge's House,* with an intertextuality similar to that of Pauline Clarke's *The Return of the Twelves*—seems to belie this comparison. Cassedy's books do, however, share one of the literary virtues of Blume's stories: an absolute ear for preadolescent dialogue in all its cruel scatological glory and for the sententious and cruelly insensitive speeches of those many uninspired adults who attempt to deal with them. This is only one of several scenes that illustrate Cassedy's talent for marvelous contrapuntalism:

"People who lose things," Miss Pimm told her, told the class, too, "don't deserve to own them in the first place."

"Remember when she lost her shoes?" Daisy whispered.

"And she had to go to assembly in her boots?" Charlotte whispered back. "And one fell off during the salute?"

"Except she didn't call them boots, she called them something else."

"Galoshes."

"Galoshes! That's the most disgusting word I ever heard. It sounds like something animals eat."

"Like something swine eat," Claire put in.

"Like something *she* eats."

"Hey, yeah. Guess what Goose eats for breakfast every day? Galoshes."

"*Cream* of galoshes, with mushed-up bananas on top, and turnips."

"No, kale."

"Lucie," Miss Pimm said, "suppose there had been a sum of money in that envelope. Think what misery your carelessness would have caused."

"Yes, Miss Pimm. I'll find it in just a moment." (50–51)

Cassedy also shows a clear eye for the physical manifestations of preadolescent distress, combined with an ability to capture the fresh perceptions and humorous musings of the intelligent and talented child.[14]

Spielstädte

E. Nesbit (1858–1924), a grand supporter of imaginative play in both her realistic and fantastic novels for children written in the early 1900s, might be horrified at any attempt to psychologize her texts. Still, a work like *The Magic City* lends itself to Winnicott's theories and perhaps fits them better than do the works of Sylvia Cassedy.

I find it hard to imagine Nesbit, who prided herself on being a tomboy, writing a doll story like Cassedy's or Godden's fantasies. In Nesbit's *Enchanted Castle* (1907), for instance, two children, tired of the strenuous magical adventures they are having, decide to find respite in doll play; as one says: "'We'll do the babiest thing we *can* do the minute we get home. We'll have a dolls' tea party. That'll make us feel as if there wasn't really any magic'" (147). Nesbit was not fond of dolls. Although Nesbit, like Potter might have had problems depicting dolls coming to life, she did in *The Enchanted Castle* toy with ideas of creation of a living being. The children literally create an audience for themselves: "The seven members of the audience seated among the wilderness of chairs had, indeed, no insides to speak of. Their bodies were bolsters and rolled-up blankets, their spines were hockey sticks and umbrellas. Their shoulders were the wooden cross-piece that Mademoiselle used for keeping her jackets in shape; their hands were gloves stuffed out with handkerchiefs; and their faces were the paper masks painted in the afternoon by the untutored brush of Gerald, tied on to the round heads made of the ends of stuffed bolster cases" (107).

Nesbit, whose fantasies often revolve around wishes that come true in far-too-literal ways, shows these "Ugly-Wuglies" coming to life in response to a wish on a magic ring. And it is not a pretty sight. The righting of this magic takes a number of adventures that include letting loose one of the "respectable" Ugly-Wuglies on London, where he clearly fits right in as Mr. U. W. Ugli, Stock and Share Broker—a transformation from empty old clothes to financier that Nesbit, one of the founding members of the Fabian society, apparently finds all too likely.[15]

One of Nesbit's friends from the socialist days of the 1880s was H. G. Wells. Both Nesbit and Wells later became intrigued with the idea of building, with the help of their children, elaborate models with which to play out equally elaborate scenarios, of the type H. G. Wells describes in *Floor Games* and *Little Wars,* his semiphilosophical how-to books. With *The Magic City*, Nesbit, by contrast, takes her Spielstadt and turns it into children's fiction. She there creates both magic and transitional space for her protagonist, orphaned Philip, and an opportunity for Philip to resolve imaginatively his sense of helplessness when his older half-sister, Helen, temporarily deserts him, leaving him in her new husband's house to deal with a new younger sister, Lucy, and a strange staff of servants, including an officiously cold nursemaid.

For this modern reader, the situation Nesbit creates is clearly a "family romance," heavily fraught with delayed oedipal tension. Helen, who is twenty years older than Philip, has been in loco parentis for many years and has proven a totally attentive parent: "She gave up almost all her time to him; she taught him all the lessons he learned; she played with him, inventing the most wonderful new games and adventures. So that every morning when Philip woke he knew that he was waking to a new day of joyous and interesting happenings. And this went on till Philip was ten years old, and he had no least shadow of a doubt that it would go on for ever" (1–2).

Into this edenic space comes a man "who was not one of the friends they both knew" (2). This person, whom Philip persists in internally dubbing "that man," devastates Philip, who does not know how to fight off this rival and largely displaces the oedipal conflict onto sibling rivalry with "that man"'s daughter: "He had to be polite to that man. His sister was very fond of that man, and this made Philip hate him still more, while at the same time it made him careful not to show how he hated him. . . . But there were no feelings of that kind to come in the way of the detestation he felt for Lucy" (8).

The change in their lives, so desirable to Helen and her suitor, seems to come about unduly quickly also, before Philip can marshal even the tactics of denial.[16] In spite of Nesbit's clear perception of the shock to Philip's system and her recognition of children's needs and longings, she is herself the product of a Victorian upbringing that does not regard children's priorities as capable of overriding familial plans, particularly those of the father.[17] Moreover, she is clearly more interested in writing a fantasy than a problem novel. So within the magic space created, she grants Philip all sorts of fascinating compensations and successful tests of his masculine competitiveness, which is expected to amply make up for Helen's temporary lapse in concern for him, as well as better prepare him to accept a father after years of edenic postponement of oedipal rivalry.

The fantasy does not have the vagueness that prevails in Cassedy's works, where ghosts and transatlantic connections form only a small, magic complement to the protagonists' compensatory or wish-fulfillment fantasies. Veteran fantasy writer that she is, Nesbit establishes her premises about the nature of the fantasy world that appears in and around the Spielstadt. The reader learns these rules at the same time as Philip does, as he interacts with the characters within the world. For Philip, unceremoniously dumped in his rival's house after the marriage, emphatically rejects the friendly advances of his new stepsister, Lucy, and after being left to his own devices with only the attendance of a disagreeable nursemaid, builds himself a compensatory structure into which by the rules of the fantasy he is allowed to enter.

He is also permitted all sorts of delights in the transformation of found objects into elaborate buildings, like the temple that is the first of his creations after he decides that Lucy's building bricks seem able to make only dull, factorylike buildings. The temple includes a bronze Egyptian god, with two silver candlesticks topped by chessmen as pillars, a pair of elephants from a Noah's Ark flanking the entrance, and "twenty-seven volumes bound in white vellum with marbled boards, a set of Shakespeare, [and] ten volumes in green morocco. These made pillars and cloisters, dark, mysterious, and attractive" (16). The rules of the fantasy also allow a variety of other settings for Philip's various adventures; even the sand castle and huts that he and Helen once built at the seashore reappear here, as well as an imaginary island created for just the two of them, of which Helen has made elaborately detailed maps.

Even more important, however, are the rules for entrance into the Spielstadt, which permit first Lucy and then a mysteriously veiled woman to enter this space after Philip does and which eventually draw in a dreaming Helen, as well as Caesar and all his legions (from a Latin book used in one building). The presence of Lucy, in particular, removes the fantasy from the realm of purely psychological fantasy, where the other characters, even if they are real people, are mere projections of the protagonist's psyche. By contrast, Philip has no control over Lucy's entrance or behavior; in fact, he leaves her behind in the magic space when he unchivalrously runs back to the real world to escape a danger to both of them. His return to rescue her when the whole household is frantically in search of her—she is now missing from reality— is the beginning of his psychic transformation and acceptance of a changed external reality.

In order to bring this about Philip must prove that he is indeed the anticipated Deliverer of the extended spaces Helen and he have created together,

"'Lor', ain't it pretty!' said the parlour-maid." From *The Magic City*.

whose created inhabitants have gotten into some trouble on their own. Lucy's presence is again necessary, for after she plays the part of a princess in the first of the seven knightly tasks that he is given, she refuses to assume the princess's passivity. She serves as a female corrective to the masculinist assumptions of the chivalric romance conventions on which Philip's testing is based. Indeed, she is responsible for accomplishing at least two of the tasks assigned him. Balanced against Lucy, however, is a veiled woman who appears on the scene as Philip's rival to the role of Deliverer. As "Pretenderette," she tries to interfere with the completion of the tasks until, defeated, she is unveiled to reveal the unpleasant nursemaid. Her punishment is to remain in the Spielstadt, "learning to be fond of people" (333).[18]

The various tasks and their solutions involve Philip and Lucy in complex fantastic adventures, among them freeing two populations of oppressed Spielstadter. In one case, Helen, who has come into the space in a dream, and Philip give up their special island to a group of child settlers. In most cases, both Lucy and Philip are aided by a talking parrot, a hippogriff (a flying white horse let loose from a book of fantastic creatures), and two dachshunds, Brenda and Max, whose personalities parody the self-indulgent, pampered female and the indulgent, strong silent male, respectively. In the novel's foreground, Philip must make friends with Lucy and fight the nursemaid (who seems like a "bad mother" figure who has taken the place of Helen). But what makes the Spielstadt true transitional space is what is in the background. In accordance with his delayed oedipal conflict, Philip is forced to deal with older male figures in the course of all these adventures. These men generally prove to be unthreatening. Mr. Perrin is a carpenter from his childhood who has entered the Spielstadt by virtue of having made some of Philip's toys; Mr. Noah, the Spielstadt's patriarch, comes from Philip's ark and early supports Philip; Caesar himself assists in the final defeat of the Pretenderette. Notably, although all of the tasks involve problem solving, none of them contains violence except the first, where Peter pretends to slash at an enlarged toy dragon but really simply removes the key that enables it to move. In the last battle, Caesar is required to get all of the participants from both sides back onto their proper pages *intact*. Philip, who like many of Nesbit's young boy protagonists is fond of telling his female cohort to "Be a man!" in tight situations, thus experiences a sense of having proved himself to be a man among men without violence—ready now to deal with "that man," Peter Graham, husband to Helen, Philip's mother/sister, and father to Lucy, his stepsister/helper.[19]

To drive this point home, a rather overdetermined scene takes place just before Philip and Lucy's return to the Grange—a scene that for me violates the fantasy premises (regarding how people are allowed to enter the city) somewhat so as to emblematize the "absent father" in his benevolent guise: "And now Caesar stood facing the children, his hand held out in farewell. The growing light of early morning transfigured his face, and to Philip it suddenly seemed to be most remarkably like the face of That Man, Mr. Peter Graham, whom Helen had married. He was just telling himself not to be a duffer when Lucy cried out in a loud cracked-sounding voice, 'Daddy, oh, Daddy!' and sprang forward" (328). Caesar/father disappears, however, in the dazzling light shining on his armor.

This scene also has the unfortunate effect of reminding me that the female side of the oedipal formula has been largely neglected in this fantasy, which provides transitional space for Philip, in the comforting presence of a parental figure with whom to do some male bonding, but assumes that Lucy can make transitions on her own. Indeed, Nesbit has a tendency here as elsewhere to depict the female child as stronger and in some ways more resilient emotionally than the male child (see *The Railway Children,* in particular), who needs more help to come through childhood crises. And characteristically, the nature of these emotional crises exists primarily in the silences and secrets of Nesbit's texts so that imaginative play and fantasy become their signifiers.

For Nesbit herself, who imagined that a socialist world of the future would not retain the ugliness that she perceived in industrialized England, Spielstädte also might signify utopian desires with a pastoral tinge; these longings show up in *The Magic City:*

After dinner Mr. Noah took them for a walk through the town "to see the factories," he said. This surprised Philip, who had been taught not to build factories with his bricks because factories were so ugly, but the factories turned out to be pleasant, long, low houses, with tall French windows opening into gardens of roses, where people of all nations made beautiful and useful things and loved making them. And all the people who were making them looked clean and happy.

"I wish we had factories like those," Philip said. "Our factories *are* so ugly. Helen says so."

"That's because all your factories are *money* factories," said Mr. Noah, "though they're called by all sorts of different names. Everyone here has to make something that isn't just money or *for* money—something useful *and* beautiful."

"Even you?" said Lucy.

"Even I," said Mr. Noah. (161–62)

And after thus expounding the labor theory of value, he goes on to tell them what beautiful laws he makes: "'Everybody must try to be kind to everybody else. Any one who has been unkind must be sorry and say so.'" When Philip inquires about broken laws, Mr. Noah then produces this incitement to civil disobedience: "'Beautiful things can't be beautiful when they're broken, of course. . . . Not even laws. But ugly laws are only beautiful when they *are* broken. That's odd, isn't? Laws are very tricky things'" (162).

Nesbit, the Fabian artist, also, in Winnicott's terms, "gathers objects or phenomena from external reality and uses these in the service of some sample derived from inner or personal reality" (*Playing and Reality* 51). The beautiful factory within the Spielstadt that comes to life at night is her evoked dream.

8 The Animal-Toy League

"Of course, the dolls and animals feel things the most," said Joan. *"I don't think the chairs and balls and things will mind."*

"I don't know," said Peggy. "They'll feel it—but, of course, the dolls and animals most."
—Mrs. H. C. Craddock, *Peggy and Joan*

The little wooden doll was seldom lonely, for there was always someone to talk to. The mice in particular were great gossips. . . . The spiders, too, were good company, but they were inclined to be narrowminded, and dwelt too much on their own affairs.
—Margery Williams Bianco, *The Little Wooden Doll*

In chapter 6 I described how at the end of Kenneth Grahame's "Sawdust and Sin" (1895) the family's black retriever, Rollo, emerges from the underbrush and runs off with Jerry, the Japanese doll. The narrator of this story, reminiscing about spying on his younger sister as she delivers a confused version of *Alice's Adventures in Wonderland* to her dolls, fits Rollo's predatory act into his own sexually titillating daydream. In his youthful fantasy, the narrator attributes provocative and seductive motives to the English doll, Rosa, and appropriately naughty responses to the sly foreigner, Jerry. The payment for Jerry's sexual receptivity is to be carried off by Rollo, as devil figure, while Rosa and the child voyeur in this scene (as well as the salacious reminiscing narrator) go free.[1]

Attacks like Rollo's are commonplace in eighteenth- and nineteenth-century texts starring animated toys or other objects, especially those given the power to tell their own stories. Cats, dogs, and rats, in particular, become the apparently natural antagonists of animated protagonists—or at least instruments of capricious fate. In these early stories, the animated toys obvi-

136

ously feel none of the kinship with the generally nonanthropomorphized animals that they tend to feel with human beings. In later texts, however, a trend in the opposite direction emerges: anthropomorphized animals and toys share a relationship from which humans are often excluded. The texts I examine at the end of this chapter, Margery Williams Bianco's *Poor Cecco* (1925), and Carolyn Sherwin Bailey's 1947 Newbery Medal winner, *Miss Hickory,* neither well known to modern readers, epitomize this trend.

Western theological and secular philosophies with regard to the relationships between humans and animals (as well as the literature that reflects those philosophies) have varied over the centuries as well, and males and females within them have sometimes been considered to have diverse relationships with nature in general and with animals in particular. I shall briefly look at this intellectual history, as well as at some earlier toy narratives, before examining the two twentieth-century texts, which between them offer interesting contrasts in their depictions of female toy protagonists relating to animals within, respectively, a carnivalesque and a natural world.

Transitions in Toy-Animal Relationships

In earlier stories, misadventures with animals are common. They are part, for instance, of the Kilners' late eighteenth-century toy memoirs. Mary Ann Kilner's Pincushion is separated from her second mistress by the playfulness of a kitten who manages to wedge her under a bookcase; later, after being tossed out into the chicken yard with the table crumbs, Pincushion is pecked by the chickens and pitched under a tub, her final resting place, by a rooster. Dorothy Kilner's Whipping Top observes the cat's predatory behavior with mice before being himself pushed off a back shelf by the cat, an act that permits his rediscovery by and eventual return to his original master. Finally he is carried away by a dog, who sends him downstream to his ignominious, muddy resting place. Grahame, writing over a century later than the Kilners, facetiously uses the arrival of the black dog as a reminder of the wages of sexual sin. In contrast to Grahame's flippancy, the changes of fortune brought about by the intervention of animals in toys' destinies become, for the Kilners' protagonists, serious occasions for self-lacerating and homiletic comments to young readers, as in the closing lines of *The Adventures of a Pincushion*: "The catastrophe which has reduced me, was entirely unexpected; and should teach them, that no seeming security can guard them from accidents. . . . Therefore it is a mark of folly, as well as of meanness, to be proud of these distinctions, which are at all times precarious in enjoyment, and uncertain in possession" (72).

In a similar fashion, the narrator-protagonist of Mary Mister's *Adventures of a Doll* (1816), left behind one day at a farmhouse, is attacked by rats and put in peril by a mischievous cat. Later, a boy ties the doll (now his sister's) to the tail of a dog, which buries her and digs her up later. This is not her terrible end, however, but merely one of those picaresque experiences common to literary dolls. Richard Horne's *Memoirs of a London Doll* (1846) shares such escapades: the narrator-protagonist, Maria, wrapped up in a burning carpet and thrown out the window, is rescued by a large dog; later in her adventures she is knocked into the crowd by a dog at a Punch-and-Judy show, confused with one of the puppets, and then traded to a peddler.

The deus (or Satanus) ex machina aspects of these aggressive animals are evident: they interact with the toy characters simply as natural instruments of the toys' picaresque fates. Any other relationship between animals and toys goes unconsidered in the early works. These toy characters offer object lessons meant to be internalized by the young, just as anthropomorphized animal characters, the stars of fables, have similarly functioned throughout the history of cautionary literature. At the same time that the Kilners were writing their didactic toy memoirs, Sarah Trimmer, in her *Fabulous Histories Designed for the Instruction of Children concerning Their Treatment of Animals* (1786) was using the memoir form with animals as narrator-protagonists to dramatize the plight of animals at the hands of human beings. Yet the possibility that animals and toys—both objects in the eyes of humans and with perhaps similar stories to tell—might join together to make a society that excluded humans (either accidentally or deliberately) is not part of the fantasy vision of these texts.

Indeed, little communication of any kind takes place between originally inanimate characters and other nonhuman characters in many of the better-known stories for children through the early nineteenth century. At mid-century, however, the relationships between animal characters and animated characters begin to become more complex, partly because of the use of animals' mythic associations in literary fairy tales. So the fish that swallows Andersen's Tin Soldier during his adventure in the sewers is not just a means of transporting him back home but a type of Jonah's whale, which introduces the death-and-rebirth motif, foreshadowing the Tin Soldier's later trial and transformation by fire. We also glimpse in this story another kind of relationship between toy and animal—although it is hostile and undeveloped—when the Water-Rat asks the Tin Soldier for a toll and the soldier ignores him. The possibilities of communication are here opened up, but not followed through.[2]

Not until *Alice's Adventures in Wonderland* (1865) do animate and inanimate nonhuman characters seem to interact at the same level of fictive "reality" in the nightmarish underground world into which the human girl intrudes. Fashionably dressed animals like the waistcoated Rabbit appear in Wonderland, and animated playing cards walk among them and form the hierarchical society into which both recognizable (rabbit and dormouse) and fantastic (mock turtle and griffin) species manage to fit. The philosophical influences on Dr. Charles Dodgson have been much investigated; prominent among them is the shock administered to both the intellectual and ecclesiastical worlds (which were still related in the British universities like Dodgson's Oxford) by the publication of Charles Darwin's *On the Origin of Species by Means of Natural Selection* (1859).

The reassuring dream frame of Carroll's story clings to the orthodoxy of his Anglican training; nevertheless, Alice's experience underground reveals a fascination with who *eats* whom that may be a reaction to the Darwinian concept of survival of the fittest. In addition, his relativistic view of time and space and his notions of the slipperiness and arbitrariness of language belong to the fields of mathematics and logic that Dodgson professed. Although these aspects of Alice's dream replicate dream strategies they also suggest Dodgson's underlying uneasiness with the established hierarchies of the Anglican orthodoxy—and, indeed, of the Judeo-Christian tradition of Western thought.[3]

The Man-Beast Hierarchy in Western Thought

The most immediate effect of Darwinism, seen in *Alice in Wonderland,* was to give an extra satiric twist to the use of animal characters to stand for human vices and virtues, as they had done in folktale and fable. Many of these earlier tales originated in pantheistic cultures where animal divinity and ancestry were firmly embedded in a mythic past. In postclassical Western literature, these tales were considered not theologically authoritative accounts of origins and spiritual history, like the Holy Scriptures and Testaments, but mere myths, folktales, and fables, taken literally by "primitive" peoples. Without spiritual resonance, the stories could be used to present morals for everyday life; in them, anthropomorphic animals offered examples of appropriate or inappropriate behavior and as such functioned didactically in conformity with a monotheistic tale of genesis in which a human being, Adam, was created in the image of a single male god, was given dominion over the animals, and was finally enabled by this god to give intercostal birth to his own mate, Eve.[4] According to this same codex, the Judeo-Christian Bible, another human, Noah, later saved two animals of every species from a worldwide flood. Animals—sometimes themselves divine in pagan religions—

became, therefore, the objects in a subject-object relationship in which by divine right man was always the subject; therefore, although animals might be used metaphorically to represent human vices and virtues, they were not to be seen as even distant, "black sheep" relatives of humans. The distance between human and animal was further enlarged by the distinctions between the mind, soul, and body that so concerned Christian commentators.

This gap between man and beast has not gone unquestioned. In *The Happy Beast in French Thought of the Seventeenth Century* (1933), George Boas describes a challenge to this way of thinking in the form of primitivism. According to Boas, the French primitivists were men who not only "looked to their pre-civilized fellows as exemplars of human conduct," but who sometimes "turned their admiring glances below man and found the true models in the animals" (1). He calls this philosophy "theriophily," and notes that in this line of thinking "natural" is always superior to civilized (which becomes regarded as *over*civilized and effete). Michel de Montaigne (1533–92) and especially his disciple Pierre Charron (1541–1603) are associated with theriophily.

When what Boas calls the implied ethics of this philosophy were taken seriously powerful opponents arose, among them René Descartes (1596–1650), who "insist[ed] that not only do the beasts lack reason but also that they lack a soul, their acts being purely mechanical" (2). Cartesian philosophy reinforced the perceived differences between man and animal in Western philosophy. Descartes's dictum *Cogito, ergo sum* was interpreted to mean that animals, who did not think—in the limited ways Descartes defined thought—and human beings, who did, could hardly be said to exist on the same plane. In spite of Descartes's attack, the work of Jean-Jacques Rousseau (1671–1741) managed to keep alive the flame of the earlier French primitivism, at least to continue the claim that the growth of civilization had corrupted "natural" goodness. Madame Le Prince de Beaumont's early eighteenth-century version of "Beauty and the Beast," for example, shows a lingering preference for the natural over what passes for the civilized in high society. The Beast, at one level in this tale, certainly represents a civilizing influence closer to the vision of the theriophilists than to that of Descartes.

During the eighteenth century, the influence of Locke's *Some Thoughts concerning Education* (1693) made the good treatment of animals an important touchstone of the development of a good human being. Followers of Locke, however, integrated his views into a strongly theological stance emphasizing hierarchical differences; Sarah Trimmer's *Fabulous Histories,* for instance, expressed her concern to "point out the line of conduct which ought to regulate the actions of human beings toward those over whom the

SUPREME GOVERNOR hath given them dominion" (quoted in Pickering 21). Nonetheless, later Lockean followers writing for children sometimes slipped into a position close to that of the primitivists.[5]

Of course, Darwin's theories challenged the dominion of man over the animals in emphasizing humans' evolutionary development from animals. At times Darwinians retained Cartesian distinctions on the basis of intellect, however, even though they deemphasized Descartes's mechanistic view of animals. And in the late nineteenth century both Cartesian and Darwinian ideas seem to be assimilated into toy texts. In Collodi's *Pinocchio* moral and intellectual development is depicted as a metamorphosis from one species to another. The central metamorphosis is the change from wooden puppet into boy, effected by a combination of external love and guidance, internal growth, and magic. In *Pinocchio* the relationship between animal and puppet is extremely complex. As in the old fables, animals—the anthropomorphized sly Cat and Fox, for instance—can operate as the puppet's worst enemies and thus teach him a moral lesson. Other animals, like the dogs, can be instruments of fate, transporting Pinocchio where he does not want to go. The shark resembles the fish in "The Steadfast Tin Soldier" (and the leviathan in the Old Testament). In *Pinocchio,* however, unlike the older toy stories, the relationship between toy and animals is reciprocal. Moreover, this relationship exists, as it were, within the puppet: Pinocchio has the potential to change either into a human being *or* an animal. Not only can he be made to take the place of a watchdog but, like his human playmates, he can change into a real donkey—and does so, along with his human buddy, Lampwick, when he regresses to an intellectual and moral level that Collodi considers bestial. Collodi is, in his depictions of possible "regressive" or "progressive" metamorphoses, still working within the Judeo-Christian tradition in which humankind is intellectually and morally superior to animalkind; in his fantasy, however, Collodi manages to break down the barriers between species, and between animate and inanimate creatures.

Other writers challenged man's superiority to animals in more extreme terms. In the late nineteenth century, a prominent line of Western thought—especially among those British intellectuals, artists, and writers who viewed the results of the Industrial Revolution with dismay—held that man's distance from an animal past did not denote progress. Like the seventeenth-century theriophilists and Rousseau, these thinkers were concerned with man's alienation from a natural, almost edenic, heritage for which civilization (and its discontents, as they were soon to be called) might prove to be a weak substitute.[6]

Certainly the writings of Kenneth Grahame—if not his "Sawdust and

Sin"—could more consistently be seen to exude a longing for a past in which humans and animals communicated equally and freely. Long before his animal novel, *The Wind in the Willows* (1908), which blurs the distinctions between humans and animals at the same time it pretends to find in the animal world a simplicity lost to human beings, Grahame was writing essays that expressed a certain neopaganism. One aspect of this was his projection of a golden age—not the biblical Eden when man named and ruled the beasts—but a period of free communication with animals.[7] Grahame resembles a number of British writers of his time, many of whom handled the longing for reunion with animal nature in more sexual and violent terms than he.[8] Freud, writing soon after, gives due recognition to "animal" needs of human beings, at worst neurotically repressed and distorted, at best—in society's eyes if not Freud's—channeled and sublimated into the arts.

In spite of this apparent trend toward desiring closer relationships between animals and human beings, I do not claim that a similar sentiment expressed itself immediately in nineteenth- and twentieth-century toy literature. Relationships between toy characters and human beings are themselves diversely complex. A case in which animals and toys do *not* unite is Beatrix Potter's *The Tale of Two Bad Mice,* discussed earlier. Potter's story subverts social norms but uses toys to stand for these norms; animals alone act subversively. Children are encouraged here to identify with the hearty if naughty animals rather than with the overcivilized dolls. Potter makes invidious distinctions between toy and animal characters in her fantasy world. In contrast, in *The Velveteen Rabbit,* Margery Williams Bianco emphasizes alliances between them, as well as possibilities of metamorphosis from toy to animal. In her *Little Wooden Doll,* quoted as an epigraph to this chapter, she shows affection between toys and animals.

Significantly, in Bianco's books animals and toys can communicate directly, while children and toys cannot—a fantasy premise characteristic of many modern works. One can see this convention at work, for instance, in Margaret Baker's *The Shoe Shop Bears* (1963). There the three teddy bears—who silently allow themselves to be manipulated by child customers all day—read diagrams of the human foot or play hide-and-seek at night, eagerly awaiting the visits of three cats, Hobson, Big Tom, and Little Tom, who "brought the bears all the news of the town" (19).[9] As I have already demonstrated for *Hitty* and *The Return of the Twelves,* other kinds of communication and allegiances between toys and nonhuman creatures are formed in such twentieth-century fantasies. Russell Hoban's *The Mouse and His Child* (discussed in detail in the next chapter) achieves even greater complexity in this regard and makes almost purely allegorical use of its sole human character, the tramp.

The Female Animal

In reading certain texts, Carolyn Sherwin Bailey's *Miss Hickory* in particular, I began to connect toy-animal relationships with one aspect of the man-beast dichotomy in Judeo-Christian thought.[10] For in the dualistic (and hierarchical) polarity of "mankind" versus animal, "woman" is frequently aligned with the beast and considered similarly marginal and less than human. This masculinist view makes a feminist critique significant in considering nonhuman nature in the form of animal-toy relationships.

When I first became acquainted with *Miss Hickory,* I thought it a strange, intriguing, but disturbing book. In it, the title character, "a country woman whose body was an applewood twig and whose head was a hickory nut" (7), goes back to nature with a vengeance. Not only does she fraternize almost exclusively with animals rather than humans but her final transformation is neither animal nor human but vegetable—a transformation almost the exact reverse of Pinocchio's. This transformation, which obliterates the protagonist's well-developed personality, makes her at the end an object rather than a subject in her own story. It was therefore a relief, at about the same time, to come upon *Poor Cecco,* a work of Margery Williams Bianco's that also involves a relationship between toys and animals that excludes humans but that, like *Hitty,* honors the subjectivity of the female toy protagonist.[11] Not as well known as *The Velveteen Rabbit, Poor Cecco* is far less sentimental. And, as Peggy Whalen-Levitt points out, it foreshadows, in the character of Jensina, "the feminist treatment of female characters in Bianco's later works of realistic fiction" (65).

In spite of their differences with regard to female characters, Bianco and Bailey share an intense interest in both living toys and anthropomorphized animals, an interest that is not expressed only in the books considered here. In many of Bianco's books toy characters, like the characters in Milne's Pooh series, are fully animated and are modeled on both her own and her children's toys. Bailey takes *Miss Hickory* from a doll of her own childhood; in an earlier book, *Tops and Whistles* (1937), old toys displayed in museums prompt stories about the periods in which they were made, which use a moderate amount of animation and make many of the toys conscious if passive observers of their surroundings, in the manner of *Hitty*. Following *Miss Hickory,* Bailey began to write animal fantasies.[12]

Bianco and Bailey are also roughly contemporary: Bianco was born in 1881 and Bailey in 1875. The latter lived until 1961, however, and *Miss Hickory* was published two years after the death of Bianco. Both writers were alike as well in being born into middle-class, intellectual families and educated at home in their early years. The course of Bianco's and Bailey's adult lives ran rather differently thereafter, however, and these personal differences could easily have influenced their ideas about sex and gender. Nevertheless, rather than arguing biographically, I suggest that so volatile has been "the woman question" over the course of the twentieth century that changes in the cultural climates between 1925 and 1946, when *Poor Cecco* and *Miss Hickory,* respectively, were published, do much to illuminate the contrast in the destinies of their female protagonists and their relationships to the natural world represented by animals.

Poor Cecco Rides Again

Poor Cecco's male hero is a wooden toy dog, whose name is taken from the toy dog owned by Bianco's two children, Cecco and Pamela.[13] The adjective *poor* may have been given the actual toy as well, because of its battered state, particularly its broken tail. From the first, however, Poor Cecco's leadership qualities seem to belie his name. He is the roving yet protective adventurer, who at the story's opening rescues his fellow toys from the cupboard where they have been locked up by Murrum, the house cat, who considers them "'a wretched noisy crowd. . . . Night after night prancing and singing all over the house!'" (17). This rowdy behavior, so typical of the nightlife of toys, has interfered with Murrum's mousing, as he complains to Toad, "the old nightwatchman, with brown wrinkled coat and speckled vest . . . [who] blinks up through his gold spectacles" (16).

Later, Murrum is to act again as satanus ex machina with the toys, but, in the course of the book, animals and toys interact in a variety of ways. The depiction of the animals, as epitomized by Toad with his gold spectacles, is as anthropomorphized and fantastic as that of the toys, so that the nonhuman animate and inanimate interact.[14] Anthropomorphization is extended to all sorts of objects; the toys that emerge from the toy cupboard are all granted mobility, feelings, and desires. Included are the toy wagon and Ida Down, who is "flat and square, dressed in pink satin with a silk cord all around" (24; in the first edition, Arthur Rackham sketches her as an eiderdown cushion with "IDA" embroidered upon it). Ida, who spends most of her existence being sat upon, is described as follows: "Romantic by nature, she was doomed to spend her life listening to other people's confidences. No one ever thought of falling in love with her, and yet she had all the qualifications for an ideal wife" (31).

Intimate relationships prevail among this diverse group of toys, who like the dolls in Rumer Godden's *Dolls' House* must accept each other through proximity, if not by choice. But, in contrast to Godden's dolls, who form a nuclear family founded on the whims of their owners, these toys themselves choose to become somewhat quarrelsome friends and potential mates, uninfluenced by human projection.[15] Grace, a doll, has just been married to the taciturn Harlequin; Virginia May, the other doll character, has her "turn to be married" coming up. So limited is their society, that "the only person they could think of for her to marry was Bulka, whom she couldn't endure" (24). Bulka is the rag puppy, rather a crybaby, who quarrels at first with the imaginative toy dog Tubby; in the course of the narrative their mutual affection becomes clear. The toy lion woos Anna the lamb, whose feet are permanently fastened to a "little green meadow, that she always carried about with her" (24). He offers to bring her back to the jungle as his queen. Reluctant, she indicates, much to his disgust, that she has made a vow never to leave her meadow. Among the eligible toys introduced to us at first, only Poor Cecco seems to stand unattached above the matchmaking—the stance of the traditional adventurer-hero.

Faced with some heavy-duty nursing and unwanted concern over his broken tail, Poor Cecco entices Bulka, another mobile if inexperienced young male dog, to explore the world with him. Their journey occupies much of the center of the text. During the course of their initial adventures, they find themselves in an ash heap where they meet a little wooden doll, Jensina, who was brought up by the gypsies and inadvertently dropped behind to survive on her own, as dolls frequently must. Like Hitty, Jensina is a survivor, although she has considerably more mobility than Hitty (she, at least, has jointed limbs). Jensina is able to offer the adventurers the hospitality of her makeshift but cozy home, but she is not so domestically inclined that she is not eager to join them when asked by Poor Cecco.

But Jensina is a creature of strong moods. She has inadvertently come into possession of a special totem, "the tooth of Grimalken" (a cat killed by the rats' legendary hero), and although the rats pursue them, she determines not to return it because the rats fought with Bulka over a necklace of blue beads and harassed them on their journey. Indeed, throughout the course of their adventure, one is struck with Jensina's volatility, in contrast to Poor Cecco's steady, almost phlegmatic character; she is full of passion and fire—terribly insulted and sulky when some moles will not include them in a dancing party, yet warm and talkative with Mrs. Woodchuck, for whom she does one hundred and thirteen bushels of laundry that have accumulated since Mrs. W. decided to take in laundry to help out her temporarily unemployed mate. Even though the chapter in which she does this is rather domestically entitled "Jensina Proves a Born Housewife," Jensina makes a formidable heroine, lacking the heroine's traditional passive helplessness—she earlier subverted that role by "taking off her frock for greater freedom in walking" (71).

After more adventures the three of them return home, where they discover all is not well—traditionally reentry is never completely smooth for the hero. Murrum has taken his revenge on Poor Cecco and the toys for interfering with his mousing by dropping Tubby into a large hollow tree trunk. But Tubby herself is a strong character, despite her tendency to dream about a compensatory retreat called Tubbyland. In the tree, she makes the acquaintance of the resident squirrel family and earns a meal by teaching the squirrel children. And after various difficulties, the toys finally identify the tree in which Tubby is imprisoned and puzzle over how to rescue her.

Jensina, who has received rather a cool welcome from Grace and Virginia May, holds the key (or the tooth?) to the rescue. When she hears that the two shadowing rats are waiting outside the house, she conceives of the perfect plan, which brings all the diverse elements of the story together. She negotiates with the rats: she will return the tooth if they will gnaw a hole in the tree to let Tubby out. It works. A peace treaty is signed with the rats. Tubby emerges into the waiting arms of Bulka. A wedding is in the offing.

The last celebratory chapter, Tubby and Bulka's wedding, signals not only the culmination of an adventure story, but a romance ending in which harmony is restored among all of the creatures, living and animated—*without* human beings (who—with the exception of a blind man with a dog whose begging Poor Cecco and Bulka take over briefly and a mail deliverer who gives the toys a ride—hardly exist in the narrative). Even the greedy, unpopular Money-Pig, who had hidden all the notes Tubby sent Bulka from her imprisonment before being killed trying to steal pennies, is brought back to life by an amateur glue job on patient Ida's part (how she applied it without hands is an unsolved mystery). He cannot eat any more pennies since his slot is now crooked. The final chapter threatens to be the kind of hymenal celebration characteristic of the multiple weddings of Shakespeare's romances. This harmony remains undeveloped, for woven into the texture of the story are certain antiromantic, as well as feminist threads. These consist not only of such sly remarks as the narrator makes about Ida Down's supine suitability for wifehood, but reluctance on the part of the characters themselves.

Early in the story, Virginia May, whose protests are attributed to jealousy by Gladys, states: "'Domestic life is boring . . . and what's more, it makes people stupid and conceited. I intend to keep my independence'" (31). Anna the lamb has, of course, been holding out rather nicely against the Lion's blandishments. This particular situation does resolve itself in favor of romance, when Anna falls into a hole dug as an unsuccessful trap for Murrum and is rescued by the Lion. They decide that they too want to get married at Tubby and Bulka's wedding. Here, however, Poor Cecco puts his foot down: "'Nonsense! . . . One wedding at a time! It's Tubby's turn today, and besides there are no more gifts ready. Anna has spent all the summer shilly-shallying

"The leader of the rats held out a folded yellow paper. 'Sign on the dotted line, please,' he said." From *Poor Cecco*.

on account of that stupid green meadow of hers, and now she must just content herself with being engaged for the present!'" (173).

In one familiar version of the tradition of adventurer-hero the cowboy finally disappears—riding off alone into the sunset leaving the sighing maiden behind. Poor Cecco's reluctance to participate romantically is well within this tradition, which seems at first to govern the final scene of the story:

In a pause in the music Poor Cecco stood by Jensina, gazing at the happy throng.
"Isn't it nice?" he said. "Oh, Jensina, how well everything has turned out! Look at Tubby! Look at Bulka, all over cake crumbs! Really, it almost makes one feel—"
"Yes?" murmured Jensina, gazing slyly up at him. She was thinking of what the policeman rat had said. [The rat had assumed that she and Poor Cecco were romantically involved and had wished them good luck—the first hint of such an alliance.]
"—makes one feel like standing on one's head!" finished Poor Cecco somewhat hastily, for he had caught the look in Jensina's eye.

Lest anyone feel, however, that Jensina has lost her heart to the elusive hero in traditional heroine fashion, read on:

Jensina's natural common sense returned to her.
"You needn't think *I'm* in a hurry to get married either," she retorted instantly, "because I'm not. I much prefer a life of adventure and combat."
"And from what I know of you," Poor Cecco gallantly returned, "you're likely to get plenty of it! And now I must go and dance with Tubby." (175)

Poor Cecco's recognition of Jensina's sincerity is appropriate to what has already been learned of her, especially from her resolution of the conflict with the rats. When she had declared her intention to treat with them, she and Poor Cecco had had the following exchange: "'Oh, Jensina, aren't you afraid? Let me go!' he entreated. 'No,' replied Jensina firmly. 'I took the Tooth, and it is I who must bargain with them. But you may keep quite near me,' she added" (161).

The flexibility with which Bianco uses conventional material is notable. Bianco's work concerns breaking down barriers between animate and inanimate, species and species (the lion and Anna the lamb are engaged to lie down together). The rats become friends with the toys; and if Murrum has been chased out of the garden another cat, like Mrs. Greypaws, who early in the journey sewed up Bulka, would certainly be welcome. In *Poor Cecco,* Bianco creates a carnival atmosphere that thus denies the simple dichotomy underlying most sexist thinking. The story often accepts conventional male and female roles, but suggests that they are just that—conventional—so that even when Jensina is shown to be a "born housekeeper," she is also shown to be a born adventurer, ready at a moment's notice to strip down for action and take to the road. Both the male Bulka, the crybaby, and the female Tubby, the dreamer, are allowed successful adventures, even though both also have to depend on others to rescue them.

The fantasy delights as much in unreason as it delights in unreality and the unnatural. Much of the humor of the text comes from watching Poor Cecco first try to reason on the basis of false premises and then give up in favor of empirical testing, as when he attempts to draw a map of where he and Bulka have been on their journey and obviously blunders on with no notion of graphic requirements. Neither he nor Jensina is good at planning, although she is the more successful because she does not try to reason things out. The near-exclusion of humans in favor of the creation by the anthropomorphized animals and toys of their own relationships, which play off of but are not confined to human conventions, serves to break down such stereotypes, many of which have elsewhere been elevated to literary archetypes.[16] Music and dancing appear often in this text and contribute to the carnival and celebratory atmosphere that at the same time defies logic and suggests that what society often considers natural is reductionist and narrow.

Miss Hickory Rides for a Fall

In contrast, most of the energy in *Miss Hickory* goes toward reviving the reductionist "natural," especially as it applies to the adult female. The text begins with the withdrawal of human beings from the scene. The remaining characters include an anthropomorphized doll, made of natural materials— an apple-wood twig "formed like a body with two arms and two legs, hand[s,] and feet" with a hickory nut head "that had grown with an especially sharp and pointed nose" (9)—and the somewhat anthropomorphized animals and birds that inhabit the farmland around Great-Granny Brown's New Hampshire house.

Acting as a messenger, Crow brings devastating news to Miss Hickory, who, as the narrator announces, might be perceived by others as "a country doll, made by Miss Katurah who kept the notions store in Hillsborough, and given to Ann," but who is, the reader must know, "a real person" who lives in a house "made of corncobs, notched, neatly fitted together and glued" under the lilac (10). Crow announces that both Great-Granny Brown's warm house to which Miss Hickory's protector Ann traditionally brings Miss Hickory and her own corncob house will be closed for the severe winter. Miss Hickory will have to make changes in her life, including leaving her beloved house, in order to survive the winter. She responds by denying the circumstances and insisting on checking them with Mr. T. Willard-Brown, the barn cat. Crow attributes her denial to her "'hard-headedness,'" a pun that will become thematic, although a scene of Miss Hickory's crying suggests the desperation behind her stubbornness. Mr. T. Willard-Brown affirms and, moreover, while he takes Miss Hickory to the closed house to show her, Chipmunk moves into her little corncob house and eats the berries she has gathered.

Miss Hickory's life throughout the following winter takes on a pattern as familiar to the children's story as the adventurer-hero's journey of *Poor Cecco*: that of the Robinsonnade, in which the inexperienced, abandoned (often orphaned) survivor gets by in the natural world, just as Robinson Crusoe did, finding food, clothing, and shelter through ingenuity and pluck. The seasonal substructure, in which the plot moves through the year from fall to spring, noting natural changes and seasonal rituals, is also familiar in children's novels.

Miss Hickory does find some advisers for this new life, Crow among them, who carries her to the orchard and an old apple tree, in whose crotch she finds a "large and deep nest" (29). In order to recognize its attractions, she must, as the unsympathetic Crow advises, have a change of heart: "'You have been living for two years with those who feel that they need a grocery store, a Ford car, a stove, and storm windows. You have grown soft'" (25). Leaving her in the tree, the Crow gives her one more piece of seemingly gratuitous advice: "'*Keep your sap running*'" (30).

The question of shelter being apparently settled, Miss Hickory turns her attention to clothing. The narrator informs us that "in spite of her stiff twig body and nut head, Miss Hickory was intensely feminine" (35). She is also becoming "not nearly so dependent upon store goods as when she had been living in the corncob house under the lilac bushes. . . . She had taught herself how to stitch and tailor with pine needles" (36). She does such a good job of making herself an outfit out of beech leaves, moss, berries, and fern down that she looks "years younger." Squirrel, passing by, indeed thinks her "enchanting," and greets her with "'Hi, cutie!'" She replies rather acerbically: "'Mind your manners, my lad!'" and calls attention to his "'scatterbrained ways'" (37). And, although she holds her own in conversation, Miss Hickory, with her nut head, finds his concern with *nuts* a frightening one, especially when she discovers that he lives in an inherited hole in the foot of her tree. Squirrel, who is rather profligate and forgetful about nutgathering in the fall, is only in a playful, not a hungry, mood at present.

By this point, readers can see that in some ways Miss Hickory seems a protagonist not unlike Jensina: relatively competent at taking care of herself, while being both moody and articulate. Her conversations with her animal friends suggest a judgmental personality, with a tendency to call attention to their weaknesses. Under the circumstances of her new life, her hardheadedness is not a bad attribute. Significantly, in Bailey's acceptance of the Newbery Medal, she describes Miss Hickory in terms of a common stereotype: "She is a plain-spoken, sharp-tongued spinster, and one can never be sure what she may say" (239).[17] In line with this description, Miss Hickory next organizes the complaining Hen-Pheasants—who are apparently driven from the feeding grounds and common nests by the Cock-Pheasants in the fall—into a Ladies Aid Society that will not only make quilts but feed together. Following this spinster stereotype too is Miss Hickory's new idea: to become a schoolteacher in the spring.

As winter progresses, Miss Hickory discovers a harmony prevailing then in the animal world, a harmony that prepares the reader for the visionary chapter "Now Christmas Comes." In spite of her new experiences, Miss Hickory appears still to suffer somewhat from her own nutty hardheadedness. She almost misses the Christmas Eve celebration because she refuses to believe Squirrel's description of the annual gathering in the barn of all the animals to see "the wonder": "'In one of the barn mangers, the animal to whom it belongs finds the wonder. In the fresh grain of his manger, at midnight tonight, there will be a small hollow, although the straw and oats were freshly laid and not touched. It will be the shape of a baby's head and body'" (70). Miss Hickory is as immune to Christmas miracles as the unreformed Scrooge until she awakens to the vision of animals of all descriptions —exotically foreign as well as domestically familiar—in procession toward the barn. But she is too late arriving so that she is excluded from experiencing the wonder: "They had all, except Miss Hickory, seen the golden imprint in Wild-Heifer's manger." Miss Hickory is left feeling there is "'really something wrong with [me]'": "'I should have paid heed to Squirrel,' she thought. "'I might have seen inside the manger in the barn, but I was hardheaded'" (77).

Seasonal rituals continue, with Miss Hickory more centrally involved, and by spring she begins to feel her sap rising. Crow persuades her to be somewhat less judgmental by taking her for a wild ride to see all of the wonders of spring. Subsequently, thinking on April Fool's Day that she is helping bullfrog get free of the ice, she helps him get rid of his old skin, an annual spring ritual that foreshadows her own rebirth. Yet, her thoughts on spring still run along old, anthropomorphic patterns despite Crow's advice to forget them. She decides first to clean house and then to make herself a new spring outfit and discovers that she has changed physically: "Her legs that showed to the knees below her short play-skirt seemed more shapely, brown, and plumper" (104). Nevertheless, her spring happiness is short-lived, for one day she returns to the nest to find Robin and his family occupying it. Deciding that she can probably safely occupy Squirrel's hole, she discovers improvident Squirrel weak and dying of starvation. She goads him by calling him a witless

"And with that final bitter remark Squirrel took off Miss Hickory's head." From *Miss Hickory*.

fellow and a wastrel. Squirrel is given strength by rage. He points out that he has hitherto refrained from eating her nut head—*which he then proceeds to do,* all the time reproaching her for the things she has missed by being so hardheaded. Her head, which briefly continues to think, agrees with his analysis. It finally notes self-reflexively, "'You lived selfishly all your life. You wouldn't even give away your hard head'" (112).

The headless doll, whose "body felt more alert and capable than when it had been hampered by a nut head"(112), manages to stumble out of Squirrel's hole, scaring him so much in the process that he is reformed from carelessness in nut gathering forever more. She climbs the apple tree past the nest to a spot "where the sun would be stronger, the winds higher and the rains could be her shower bath" (113). There, she begins to feel "knobby, as if she were budding. Her warm sap, like lifeblood, seemed bursting through her body and as she went on, higher and higher toward the top of the tree, she had a feeling of being really at home, as though she belonged there." She finally stops and remains in "a wide upper crotch in the apple tree" (115).

In the final chapter, Ann returns and mourns the loss of her doll, who was "a real person"; Timothy-of-the-Next-Farm, who built Miss Hickory's corn-cob house, finds this silly. He suggests that Ann join him for a walk through the orchard, where a crow seems to lead them to an old McIntosh tree suddenly blooming after years of infertility. Crow appears also to be directing them to the uppermost branches; when Timothy climbs up he discovers a new "scion" but cannot figure out who has put the graft on the old tree "'to start it blooming and bearing again'" (120). When Ann climbs up to join him, she thinks that the scion looks like Miss Hickory "up to the neck." Crow, meanwhile, is amused that human beings seem to need everything explained. "As for Miss Hickory, who had been a scion all along without knowing it, she felt completely happy. She would never have to do any hard thinking again. She had a permanent home at last and some day she would give Ann, who had recognized her, a big red apple" (122). The book ends on that presumably happy note—with Miss Hickory fused with nature and content in her fertility as she has never been before.

Some of the reasons why the story won the Newbery are obvious. Like Bianco before her, Bailey knows how to take a traditional form and make it her own, for although she uses the Robinsonnade framework, she deviates from it. She does not make it into a the kind of bildungsroman where the protagonist develops a *mastery* of nature (as Crusoe turned his island into a home fit for a bourgeois preindustrialist), but instead has Miss Hickory learn to adjust to nature. Thus, unlike Pinocchio, Miss Hickory becomes "real" in a rather original way, abandoning her "personhood" for a role in the renewal of the natural cycle, affirming her "essential" vegetable state. The role of humor in Miss Hickory's snappy exchanges during her period of "sharp-tongued" spinsterhood combined with wordplay of the type in which Bianco also indulges—significant puns, for instance—are all features many find attractive.

Probably most important is the lovingly depicted setting of the New Hampshire countryside, which Bailey obviously longed for despite its austerity. And her witty, anthropomorphic use of animals, which stays close to their basic nature without sentimentality, is obviously another attractive quality (beautifully captured by illustrator Ruth Gannet). In her animal portrayals Bailey seems closer to Potter than to Bianco. Indeed, she is even more severely naturalistic than Potter, since none of her animals wear human clothes, eat cooked food, or use much furniture. The fantasy premises are limited and severely practiced, using few departures from consensus reality.

Only two gifts are given the animals: the gift of speech and, interestingly, the gift of faith in the wonder of Christmas.

The creation of the Nativity scene is the closest Bailey comes to the notion of carnival, where barriers between all creatures come down, even—since Squirrel's dead mother seems to be present—between the living and the dead. Coming in the middle of the text and surrounded by chapters devoted to naturalistic seasonal rituals, "Now Christmas Comes" has some of the same visionary quality as Kenneth Grahame's "Piper at the Gates of Dawn" chapter at the center of *The Wind in the Willows*. Grahame, however, celebrates a pagan god, Pan, the protector of animals, while Bailey fuses Christianity with a similar vision of natural, almost pre-Adamic harmony—which was no doubt comforting at the end of World War II.

Less sentimental and more naturalistic than Grahame, Bailey is also willing to recognize nature as savage. In Grahame's work, only the inhabitants of the Wild Wood are guilty of disharmonious behavior (give or take Toad's vagaries); Bailey's major animal characters, Crow, Squirrel, and Mr. T. Willard-Brown, have a number of habits to answer for—and sometimes they answer for themselves; says Crow to Miss Hickory's complaints of his thievery: "'Suppose I do eat the neighbors' corn? I eat bugs too. What if I can't sing like a thrush? I'm the first bird to spread the word of the spring thaws. And I have no hard feelings that I, Starling, English Sparrow, Hawk and Owl can be shot at whenever we can be found close enough'" (89). Only Miss Hickory among them is judged and found wanting in behavior and mode of existence.

In addition, for the reader of the late twentieth century, Bailey shows a sense of ecological balance and self-sufficiency. Crow's words to Miss Hickory about dropping her desire for store-bought things and learning to live on the land fit well into present notions of a necessary retreat from destruction, pollution, and overdevelopment of the natural landscape.

Why then should I find the text disturbing? Are not feminists equally concerned with ecology and all the other good notions of natural harmonies and balances that seem to emanate from this text? In reply to these questions, I would have to say that a natural harmony that is restored by a scene that I read as a rape is no harmony to me—and that is how I read Squirrel's beheading of Miss Hickory.

In commenting on the story, I have taken pains to bring out those elements on which such a reading can be based: Bailey's own view of her character as a plainspoken, sharp-tongued spinster, whose head is hard and whose nose is sharp, who is yet "intensely feminine" in a conventional way; Crow's unsympathetic admonition about keeping the sap running; Squirrel's aggressively "playful" approaches beginning with the salutation "'Hi, cutie!'" and continuing with his entry into her nest; Miss Hickory's forming the Ladies' Aid

Society for selfish reasons—it "'pleased your vanity'" her own head says to her in its disconnected state; Miss Hickory's inability to see the Christmas vision so headstrong is she; the description of Miss Hickory's newly rounded legs in her spring outfit; Squirrel's self-righteous aggression in the face of Miss Hickory's scolding; Miss Hickory's guilty head filled with self-hatred and her invigorated body after the beheading, when she is alliteratively described as "headless, heedless, happy Miss Hickory" (113); and, finally, her subsequent fertility. All these add up to a masculinist scenario (frequently internalized by women as well) of the justifiable rape of an overtalkative, stubborn, misguided, barren old maid, who is really just "dying for it" and for whom it will be the perfect cure for both her imperfections and her ungrateful discontent with the conditions of her life.[18]

I do not believe that either Bailey or those who chose the book for the Newbery Medal had any notion that it could be read in these terms. But in 1947, this country was not only celebrating the end of a vicious war but in the midst of a retreat from the gains of the women's rights movement of the early twentieth century and the independence virtually foisted upon women during that war. Jensina's volatile behavior and her rejection of marriage in favor of action and combat would just not do as it had a few years after the granting of women's suffrage.[19]

A prettied-up version of my harsh analysis of Miss Hickory's situation that cited Freud's "anatomy as destiny" and "penis envy" theories in an oversimplified way would come close to describing the "feminine mystique" dominating the late forties that is defined by Betty Friedan in her groundbreaking book of 1963. Such a version might well have been accepted by both award winner and award givers.[20] As Friedan shows, between 1939 and 1949 the depiction of the career woman changed in popular women's magazines. Honored in stories during the thirties in partnership with men, the career woman is denigrated and despised in the same journals by the end of the forties. In her place is put the self-sacrificial wife, mother, and happy housewife busy with her labor-saving devices, the sale of which was so necessary to the reversion to a peacetime economy and to the advertisers in the journals.[21] Looking at Miss Hickory as "a real person" (as Bailey describes her), not just as a country doll, I consider her a victim of this trend. Indeed, she is a particularly good exemplar of it because the scene in question masks the male violence in a cloak of righteousness and activates the female guilt prevalent in victims of rape, attempting to convince the reader that what happens to Miss Hickory is natural, harmonious with nature's plan for propagation. Her virtual rape is shrouded in the feminine mystique.

As such, the scene and its denouement indeed relegate women to the body, according to any debate that dichotomizes the body and soul. More important for my concerns in this chapter, the text's version of naturalism, like some versions of the animal-human dichotomy, consigns women to the non-human (and Bailey takes her female toy character one step farther down, to the vegetable). Bailey has managed to create a text that gives many different messages about women's place, in all probability both intended and unintended. Bailey's admiration and love for animals and nature is almost primitivist; yet the Christian tradition to which she adheres has been used to keep women, like animals, which are considered to have no souls, under the domination of men. Moreover, Miss Hickory, the toy that becomes real and interacts with talking animals on an equal basis, does not change from "a real person" to an animal but to a vegetable. This fact is enormously significant: as a vegetable she needs no head and has no apparent desire to communicate or relate to others, animal or human, except in giving up her fruit. Reversing the usual development in toy narratives—where toys that come alive often share their subjectivity with animals who are also perceived to have a subjectivity that is undetectable to humans—Miss Hickory regresses from subject to object.[22]

Bringing in humans at the end further complicates the signals given. Ann, responding to Timothy's notion that she is too old to play with dolls, presents a *relational* level of female consciousness that can be honored: "Ann turned on Timothy. 'I can't forget Miss Hickory. She wasn't just a doll. She was a real person. . . . I don't forget my friends, Timothy, and you ought to know that'" (117). Nor does Ann play the helpless female at the foot of the tree while Timothy climbs to the top; she is up there with him to see the scion. Timothy himself briefly seems as attuned with nature as was Dickon in *The Secret Garden,* for it is he who seems to understand the animals. His whistle brings the crow to lead them to the tree. Finally, the scion's conscious wish to produce a red apple for Ann seems, in this context, an example of the pathetic fallacy in which humans childishly project their own needs and desires on nature; the scion's response sends a message of human's dominion over nature somewhat at odds with the story's vision of nature elsewhere.

My complaint is not, however, with the book's inconsistency; *Poor Cecco* gives all sorts of diverse messages too. The shock of the image of the headless woman—maimed, silenced, and grotesquely vigorous—is what disturbs me.[23] Bailey could not use the excuse that Miss Hickory is "only a doll" to justify this figure. On the contrary the narrator, as well as Ann, has taken great pains to develop Miss Hickory's personality, in order to convince the reader that this doll is indeed a real person.

9 Beyond the Last Visible Toy

"We aren't toys anymore," said the father. "Toys are to be played with and we aren't."
—Russell Hoban, *The Mouse and His Child*

In the process of imagining toys coming alive, writers of the last two centuries have experimented with many different narrative forms common to both children's and adult literature: autobiographical and picaresque memoirs; literary fairy tales, tales of child development; depictions of domestic life, friendship, and love; and Robinsonnades of survival in nature—as well as mixtures of these forms and of others, the adventure story in particular. The three novels that I have chosen for this penultimate chapter—Dean Koontz's *Oddkins* (1988), Richard Kennedy's *Amy's Eyes* (1985), and Russell Hoban's *The Mouse and His Child* (1967)—all published within a twenty-five-year period—feature toy protagonists, primarily male, engaged in the kind of adventure story that is usually labeled a "quest narrative."

Such quests, outlined by literary critics and scholars like Joseph Campbell, in his *Hero with a Thousand Faces,* concern the development of heroes who make journeys, pass or fail qualifying tests, and strive to achieve their various goals, gathering good helpers and friends—always confronting their evil enemies in battles that are rarely of wits alone. Generally, quests also examine the nature of life and death and speculate about whether good can survive violent danger and injustice in imperfect worlds. Personal rewards usually come to the hero, but he also manages to improve the world around him, demonstrating his good leadership in the process of the quest.

Whatever their general likenesses in adopting this underlying structure, each of the toy novels considered here is ambitious in its own way to explore the limits of the toy story, and each merits close reading and examination for its individual qualities, as well as consideration under the rubric of the quest narrative.

Goodfellas and Badfellas

I am not one to sneer at the power of formulaic writing. Like John Cawelti in *Adventure, Mystery and Romance: Formula Stories as Art and Popular Culture,* I am struck with how a good formulaic writer can play variations on themes that pick up and reflect cultural values. Cawelti characterizes "the special artistic quality of formulaic literature" as the result of "striking a balance, appropriate to the intended audience, between the sense of reality and mimesis essential to art of any kind and the characteristics of escapist experience: an emphasis on game and play, on wish-fulfilling forms of identification, on the creation of an integral, slightly removed imaginative world, and on intense, but temporary emotional effects like suspense, surprise, and horror, always controlled by a certainty of resolution" (34).

Dean Koontz, a bestselling writer of science-fiction suspense-horror tales, moved for the first time into the toy narrative with *Oddkins: A Fable for All Ages*. In contrast to Kennedy's and Hoban's tales, Koontz's story is simple philosophically, with obvious popular appeal that excites and fulfills formulaic expectations. Beginning with the evocation of a dark and stormy day in November that becomes an even more bitter night of urban adventure in which the forces of Good and Evil clash, and the good toys emerge victorious, Koontz plays variations on culturally dominant concerns.

Two types of toys are pitted against each other; their depiction evokes the hopes, needs, and forbidden desires of our times. Stuffed toys representing animals are the forces of good, the *Leben* toys, created by Isaac Bodkins, who dies without appointing a successor. Their evil enemies, the *Charon* toys, emerge from the subcellar of Bodkins's old home hoping to make one of their kind the new toy maker. These toys from hell, from whose boatman-guide they take their name, form a mixed group representing among them human, animal, and mechanical types. Whoever wins the fight to fill the post of toy maker will determine not only the type of toys created but the fate of the next generation of children, letting loose, as it were, the forces of either light or darkness upon the innocent. Contemporary concerns about the toys commercially available to children are thus apparent.

Actually, the struggle goes beyond the parental need to find appropriate toys for children. For the good, Leben, toys—nicknamed Oddkins by "Uncle

Isaac" Bodkins—are actually capable of saving "special" children who are destined to contribute to society. These children, as Uncle Isaac tells the toy leader, Amos, "'must face enormous problems or . . . must live through a terrible sorrow'" (4). Perhaps a child whose parents mistreat him will find in the Oddkin a secret friend, for the Oddkins actually come alive, although the child forgets this when it no longer needs them. At that time "the magical life" "drain[s] out" of these stuffed animals, so that their "secret conversations and adventures . . . seem to have been fantasies, mere games that the child . . . played in more innocent days before growing into the no-nonsense world of adults" (5). They are thus transitional objects, acceptable in youth, but here considered fetishistic in later life. No adults other than toy makers are supposed to see the Oddkins come alive.

Although the evil Charon toys are horrible, they do not have as specifically influential or complex a role to play. They are likely to shake a child's trust in life in general, for they have the power to hurt it physically and are endowed with a malicious need to do just that. They have no redeeming virtues, being self-centered and unable to help one another; no honor prevails among these thieves of trust. Their instructions come from the voice of an evil figure who reveals himself—in shifting embodied forms—only to a newly released criminal, who learned to make toys while serving time. Called Nick Jagg, the criminal is recruited, by what appears to be the devil himself, to become the next Charon toy maker.

The plot requires that a group of the good toys, led by the teddy bear, Amos—who wears on his sweatshirt the leadership symbol of Alpha and Omega bestowed upon him by Bodkins—leave their comfortable country home and journey to the city where dwells the good toy maker, Mrs. Shannon, whom Bodkins wanted to take his place. The Oddkins group is individuated: besides Amos, they are Burl, an elephant who dreams of the African veldt; Skippy, a rabbit addicted to television comedy with hopes of becoming a stand-up comic; Butterscotch, a female dog whose sweetness, gentleness, and righteousness are the opposite of "bitchy"; Patch, a cat dressed up as a musketeer who longs for romantic adventure; and finally, Gibbons, an animal of indeterminate species but with a "wise and scholarly" look fitted to his role as Oddkins historian, like his near-namesake. Each has an opportunity to display courage during the course of the adventure. Although all of them have teeth and claws, such appendages are made of soft materials like Patch's rubber sword; none is armed with anything hard that can be used violently.

On their trail throughout the journey are the armed Charon toys, led by Rex, a dandified male marionette with a swordstick. With him are Lizzie, a sexy female puppet who carries a burning cigarette in a holder; Stinger, an outsize bee with a face like a man and a telescoping stinger at the other end;

Jack Weasel, a jack-in-the-box with a "wickedly painted clown's head" (26), who plans to capture the Oddkins and suffocate them in his box; and a metal robot, Gear, who longs to tear the soft toys apart with his "lipless mouth . . . toothed like the jaws of a steam shovel" and his "frighteningly powerful" hands (23). The physical odds therefore seem to be against the soft toys and in favor of the nightmare troupe, who embody adult fears of "degenerate" sexuality, monstrous insects, the physically "abnormal," and the mechanical. Fortunately, however, like the evil power behind the Charon toys, Bodkins, while perhaps not as godlike, has an influence over the universe that lingers after his death and to some extent protects his "children," the Oddkins, on their quest.

Yet the victory over evil will not be easy. Nick Jagg is on his way from prison to the city planning to buy the toy business from Bodkins's nephew, Victor. Victor Bodkins seems prematurely elderly, preoccupied by the pursuit of worldly riches, in contrast to his uncle, who never grew up properly, in Victor's opinion. Victor is pulled into the struggle against his will. Ruminating about his uncle's "childish belief in miracles and the goodness of other people," he almost runs over the Oddkins and then tangles with their menacing toy followers, who momentarily disable him. Hoping to dispel this fantastic intrusion on his "ordered and logical" complacency and regain a "life without magic and mystery" (53), Victor turns away from his uncle's property, which he is planning to develop, and heads back toward the city.

Thus, everyone important, toy and human, is heading for the same place in an urgent journey that emphasizes the excitement of the pursuit as much as it does the importance of the quest. A battle must be joined before victory for the protagonists can be proclaimed—the good cannot succeed by turning their backs on evil and running away. As is true of quest narratives, the place of battle is significant. Where else should Amos and his little saving remnant take their stand but on "the vast third floor" of a nocturnally deserted department store, which is "divided among the sporting-goods, home-entertainment, and toy departments" (126)? And when Skippy is captured in a foray in home entertainment, suggesting an ironic comment on his ambitions for a television career, the Oddkins regroup to the toy department in order to "arm" themselves to rescue him, while Skippy besieges his captors with a line of patter.

Surprise and ingenuity predominate. The lethal weapons from the sporting goods department recoil against the Charon toys who try to use them. The Oddkins, in battery-powered toy automobiles with a gun that shoots ping-pong balls, gain a new advantage. (Although squeamish about both technology and weaponry they finally admit its necessity.) They run over and destroy Lizzie, lock Jack into his own box and throw him down the escalator, and then, retreating to the fourth floor chased by Gear, send housewares down upon the robot. Alarms sounded in the store attract not only the police but Victor, who is still searching for the Oddkins. He has had a brief encounter with Nick Jagg in which another fleeting glimpse of Oddkins makes him ignore Jagg's suitcase full of money in favor of his uncle's alternate vision. Victor (whose name proves prophetic) arrives providentially to help the Oddkins defeat the Charon toys, although Amos suffers what seems to be a fatal mangling. Victor scoops up the toys to take them to Mrs. Shannon's.

The denouement has Rex, who has failed his evil master, destined to remain down below in a kind of hell by his master's side, worked by him with strings, rather than as a free-roaming agent. Up above, the Oddkins reach the toy shop, known as Wondersmith, run by Mrs. Shannon—a young, childless widow, who experienced the empathy of an Oddkin lion in her own difficult childhood. There the toys undergo needed repairs. Victor—converted to wonder and magic—sympathetically participates (and is obviously attracted to Mrs. Shannon). Yet Amos cannot be revived, it seems, despite Mrs. Shannon's skill in replacing the animals' missing parts with stylish and humorous substitutes. (The metaphor "the stuffing seems to have gone out of him" is literal here.) Not surprisingly, Butterscotch, whose maternal manner has been evident throughout, is the one to discern the extreme solution needed: to replace Amos's original magic stuffing with some of her own. Each of the other Oddkins then donates some of its stuffing, for self-sacrifice goes beyond familial relationship. As Burl says, "'There is nothing more magical than the love that exists between friends. Nothing finer or more powerful. When we give Amos a small portion of our stuffing, a little piece of ourselves, we'll be giving him love, and maybe love can make this miracle work'" (176). And indeed it does.

This formulaic text is not one to leave any ambiguities. Starting with Bodkins's death, questions about life after death have been on the Oddkins' minds; they are revived by Amos's near destruction when Burl wonders, "'What happens to an Oddkin when the life goes out of his body? What happens to his soul? What has happened to Amos's soul?'" (164). Skippy theorizes that an Oddkin's spirit goes to heaven "'just like a human spirit. I mean, after all, God must like toys as much as everyone else does. Right? So what I figure is, we go to Heaven where we play with God and give Him pleasure for all eternity'" (164). Certainly, the fateful intervention in toy and human affairs throughout this narrative suggests a governing divinity, which gives further support to Skippy's "'lovely thought'" (164). For worried readers an even more delightful compensation for the Oddkins' future loss of magic is found in the surge of knowledge that Mrs. Shannon feels as soon as she agrees to become the new toy maker. Like the Velveteen Rabbit, all the stuffed toys will be reborn or metamorphize as real animals in order to "'experience the joy of being fully alive'" (179) and, moreover, once their lives as real animals are over (unlike the Velveteen Rabbit they are not to be real animals "'forever and ever'"), the Oddkins will return to toydom and go up to heaven because God "'*loves* toys'" (181).

As the storm dies down into a snow that presages the Christmas season to come and transforms "the grimy city into a clean white fantasy land" where many of the toys will go out to fulfill their vocation as companions to needy children, Amos speculates that there are no endings, only beginnings. And Koontz pays his respects to Jimmy Stewart and his Christmas crew in Amos's last words, "'Isn't it a wonderful life?'" (182). Indeed, only a cynically grumpy reader would remain entirely uncharmed by *Oddkins*, reassuring as it is that city and country, department store and toy shop can live side by side, and imaginative vision will win over the capitalist real-estate developers like Victor. Moreover, neglected and abused children and wounded teddy bears alike have someone looking after them in a world where good and evil prove not so hard to separate. Uncle Isaac, if not a fatherly god himself, looks down from heaven, providing a counterpoint to the toys from hell. Needed comfort in troubling times rests in the re-creation of a cosmos that is not indifferent to human fate. In this universal design, imaginative humans are the dominant species and toys sacrifice themselves to help abused children—as dolls sacrificed themselves in nineteenth-century toy narratives.

Oddkins is stylistically sophisticated. The dialogue is very funny and the character of comedy-struck Skippy is particularly delicious. The narrative is also verbally playful, eschewing formulaic language in favor of "natural" good taste. Amos's chronic recitation of the poetry of Rupert Toon, whose style runs to easy rhymes and greeting-card sentiments, is met with appropriate derision. When the Oddkins discover that Toon is actually Amos himself, their friendship and relief at his resurrection temper their reaction, but do not redeem Toon's verse.

In an interview in *Writer's Digest* that appeared shortly after *Oddkins* was published, Koontz talked about his wish to cross genre boundaries and write books that meld "'elements of mystery, suspense, science fiction, horror and adventure,'" endowed with what he terms a "'mainstream sensitivity,'" that will affect the reader along a wide emotional continuum (Wiater 37). Certainly, in *Oddkins* Koontz addresses both adult and child desires.[1] Combined with the high degree of closure that the text provides and its emphasis on anthropomorphized animals of a type as likely to appear in television commercials as in the shows they sponsor, the illustrated text gives the impression of a television holiday special, for which, gathered before the screen, the same mixed audience of "all ages" is assumed. Neither the deeper structural

formulas nor the surface philosophy of *Oddkins* afford the complex ambiguities prevalent in the other two texts.[2]

Mother Goose Goes to Sea

In *Oddkins*, metamorphosis into real animals is a neat reward for the soft toys,
without much ultimate significance except that it shows an affinity with
benign nature that is deeply desired in our technological age. Metamorphosis
and reverse metamorphosis of inanimate and animate raise central philosophical questions in Richard Kennedy's *Amy's Eyes*, which seems, like both
Oddkins and *The Mouse and His Child*, to be a quest narrative addressed to a
mixed audience of children and adults but, in this case, with considerable
bias toward the latter.[3]

In an earlier picture book, *The Porcelain Man* (1976), Kennedy (unlike
Koontz, marketed as a writer for children) dealt briskly and playfully with
metamorphosis, allowing a browbeaten young woman to fashion from the
shards of a porcelain vase first a porcelain lover and then a porcelain horse
that permit her to escape her overprotective and exploitative father and find a
flesh-and-blood man. *Amy's Eyes* goes deeper into the significance of metamorphosis and the human quest for meaning; in doing so, it nostalgically
withdraws to a world of sailing ships, pirates, and buried treasure that was
already fading when Robert Louis Stevenson wrote *Treasure Island*, some
hundred years before. In addition, *Amy's Eyes* portrays a world that focuses
upon orphanages and homes in which little girls are tormented, as they
were in even earlier nineteenth-century novels (and, alas, probably in late
twentieth-century institutions or homes). Perhaps aiming for one version of
"timeless universality" in its pre–twentieth century setting, this text differs
from the two others considered here in its avoidance of a direct confrontation
of the conflicts and anomalies in twentieth-century society and in a technologically sophisticated world.

The early chapters of *Amy's Eyes* suggest that the relationship between
child and toy will be more central than it is in *Oddkins* or *The Mouse and His
Child*. An unemployed tailor, bereaved by the death of his wife in childbirth,
sets out to make his fortune at sea, leaving his infant daughter, Amy, on the
doorstep of St. Anne's Home for Girls. With her in a basket are a loaf of bread
and a sailor doll, "tattooed" in embroidery with the sign of a needle and
thread and the words, "The Capt." But what begins as Amy's story evolves
relatively quickly into the doll's story when Amy, after bringing the doll to
life, is deprived of him through the machinations of Miss Quince, a spiteful,
sour teacher at the orphanage. In spite of the efforts of the sweet, loving Miss

Eclair, Amy then gradually becomes a doll herself. This role reversal, in which the doll captain becomes a man and the girl becomes a doll, is one of the most interesting and, to me, troubling aspects of the story: interesting because Amy's metamorphosis in particular plays an important variation on the toy theme, resembling the enchantment of Drosselmeier's nephew into the Nutcracker but using the metamorphosis as an apt metaphor for the virtual emotional catatonia, the state of deep freeze, that an abused child may enter; troubling because Amy's state is prolonged and, as doll, the child is tormented and fragmented further for reasons that seem arbitrary and plot-driven, thus inappropriately abusive themselves. (In addition, the absence of her consciousness and participation deprives the reader of an attractive child protagonist.) Be that as it may, as soon as Amy enters this doll state, the doll captain takes center stage and remains the leading character throughout most of the book, until he achieves his explicit quest—treasure—and, unexpectedly, reunion with his and Amy's father, a reunion of father and son that is one aspect of male development explored frequently in quest narratives.

Within this perspective, how life may be given to an inanimate object remains a major area of investigation. Persistent concern with this kind of creation brings *Amy's Eyes* closer in this issue to the texts considered in Chapters 4 and 10 (which highlight and problematize the issue of human versus divine creativity) than to *Oddkins,* where Uncle Isaac's powers seem ordained and providential, or to *The Mouse and His Child,* where consciousness is pervasive among toys, and even other inanimate objects. In Kennedy's version of life endowment, human language imitating divine command seems to be primary in bringing conscious life into being. As Skivvy, a troubled being that the captain himself creates, says: "'"In the beginning was the Word," or something like that, perhaps'" (119). Indeed, *Amy's Eyes,* which was written if not set in a postmodern world where consciousness can operate only through language, but where any abiding relationship between signifier and signified seems largely coincidental, postulates extraordinary magical powers for certain kinds of words: those that come from the King James Bible, in which genesis from the Word is posited, as well as those originating in a text that might be called the bible of Anglo-American childhood—*The Complete Rhymes and Riddles of Mother Goose.*

Amy brings the captain doll to life by reading steadily to him for four years, primarily from Mother Goose, and explaining patiently if naively the significance of what he has heard. In addition, as Amy's only close associate in her orphaned state, the captain is "hugged and loved constantly and told the most secret things" (20)—most of which make Amy an endearingly perceptive and mischievous child whom the reader will miss later on. Metamorphosis requires only one more catalytic experience in addition: while mending the doll by sewing back his half-detached ears, Amy sticks a needle into his head. With a yell, he immediately gains full consciousness, beginning by calling her "'Sis.'" Once the process has started, "In less than a day's time he began to change into a real flesh-and-blood person" (25). Moreover, having been originally created as a sailor, he need only brush up on his sea lore; he also seems to have been created knowing his duty—an example of the inheritance of acquired characteristics in doll metamorphoses.

After the transformed captain is forced to leave the orphanage, he proceeds to grow and change enough to inherit a ship and a treasure map. Surprisingly, when the captain returns for Amy, who in contrast has dwindled into a doll, he does not seem horrified by her transformation. On the contrary, he finds her doll state suits his purposes, since Amy is more portable as doll than as a preadolescent girl, who, he rationalizes, could not have been accepted as even a cabin boy aboard the *Ariel*. And, of course, he plans to seek worldly wealth—the type of quest that so frequently results in finding something other, in addition to or instead of, what was originally sought.

Once aboard ship, the captain proceeds to people it through metamorphosis. He creates the second mate, Skivvy, from his own underwear, in an intense if abbreviated version of the way Amy created him, but with the King James Bible as reading matter. The uneasy human crew abandons their new captain before they set sail, except the first mate, Mr. Cloud, of whom the captain is suspicious, and the new cook, a mysterious veiled woman, who declares herself the former captain's Bad Sister, entitled to a share of the treasure as her inheritance. Skivvy is then sent out to buy up sailor dolls. He finds no boy dolls and substitutes a range of animals to be turned into a crew in a similar manner—returning to Mother Goose for required life-giving readings. That text provides at least one set of verses in which a ship is manned by mice and captained by a duck. Unfortunately, the duck is misled by the readings into thinking he should be captain. He helps guide the pirate Goldnose, who also seeks the treasure and who follows the *Ariel*. So frequently merged with the quest journey, the pursuit is on.

Unfortunately, the good ship *Ariel,* whose name in the Old Testament designates the desired Jerusalem,[4] ironically seethes with plots based to a great extent on the misinterpretations of the very texts that have brought many of the crew to life. Skivvy, created by scripture, develops an obsession with numerology, and reads chapter and verse as predicting an apocalyptical ending to their voyage, one he must prevent. Davy Duck develops a similar obsession with the Mother Goose rhyme that gave him life, and begins secretly creating a crew of ducks that he will bring to life by reading them the same rhyme, while attempting rather unsuccessfully to recruit other crew members (casting aspersions on those who have "lips"). A frog, who must put up with the mysterious Bad Sister's temper as cook's assistant, becomes lovesick over her, interpreting all her harsh words as evidence of her passion for him.

The captain has also to interpret a disturbing dream that suggests that his seeking for treasure, while destined to be permeated finally by a golden light, will cause suffering and grief. As is traditional, the hero decides to proceed in spite of these warnings. Having noticed in the process of his own coming to life that one of his ears, not yet sewn on and fallen to the floor in the excitement of the moment, could still hear, the captain decides to place his sister's blue button doll eyes in a bottle and lower them to the ocean floor in order to find the sunken treasure. After dropping the bottle down "five fathoms," he immediately brings to the surface not a treasure but a "golden man," blond and tanned, who turns out to be the real treasure, Amy's and the captain's long-lost father, the marooned survivor of the pirate crew. His bones have not turned to coral, however, nor his eyes to pearl, but rather, like Ben Gunn in *Treasure Island,* this father has survived his marooning to control the treasure. He would give it all in exchange for civilization and his daughter.

The reunion between father and former doll son takes place quickly, but not before Amy's eyes are lost when a large fish breaks the bottle and swallows them. Amy's plight at last comes to the fore once more when thoughts of the treasure are shoved into the background while the *Ariel* crew, not particularly gold hungry anyway, hunts for the eyes in all the big fish it can capture. Meanwhile, Amy's eyeless body, brought back to near full consciousness before the captain's rash act, must be kept packed in salt in order not to grow and develop too rapidly. Ironically, she is put in a breadbox for safekeeping.[5] And one more complexity is added to the cosmos that is created by the text. On some island, miles away, dwells a prophetic old black woman, Mama Dah Dah, who keeps a pet white albatross, into whose eyes she can look and discover what he has seen each day. The albatross, who has been dining on a large fish, brings the blue button eyes back to Mama, and she finds that she can read the narrative in them too—just about the time the big battle begins between the *Ariel* and Goldnose's *Locust,* which has managed to find its prey at the treasure site.

Yet once more Amy's plight recedes while the captain works out what he conceives as his manifest destiny, which seems to be the same as that of Skivvy and most of the toy-animal crew as well. This obligatory confrontation between good and evil is made more ambiguous by Skivvy's opposition to the captain's seeking after treasure; gradually it becomes clear that Skivvy was the mysterious hooded figure who had followed the captain earlier. When, the night before the battle, Skivvy resumes this disguise to stalk the captain, he gets stabbed by the captain and disappears before being unveiled.

Emerging wounded when the *Locust* arrives, Skivvy cuts the sail lines so that the *Ariel* cannot sail away, which the captain might have liked to do, leaving the gold to Goldnose, who at first tries to bargain for it. The confusion of the ensuing bloody battle, rather far from the scenes of cleverness that prevail in the battles of both *Oddkins* and *The Mouse and His Child,* is depicted through the various mishaps of one of the cats. Although the *Ariel* emerges victorious, all of the major toy characters as well as the pirates die.

Permeated by a sadness that comes from the funerals of the crew members, among them the Bad Sister's devoted frog (for whom the now unveiled Miss Eclair does shed a tear), a sense of catharsis nevertheless reigns in the denouement. The narrative returns to a human world that has been saved by the ministrations of living toys, more fatally self-sacrificing than those in *Oddkins*. The albatross has brought back Amy's eyes and Mr. Cloud has been proved faithful. Amy, protected in her breadbox by Miss Eclair, appears once again on center stage with no sign of suffering from her prolonged ordeal. Released, she continues to grow and questions Miss Eclair about the events that led to her assuming the role of Bad Sister, a role played by Miss Quince until she fell off the dock while attacking Miss Eclair. Possibly Miss Eclair and Amy's father will fall in love, restoring a family scene that includes a resurrected self-appointed mother, if not the sacrificed doll brother. The captain, we have been assured earlier, has as much chance as any man for an afterlife, for he and Skivvy, much concerned about this question, are convinced, after witnessing the death of a rabbit crew member, who does not turn back into the stuffed toy as they feared he would, that "they were truly men, and they would never be dolls again. . . . Now they were truly men with all the parts of a man. They had souls" (267). Meanwhile, unbeknown to these other characters, Mama Dah Dah, who has acted as deus ex machina with regard to Amy's eyes, tells her albatross that Mother Goose is her sister.

In *Amy's Eyes,* Kennedy combines the quest narrative with one traditional thematic motif of toy narratives: the concern with what it means to become or to be "real." In this case, the captain seems to accept the fact that this human realness will make him prey to all the slings and arrows of outrageous fortune to which our flesh is heir. Moreover, the captain's final adoption of the Hamletian creed "the readiness is all" also fits the conclusions reached by the main male toy protagonists in the other two quest narratives considered in this chapter. Amos the teddy bear, the mouse father, and the mouse child, like the captain, all decide that leaders must lead even if their actions have unclear goals and uncertain outcomes. As the captain puts it after experiencing his bad dream: "Away with doubt! He was not made a captain without cause. He knew how to make a decision. . . . That was his destiny. He would search [the treasure] out no matter what the dangers" (282).

Amy's Eyes fails to follow out its initial promise in the depiction of Amy's metamorphosis as the result of the numbing effect of neglect and abuse on a child, which may well leave lasting scars that are brushed aside here. And Amy remains a doll throughout the action of the story, when a boy of her age would probably have been permitted to participate in the action. Confirming this, Skivvy's assumption—that toy animals might be turned into crew members but girl dolls may not—follows the tradition of the Mother Goose crew in the nursery rhyme that created Davy Duck and the other animals, suggesting the boundaries and limitations of masculinist fantasy. I am troubled more deeply by the captain's appropriation of Amy's detached eyes and the salting of her growing body and putting it in the breadbox from which the captain himself had been helped to escape. (Even Snow White herself was only incarcerated in a glass coffin!) Such incidents also involve the text in contrived plot complications. The Mama Dah Dah-albatross episodes are among these, which, although they add a powerful, nonwhite female to the text (as well as get Amy's eyes back to her) do so in peripheral and perfunctory ways.

Amy, as doll-sister, is handled badly, but even the captain, as man-son, is not treated well. Like *Treasure Island* and traditional quest narratives in general, *Amy's Eyes* turns a quest for treasure into a quest for masculine identity; however, where Jim Hawkins is allowed a multiplicity of father figures to deal with and choose among in order to establish this identity and is permitted a future in which to practice it, the captain, a one-dimensional hero who does not really convince us that he has "all the parts of a man," is, after some patronage from Captain Kimberly, allowed reunion only with a father to whom he hands over the future, in the form of a daughter, a possible wife, and a passage home with a small fortune. The exaltation of this father figure is extraordinary; he changes in the course of the novel from a grieving, poverty-stricken tailor into a "golden man" with everything his erstwhile son has preserved and garnered for him.[6] Even Geppetto, who ends his days well cared for by Pinocchio, never had it so good.

Patriarchy triumphant one might call this novel. Early on it makes a poetic apology for the ubiquitous absence of fathers:

But here is the truth, and you shall know it now. Amy's father never returned. God only knows what happens to so many people who intend to return, but never do. God only knows what might happen to a good country tailor in a seaport town without a wife to watch over him. There are temptations and dangers in such a place, and a wild chance lurking around the lanes and alleys such as seafaring men roam at all hours. Or perhaps it is the same wild chance that follows them from the sea, a stormy and haunting wind that blows always about their heads. Indeed, there might be a dozen reasons that Amy's father never came back for her, but not one of them was that he didn't love her more dearly than anything on earth. (5)

Yes, Father takes all here. As I noted in Chapter 5, not just females but everyone without power is oppressed under patriarchal systems—like the tailor himself in his youth, and certainly like his captain-son, whose self-sacrifice is exalted in the same way that the deaths of the sons on the battle-field are. While the structure of this novel proclaims the captain as protagonist, the captain's origin as a doll that has metamorphized into a basically undeveloped man distances us from him and blurs our perception of the injustices of his becoming real only to die for his father. How quickly the waters close over his body! In *Oddkins,* the ways the toys are made to benefit humankind are clear and the rewards both on earth and in heaven specific; *Amy's Eyes* takes metamorphosis into the human realm, but it finally denies all of the toys, including Skivvy and the captain, anything but the most limited access to this realm, supplemented by a vague promise of an afterlife. The waters become much more murky than even this stirred-up text would have them. Fatherly power is given full reign while the fatherly responsibilities of those who create their own sons and daughters by stitch or word or sperm remain largely uninvestigated.

Down in the Dump

Oddkins and *Amy's Eyes* give humankind, if not children themselves, a central place in the toy narrative. *The Mouse and His Child* creates a world at the margins of the human one, reflecting human needs and desires but imagining a secret existence that humans neither control for the most part nor benefit from—a world in which animals and toys communicate with one another at a level of discourse so sophisticated that it parodies avant-garde art and academic obscurantism.[7] In creating this world for child readers, Hoban may offer an anthropomorphic blueprint for a human quest but makes no promises that the benefits gained by the protagonists extend to humankind. In thus veering from androcentricity, *The Mouse and His Child* resembles most Bianco's *Poor Cecco,* in particular Jensina's early relationship with the rats in the dump and her final negotiations with them to benefit the needs of the toys.

The vision of *Poor Cecco* that everything in the material world lives at a threshold of consciousness and speaks in a voice that is just out of human hearing—a sense shared with Hans Christian Andersen—appears also in Hoban's later picture book *La Corona and the Tin Frog* (1974, 1979).[8] This short book consists of a series of connected stories, in the first of which a tin frog wins the hand of "the beautiful lady in the picture on the inside of the cigar box lid" (n.p.). He is aided by a talking magnifying glass, a tape measure, and a seashell. Similarly, a tin horseman woos a yellow-haired princess in a "weather castle . . . printed on a card that hung by the window," although he is fearful of a monkey in a game of skill. A wooden night watchman inarticulately encourages a tin crocodile who longs to submit his poetry to the mouse who edits a literary magazine. On a night when the clock finally refuses to strike midnight and walks out from its setting on "just two little walking brass legs," all of these characters follow the clock out the open window and "into the moonlight." Even the threatening monkey that inhabits the game of skill participates in this open ending: "'They'll want me too,' he said. 'Everyone can't be nice.'" A modified form of this extreme sensibility to objects—where clocks talk but dollhouses do not—distinguishes *The Mouse and His Child* from *Oddkins* and *Amy's Eyes* as well. And the last line of *La Corona and the Tin Frog,* with its denial of the desire for universal "niceness," explains what Hoban did differently with the classic conflict of good and evil that permeates the quest in all three toy narratives considered here.

Hoban came to *The Mouse and His Child* after writing a number of popular didactic picture books about Frances the badger and her middle-class family. In contrast to Koontz and Kennedy with their stuffed toys or dolls, he chooses to use, in addition to anthropomorphized "real" animals, tin wind-up toys as main characters. The tin-toy protagonists, a mouse father and child, facing each other with hands attached and dancing together in a circle when wound, constitute initially a single mechanical tin toy that is never played with by children but kept as a wonder to be displayed by adults at Christmas time. In using them, Hoban capitalizes on our fascination and identification with such mechanical objects—a fascination he exploits every time he lectures by bringing out the original toy that inspired him and winding it up to dance for his audience. Yet at the same time, by concentrating on these characters he avoids dealing with the child-doll or child–stuffed animal relationships that are evoked by other, more cuddly, toy animals or dolls. In addition, the mechanical, clockwork aspect of such artifacts raises questions predominant in a technological society, questions with which *The Mouse and His Child* will deal much more directly than the equally contemporary *Oddkins,* especially when the wind-up toys are used to further the aggrandizing schemes of Manny Rat, who uses them as slaves, reminding the reader of similar uses of human beings—on assembly lines, for instance—*as if they were machines.*[9] Still, although Hoban moves out into a world foreign to children and goes well beyond the issues of domestic relationships that occupy his Frances series, he succeeds in bonding the reader to his tin protagonists from the first. And, appropriate to a work for children as well as adults, the text ties the audience primarily to the mouse son, rather than to the mouse father.[10]

The early pages of *The Mouse and His Child* echo traditional and familiar toy narratives, which move swiftly through the cycles of toy life from the first appearance at the gala Christmas toy store where the toys come alive at midnight, to the arrival at a home with children, to the eventual decrepitude, accidental batterings, and final trashing. The reader can recognize this cycle from *The Velveteen Rabbit,* "The Steadfast Tin Soldier," and many another popular text. Such stories also tend to deal with the "Hereafter" of rejected toys, either a "Never-never-land" like Mrs. Ewing's Land of Lost Toys or an actual dump, where the toys sometimes join together and make a new life for themselves.[11] But whatever the reader's literary background, the longings expressed by the mouse child for home and family are likely to be familiar from life as well as from reading. The prohibitions against the mouse child's quickly revealed desires are ripe for subversion.

One midnight during the Christmas season, the mouse father and child gain consciousness in the toy shop. The child asks the eternal questions of awakening consciousness: "'Where are we?'" and then "'*What* are we, Papa?'" (4). Although the father is unable to answer them, the clockwork elephant, who considers herself "part of the establishment" and virtual owner of the elegant dollhouse in front of which she paces, answers them in realistic terms, underlining their toy state and the likelihood of their being sold soon.

The mouse child is a creature of strong if inchoate desires, who immediately tries to reshape this reality to meet his needs, despite the rules of toy behavior dictated by the clock: "'No talking before midnight and after dawn, and no crying on the job.'" By protesting and crying, the mouse child manages to persuade the elephant to sing him a lullaby and then tries to appropriate her as the mama that "he knew at once he needed . . . badly." He is even able to articulate an edenic vision: "'Will you *be* my mama? . . . and will you sing to me all the time? And we can all stay here together in this beautiful house where the party is and not go out in the world?'" (7). She refuses snobbishly, describing the mouse toys as "'the transient element.'" The next day they are sold, to be displayed at Christmastime and then stored in the attic until the following year. This half-life goes on until one day the mouse child breaks the rules again and startles the family cat by crying on the job. The cat knocks over a vase that crushes the mouse and his child flat, making them fit only for the trash bin.

Joanne Lynn has described this event as analogous to Adam and Eve's "fortunate fall," in that it permits development and growth beyond Eden (22). Certainly the mouse and his child now have the dubious freedom of having nothing left to lose. They thus become like the tramp, the book's single human, whose appearances frame the story. We first see him pressing his nose to the toy shop window and dancing in imitation of the mouse and his child, and then wandering off, followed by a little dog. At the mouse child and father's darkest moment, this tramp finds the flattened toy and attempts ineptly to restore it, succeeding in making the father lurch "straight ahead with a rolling stride, pushing the child backward before him" (11). No longer dancers in a circle, the mouse and his child, placed on the road and wound up, will obey, insofar as possible, the tramp's admonition to "'be tramps'" (12). They will meet the tramp again at the end of their quest, the nature of which they only discover along the way. After this they meet no other humans, but, like Alice in Wonderland, wander through a predatory world of exploitation, violence, and—oddly—nonstop talking, where toys and animals mingle. Unlike Alice, they remain in the nightmare world and shape it to meet their evolving dreams of place, love, and power.

In these quest narratives, the chase seems inevitably tied to the quest—the forces of evil are aroused by the activity of the good. The mouse and his child barely manage to go a few yards before they are stalled. The evil antagonist, in the form of the dump boss, Manny Rat, captures them and forces them to work on his slave team of wind-up toys that forage through the trash. The dump turns out to be a well-developed bartering community whose small-animal residents cater to each other's cultured desires for the debris and garbage of an affluent society. Endowed, as he brags, with "the longest, strongest, sharpest teeth in the dump" (22), Manny rules the territory, partly through his vicious lieutenants and partly through his superior technical skill. The latter allows him to cull spare parts from disintegrating toys, which he keeps in a can labeled "Bonzo Dog Food" until they are needed, and which he uses in diverse ways.

On the way to their first assignment, a robbery of the Meadow Mutual Hoard and Trust Company, the enslaved mouse father and son, accompanied by Manny's lieutenant, meet an elderly frog who makes his living telling fortunes. This frog becomes the first of several guides for the protagonists, through his predictions about their future in uncertain, ambiguous terms. But he is also the instrument of their escape, getting the lieutenant killed and successfully confronting Manny, who has begun searching for them accompanied by the once-proud toy elephant, who too has been thrown out and then enslaved.

Having managed to evade Manny, who becomes obsessive in his pursuit, the father and son—bound together and thus sharing the role of hero—begin a questing journey, becoming involved in the small-animal and bird life and being tested many times as they continue to elude Manny. They see a territorial war between shrews and weasels in which the victorious weasels are then eaten by owls; they join the Crows' Caws of Art Experimental

"A large rat crept out of the shadows of the girders into the light of the overhead lamps, and stood up suddenly on his hind legs before the mouse and his child." From *The Mouse and His Child*.

Theatre and participate in a Beckettlike play; they experience servitude at the whim of a pedantic Muskrat who wants to practice his theories by means of others' labor; they are stuck in the pond mud along with the author of the experimental play, a giant predatory turtle named C. Serpentina, who bores them with existentialist philosophy; and, having been picked up by a hawk but discovered to be not a part of the food chain, they are dropped on rocks back in the dump, where they split into many pieces, from which they are resurrected as two separate entities.

Their circular travels away from and back to the dump afford them not only souvenirs that will help them in their final battle with Manny but knowledge, which helps them set goals and find the means, perhaps, of achieving those goals. The frog's prophecy arouses in the mouse child a vision of his original need for home and family. The father acquires the idea of territory from the war between the shrews and the weasels. A member of the drama group, Euterpe, offers them the idea of becoming self-winding. Lectures from the Muskrat on his formula "Why Times How Equals What" are given practical application in several crises.

Probably the most significant of their experiences, however, is the insight gained by the mouse child when they are stuck on the bottom of the pond with C. Serpentina. As his father begins to despair at their plight, the child finds himself staring at the label on a sunken can of Bonzo dog food (these cans have appeared throughout the story). Its label is immediately intriguing in its apparently infinite regression, showing a little black-and-white spotted dog wearing a chef's hat and carrying a tray on which appears a Bonzo dog-food can, on which there appears a picture of a little black-and-white spotted dog, and so on. Although this label has been the inspiration of C. Serpentina's play, "Beyond the Last Visible Dog," C. Serpentina cannot or will not tell the mouse child what is beyond the last visible dog. After gazing deep into the picture, he seems about to accept the nihilistic philosophy implied by the answer "Nothing," when an insect who has befriended them, Miss Mudd, strips the label completely off the can; the mouse child and his father's back are symbolically reflected in the metal. For the mouse child the answer thus becomes "'there is nothing on the other side of nothing but us.'" This answer demands action rather than fatalism.

With the help of Miss Mudd and using Muskrat's formula, as well as a coin and an acorn drum on a string acquired on their travels, they devise a way to pull themselves out of the mud—ironically, they escape only to be shattered on the dump rocks. Their fall, however, is made known to the whole area by the blue jay (who throughout the text acts as reporter, screaming out the latest headlines). Both friends and enemies rush to find them. Among the former are a toy seal from the old shop days (whom the mouse child has already decided he wants for a sister), along with her protector, a kingfisher, and their old friend, Frog, whom the child has dubbed Uncle, and who persuades a bittern to transport him there.

Manny, returned to the dump and now in proud possession of the old doll-house, sends his new lieutenant to search for them. The lieutenant arrives only after the friends have rebuilt the toys, now detached from each other, and hidden them in the trees, from which the mouse child can see Manny's new home, which he immediately knows is "'Ours.'"

For both father and son, the breakup provides the final testing and opportunity to be reborn with a new independence and identity, even before they become self-winding. At this point the father determines that they are no longer toys; they are ready to act to gain the dollhouse and free the elephant from her bondage to Manny, following their destiny as the captain had followed his in *Amy's Eyes*. Frog's oracular inspiration on first meeting the tin mice has been almost completely fulfilled: *"'Low in the dark of the summer, high in the winter light; a painful spring, a shattering fall, a scattering regathered. The enemy you flee at the beginning awaits you at the end'"* (28). Like all developing males who engage in the traditional quest, they must engage the enemy in battle, which through careful and complex planning (they have not been Muskrat's students for nothing) and the help of Frog, Kingfisher, and Bittern turns out to be a rout of Manny. Using spare parts from the Bonzo dog-food can that they have stolen, they contrive in several mechanically ingenious ways—even by altering the forms of the tin mice—to invade and conquer the dilapidated dollhouse. In spite of their cleverness, victory is almost lost to them at the last moment when Manny emerges from hiding and seems about to dismantle the tin mice with a can opener. But the frog, using a spring mechanism they have contrived, sends the lucky coin into Manny's face, smashing out the teeth about which he had earlier bragged. This act unmans Manny and he slinks away.

The mouse child precedes to arrange things to fit his desires, enlisting the seal as sister, and Kingfisher and Bittern to join Frog as uncles. Fortunately, since the mouse father and elephant have somehow fallen in love despite the physical incongruities of the match, his father plays the appropriate part by asking the elephant to marry him. A marriage is celebrated and the self-winding postponed until the elephant and seal have persuaded everybody to make the house into what they want it to be, not a carbon copy of its original bourgeois comfort, but a gaily painted, if battered survivor, resembling its toy inhabitants whose wounds have healed but whose scars remain.

A subdued Manny returns and offers to help. He finally succeeds in making the tin mice "self-winding," for he is truly a practical mechanical genius. This intriguing task accomplished, Manny's humility becomes such a strain that he tries once more to harm them by wiring the house in such a way that it will blow up. He is accidentally foiled by the elephant and electrocutes himself instead. When he somehow is revived or reborn, *The Mouse and His Child* takes a different tack from the other two texts considered in this chapter, for Manny, who has played the traditional role of the evil antagonist-pursuer, is not ejected from the paradise regained. The mouse child recruits Manny to become another uncle in the variegated household that his deep desire and faith in its fulfillment have created—and, in which, apparently, not everyone can be nice. Inclusion not exclusion becomes the order of the day; instead of a private home, the dollhouse becomes an inn for wayfaring birds. Named The Last Visible Dog, this inn carries a sign with the Bonzo dog-food label and becomes a center of culture visited by the Caws of Art and sponsoring a Deep Thought seminar led by C. Serpentina. Emphasis on community over family and individual is suggested also by the fact that when Manny's original solution to self-winding proves only temporary, both father and son decide to forgo independence and rely on their friends to wind them up. When Christmas rolls around again, the tramp, followed by his own little black-and-white spotted dog, looks into the window of the festive dollhouse and smiles; in the last sentence of the book, he then admonishes its inhabitants to "'be happy,'" apparently offering a godlike blessing.

All three of these quest narratives have endings that emphasize the restoration of order and the wish for love and care of both children and adults, but only *Oddkins* maintains that order, love, and care in this world are part of a divine plan and that society already embodies that utopian vision. The more limited interventions of both Mama Dah Dah in *Amy's Eyes* and the tramp in *The Mouse and His Child* suggest benign forces only intermittently at work. Linguistic playfulness in the latter narratives casts doubt on the ability of language to represent reality while examining its paradoxically powerful role in our lives. Yet despite the difficulties the characters have in communicating, references in *Amy's Eyes* to traditional texts, reassurances about the souls of both dolls and people, and the retreat to a nostalgic setting, combined with an omniscient narrator—who controls the text as an interested and intervening god might control the universe—provide some sense that all is really well that ends well.

The suggestive slipperiness of pun after pun pervades *The Mouse and His Child*. And this text, in all its playful parody, certainly notes the failure of philosophic attempts to make sense of the universe. Its dystopic setting, amid not only feral nature but the garbage of a technological universe controlled by the paternalistic and capitalistic Manny, undercuts any complacency about permanence and security in the society created here or elsewhere in the universe. "Be happy" makes no promises about the future. And this relatively happy ending acknowledges the necessity of endless remaking, virtual recycling, of the world to meet human desires. Hoban uses his toy narrative to mirror and exploit the uncertainties of human life as we approach the twenty-first century.

Interestingly, *The Mouse and His Child*, for all its considerations of societal marginality and its odd use of allusions to existentialist drama in a text purportedly for children, is not particularly poststructuralist or deeply experimental as a literary text. It partakes of the linearity of a quest narrative and marks time in traditional seasonal patterns. It may not provide an intrusive narrator, but it strives for unity and closure in another way: through pervasive images. The little black-and-white spotted dog not only follows the tramp but appears on the dog-food can that inspires the mouse child to contemplate infinite regression and nothingness; it connects with the Dog Star that appears in the sky during momentous occasions and with the frog's disturbing prophecy to Manny Rat that "*'a dog shall rise . . . a rat shall fall'*" (41). This image acquires symbolic meaning that, because it is part of a consciously created literary text, suggests a universe less random than existentialist philosophy might have it. The London *Spectator* review of *The Mouse and His Child* describes the book as "brilliantly plotted, so that everything is satisfactorily linked and coincidence seems like destiny." Yes.

The Mouse and His Child, again like *Amy's Eyes,* does not deviate from traditional gender depictions and notions of patriarchal family, even extended ones. Koontz, in tune with his times, makes a gesture toward feminism in designating Mrs. Shannon the next Oddkins toy maker, which suggests some fluidity of roles, although most of the book's active characters are male, and the one female Oddkin, Butterscotch, is soft and maternal while the evil Lizzie is hard and sexy, reiterating the mother/whore dichotomy. Yet fantastically lively as their imaginations are, neither Hoban nor Kennedy can imagine a quest scenario without gender roles in which females are peripheral to male bonding and development and, as characters, important largely in their roles as wives (children's literature precludes their emergence as sex objects except subliminally), good or bad mothers, and/or sisters. Both works are primarily interested in fathers and sons, but *The Mouse and His Child* at least questions patriarchal triumph in the figure of Manny and does not sacrifice the son to the father. It suggests that the child may be more alert to life's possibilities than the adult—a subversive Wordsworthian notion exploited in children's literature since the mid-nineteenth century.

Miss Mudd is an attractively sturdy little character whose longings to fulfill her potential as a dragonfly take on little sexist resonance. I find, however, that the depiction of the elephant and the seal assigns to them aggravatingly conventional roles, even though their journeys and experiences are as potentially meaningful and testing as those of the father and son. The seal has also worked in the Caws for the Arts and appeared in a rabbit flea circus; she too has listened to Muskrat, and has accommodated herself to assisting the kingfisher, acting as bait. The elephant has been punished for any initial pride and complacency. Battered in the service of child owners, she is abused by Manny Rat. Like the relationship of Squirrel and Miss Hickory discussed in Chapter 8, the dialogue of Manny and the elephant resonates with sexual innuendo:

"Good evening, madam," said Manny Rat. "Do we find ourselves quite worn out and thrown away? Do we lie here, lonely in the wintery waste, and rot? The pity of it!"

The elephant said nothing.

"Be of good cheer," said Manny Rat. "Rejoice! Help is at hand!"

Still the elephant preserved her silence.

"Surely you can speak," said Manny Rat. "You heard the striking of the town hall clock, and the hour is long past midnight."

"We have not been introduced," murmured the elephant almost inaudibly, as if she hoped to create the illusion that the words had not actually come from her.

"Ah, but we shall be!" said Manny Rat. "We shall become, moreover, close friends and intimate associates." He tried the elephant's key, but could not turn it. The spring was tightly wound and thick with rust. "What better introduction could there be," he said, "than to take you apart and repair you so you can work for me?" He produced a rusty beer-can opener from within his robe and undid the tin clasp that held the elephant together.

"Nothing more to say, madam?" he asked as he pried apart the two halves of her tin body. "Not so much as a how-do-you-do?"

But the elephant was silent. She had fainted. (30)

Manny's loss of teeth is, as I have already mentioned, an act of castration, and I do not want to suggest that he deserves more punishment and less acceptance at the end for his assertion of power through a virtual rape than for his earlier violent torture of the donkey, one of his male slave toys. Rather, after all these testing experiences, the concluding "feminine" image of the elephant and seal as concerned only with decorating and hostessing high- lights the absence of any interest in their becoming self-winding. Hoban's final sexist stereotyping of them comes when they contribute to the cultural activities of the restored inn a Fashion Forum and Homemaker's Clinic (obvi- ously not a consciousness-raising group). This depiction of female character is that of a limited masculinist fantasy, which assumes that the nature of the female quest is known and fixed in the domestic arena, and that individual experience and testing bring no essential change: to be male means develop- ment and change toward individuality in toy or flesh and blood, and to be female means waiting passively for rescue and the move toward the maternal.

Beyond Gender

One massive paradox in the use of toys as characters in literature rests in the persistence of assigning an essentialist gender to toys in the face of the absence, except for Barbie dolls, of primary or secondary sexual characteris- tics.[12] Given the fact that only clothing or hairstyle makes most toys mas- culine or feminine, let alone male or female, why are these roles not more fluid when toy metamorphoses of even more striking sorts, like those into flesh and blood, can be easily imagined? One answer lies in the very nature of our language itself: once a toy has been personified and made subjective, he or she is no longer an "it"; English has only personal pronouns denoting gender for use in telling tales about shes or hes.[13]

In addition, no repertoire exists in Western literature of tales for a gender- less or even gender-fluid toy to act in. If such narrative structures are now being conceived, these three toy texts, although relatively recently written, do not choose to embody them.[14] All three books are structured in the traditional form of the quest narrative. This form, as Joseph Campbell, rely- ing not only on mythology but Freudian and Jungian psychology, has outlined it in *The Hero with a Thousand Faces,* postulates fixed gender relationships, if not fixed gender characteristics. In it, the relationship between the father and son becomes central and the subordination of female to male is molded into the patriarchal mode. Writes Campbell:

When the child outgrows the popular idyl of the mother breast and turns to the world of specialized adult action, it passes spiritually, into the sphere of the father. . . . Whether he knows it or not, and no matter what his position in society, the father is the initiating priest through whom the young being passes on into the larger world. And just as, formerly, the mother represented the "good" and "evil," so now does he, but with this complication—that there is a new element of rivalry in the picture· the son against the father *for the mastery of the universe,* and the daughter against the mother *to be the mastered universe.* (emphases mine, 136)

Each toy text under consideration makes some inroads on the traditional. A female, Mrs. Shannon, takes over Isaac Bodkins's role in relation to the Oddkins, although she is likely to share it with the newly converted Victor. In *Amy's Eyes,* turning the myth on its head, the father regains the mastery of universe won back by his son, who does not survive his initiation. *The Mouse and His Child* centers the father-and-son relationship in such scenes as the mouse child's epiphany on seeing his reflection in the Bonzo can: "He had never seen himself before, but he recognized his father and therefore knew himself" (111). It deemphasizes, however, the traditional rivalry between father and son by having them both start from the same testing place, yet keeps the mouse child in his child role throughout the text, so that he is still gratified by the fulfillment of preoedipal desires at the end.

Reflecting our society, these quest narratives remain overwhelmingly resistant to postmodern Lacanian notions that gender is constructed rather than "natural" and fixed. One would not expect to find much toying with gender in the formulaic *Oddkins,* which can be expected, as Cawelti claims, to reflect cultural values. But even the supposedly "original" *Amy's Eyes* and *The Mouse and His Child,* linguistically interesting and philosophically speculative as they are, do little to alter the masculinist preoccupations of the "universal" quest outlined in Campbell's "monomyth." Without understanding the engendered nature of such traditional quests, it may be impossible to write a toy story that looks to the future rather than to the past for its inspiration. Writers of toy narratives, although ingenious, may have exhausted the potential of the old literary forms.

10 Life(size) Endowments: Monsters, Automata, Robots, Cyborgs

To dance with one's own masterpiece represents the ultimate transference of creative energy, the penetrating of that narrow and frustrating barrier between life and art.
—Leonard Mendelsohn, "Toys in Literature"

In the sexy passage quoted above, Leonard Mendelsohn celebrates the Walt Disney version of Collodi's *Pinocchio*. This film, Mendelsohn admits, is an "example of Disney's manhandling of yet another classic," which transforms Geppetto, Collodi's humble artisan, into a toy maker at the peak of his creative powers who lives not in the sparse quarters Collodi allotted him but in "a quite charming cottage crowded by an overplus of imaginative toys" (81). What Mendelsohn admires, however, is the carnivalesque dance of the toys that, among other foreign elements, Disney imposes on the narrative. My principal interest in this passage is in Mendelsohn's emphasis on toy making as exemplifying art, with the toy maker as consummate artist, who experiences great joy when toys take on life.[1]

Further, for Mendelsohn the act of dancing with one's own creation is emblematic of a reciprocal relationship between toy and creator. This potential for reciprocity he sees passing down through the toy so that, once endowed with life, it becomes a "force that dominates and determines those who come under its spell, acting as a creator in no less a fashion than the individual who formed its existence" (83). To Mendelsohn, toys in both life and fiction are not only products of the artistry of the artisan or writer, but also bring out the imaginative creativity of player or reader, which, in turn, brings the toy to life once more.

180

In *The Gods Made Flesh: Metamorphosis and the Pursuit of Paganism,* Leonard Barkan makes much of a similar reciprocity between master and masterpiece in discussing Ovid's version of the Pygmalion story, in which Pygmalion creates a beautiful woman out of stone, falls in love with her, and then brings her to life through his love. For Barkan, this Ovidian redaction becomes a story of a young man's rejection of nature in favor of imaginative art. Pygmalion's narcissistic act of creation is potentially comical, but almost in spite of itself, it brings about a reconciliation of art and nature through the love that the statue elicits from Pygmalion. Although, among pagans, inter-ference with nature is suspect, in this story Venus, representing the gods' reaction to such potentially defiant creativity, eventually approves Pyg-malion's actions. With her blessing, according to Barkan, artist and statue both come alive: "It is not only the statue that softens under the pressure of love but also the creator himself. Nature as a general force, and Pygmalion's own nature in particular, are seconding the artistic creation and softening the hardness of both individuals" (76–77).

I find it hard to disregard Pygmalion's basic misogyny in rejecting all natural women, even if Venus (and Barkan) excuse it. Ignoring misogyny for the moment, however, I would like to point out, as I did in considering metamorphic stories like *Pinocchio,* that Barkan's study uses the historically recurring artistic fascination with such tales as an example of the persistence of paganism, in defiance of the Judeo-Christian tradition, in Western art. Indeed, the kind of metamorphosis in Pygmalion's story is the one most abhorred in that Western tradition: human endowment of inert matter with life. And in the Judeo-Christian cosmos, human creators must placate not just Mother Nature but Father God.

Mendelsohn's account of toys in literature, while celebrating the human masculine life-giving force, ignores the Judeo-Christian prohibition of that force and does not deal with the anxiety such metamorphoses aroused and continue to arouse in cultures attracted by art to pagan concepts but required by religion to shun them. I begin in this chapter by touching on the bad character often attributed to toy makers in literature, whose activities may even seem tinged with the demonic. The works I examine more closely here, in which humans attempt to, or actually do, endow inert matter with some kind of life, are not about toys per se, yet they illuminate, I think, the aura of danger that surrounds the coming alive of toys, faint as that aura may be in stories for children. Since the beginning of the nineteenth century, literature has expressed growing concern over not only art's but science's encroach-ments on divine creativity: hubristic artist and mad scientist seek similar powers. Visions of electronic robotry and feats of bioengineering add to mechanical ingenuity to bring new vitality to coming alive narratives. These scientific achievements also revive threats of loss: both of divine control over human creation—and of human control as well.[2]

The narratives that I examine at some length here all concern toylike but not miniature automata, beginning with E. T. A. Hoffmann's "The Sandman" (1816–18), which features a life-size figure of an automated woman. The tale is troubling in the light it throws on sexual desire and repression, combined with a misogyny similar to Pygmalion's. Isaac Bashevis Singer's version of an old Jewish legend, *The Golem* (1969, 1981), with its monstrously large animated clay man, brings to the fore other disturbing elements in the creation not of miniature figures but of larger-than-life-size beings whose resemblance and danger to humans seems enhanced by their size. As in Nathaniel Hawthorne's story "Feathertop" questions of identity, power, sexuality, and empathy between humans and animated beings arise in these relatively short fictions. Their resolutions generally require the destruction of the created being.

Singer's version of the golem legend, which was written with children as well as adults in mind, considers the potential for growth and change of the created being through both development and redemptive love—an idea that dominates such children's stories as Pamela Stearns's *Mechanical Doll* (1979). Another children's tale—Carol Ryrie Brink's *Andy Buckram's Tin Men* (1966), a robot story, also offers some possibilities for development and growth, evading the issue of whether the created beings must ultimately be destroyed while faintly suggesting new ethical conflicts connected with technological advances.

Finally, Marge Piercy's novel *He, She and It* (1991), which appeared just after I had written the first draft of this chapter, raises all the right questions about creation in its account of the invention of a new biomechanical golem, a cyborg. Piercy also brings to light and violently resolves what is suggested but I think insufficiently developed by many of the other narratives considered: the troublesome issue of human, largely patriarchal, power over life and death. She displays concern with the moral choices both men and women may need to make in the foreseeable future, when what was pure fantasy in the past—the human creation of a living being other than by conception, pregnancy, and birth—may become technologically possible.[3]

Toy Makers

In spite of the commercial reality, our popular image of the toy shop remains not a factory but a cozy workroom presided over by a bustling Mr. Santa and staffed by jolly, nonunionized elves, who whistle while they work and during their work breaks imbibe milk with cookies baked by Mrs. Santa. Literary accounts of the toy shop, as workshop or retail venture, are somewhat more complex than North Pole, Ltd., although a few of them evoke that climate of familial warmth and good fellowship. The benevolent atmosphere that prevails in Ruth Ainsworth's *Mr. Jumble's Toy Shop* (1978) comes perhaps from the cozily parental toy-shop owners, Mr. and Mrs. Jumble, who seem able to communicate with the toys and lend a timely helping hand, although they do not join the nocturnal activities. And the kindly toy maker of Ursula Morey Williams's *Adventures of a Little Wooden Horse* (1938) earns the devotion of his creation, the wooden horse. Their nurturing attitude is like that of the good toy maker Uncle Isaac in Dean Koontz's *Oddkins*. Also, like Geppetto, the creator of Pinocchio, such toy makers and retailers belong to the realm of the good father.

In Florence and Bertha Upton's *Adventures of Two Dutch Dolls—And a Golliwog,* the dolls and toys are treated at midnight to delightful tastes "of human joys" and the golliwog appears as a charming gentlemanly creature. But the nocturnal toy shop is a place where anything grotesque might happen as well. As a setting, it ranges from providing freedom to indulge relatively harmless desires to giving license and reality to nightmarish, conflict-laden visions. In *The Mysterious Toyshop* (1924), Cyril Beaumont describes in detail the attractions of a wonderful new store that opens suddenly on Holborn Street in London just before Christmas, promising to meet shoppers' deepest desires. The toys it purveys are marvelous; they become the talk of the town. The fact that the accommodating clerks are rather peculiarly mechanical in their movements becomes significant enough only to make readers uneasy when they learn that the proprietor, a strange old man, invites certain special *adult* customers to a hidden room on the third floor in order to give them animated toys. When an importunate gentleman insists on visiting the old man to demand certain toys, his insistence so infuriates the elderly proprietor that he flies apart in his rage, revealing that he is mechanical, as must be his clerks.

The text manages to convey the self-importance and wrongheadedness of the visitor, who is a parody of bourgeois pomposity; nevertheless, the notion of a toy store run by life-size toys dispensing their own creations and catering to adult desires conveys more psychic unease than social satire. The sudden subsequent disappearance of the toy merchandise and the customers' bewildered storming of the empty premises further add to the charged atmosphere of potentially evil magic. The ability of the toys themselves, especially the old man upstairs, to control this magic and to manipulate adult humans by fulfilling their wishes can be frightening. Beaumont's narrator ends on a reassuring note, but the mystery of what may have gone on in the third-floor room also points to the secrets of the night and a sense of the uncanny power of playthings to turn nasty.

The magic that pervades the toy-shop setting seems to have much to do with the nature of the toy maker, traditionally male, himself.[4] And, manifesting itself in various ways, an air of the disreputable, at the very least, often hangs over the toy maker as shown in fiction. Charles Dickens, in *Our Mutual Friend* (1864–65), for instance, depicts the dwarfed and delightful "Jenny Wren," otherwise known as Fanny Cleaver, doll dressmaker, who supports her drunken wretch of a father, the toy maker known as Mr. Dolls. In *The Enchanted Doll, A Fairy Tale for Little People* (1849), Dickens's friend Mark Lemon uses a rapidly growing ebony doll to embody the evil envy manifested by a villain toy maker toward his prosperous neighbor, a worthy silversmith. In Ursula Morey Williams's *The Toymaker's Daughter* (1963), a doll escapes from a wicked creator, Malkin, and returns to him only after he has reformed, while Lottie, the talking doll in John Symonds's book of the same name (1957) runs away and becomes permanently independent of Mr. Gotobed (what a suggestive name!), the clockmaker who creates and then forces her and the foundling dog Toby to work for him. As noted in the last chapter, the spirit of the bad toy maker remains in the cellar beneath Uncle Isaac's house in *Oddkins,* a devillike power whose malevolent toys are no longer suppressed when Uncle Isaac dies. The bad father seems determined to return.

Short of Santa Claus/Father Christmas, kindly patriarchal portraits of toy makers do not pervade fiction, and the atmosphere that surrounds the bad toy maker can make the toy shop a fiercely threatening place to be, as it is in Angela Carter's novel of adolescence *The Magic Toy Shop* (1967). Although Carter, later to adopt magic realism, stops barely short of magic in this early novel, she does use the living-toy theme to create an atmosphere of fantastic possibility and psychic threat. The sadistic toy maker, Uncle Philip, through the frightening puppet shows he forces on his orphaned niece, Melanie— who with her two younger siblings comes to live over his toy shop—seems almost magically to control the fate of Melanie's family, as he has that of his young wife (struck dumb on her wedding day) and her two brothers. His relatives are barely able to shake off Uncle Philip's power in a holocaust ending that only a few of them survive.

In Carter's story, the bad toy maker seems to coalesce with the image of the bad father in an antipatriarchal tale of which hints appear in *The Toymaker's Daughter* and *Lottie.* The nightmare toy shop is associated with the same male power and phallic threat that Hoffmann evokes in his depiction of the makers and manipulators of automata, who toy with young men by manipulating their desires for the perfect female and not only make the inanimate animate but threaten to reverse—or actually succeed in reversing—the process, making the living into puppets or corpses.

Ambiguity elegantly clothes the figure of toy maker Judge Drosselmeier in Hoffmann's *Nutcracker*. Two other stories that Hoffmann wrote about the same period feature powerful old men, who are similarly associated with figures feigning life: "Automata" (1814) and "The Sandman" (1816–17). These characters, Professor X and Coppelius, respectively, are the users and vital animators of automata made by others, controlling the creations in mysterious ways and manipulating people through them—masterminds if not creative artists. And Professor X and Coppelius both seem grotesquely cruel and hostile toward the bewildered protagonists, young students drawn in by mysterious women, of which one is actually the animated figure itself. The fairy tale atmosphere that lends air and light but perhaps cloying sweetness to *Nutcracker* is withdrawn; a gothic terror of the unexplained psychic power of the apparently mechanical beings and of the evil patriarchal figures behind them takes over.

In his introduction to *The Best Tales of Hoffmann*, E. F. Bleiler calls the automaton one of Hoffmann's "idées fixes," noting his horror at "the possibility of mistaking an automaton for a human being" (xxi). Bleiler goes on to discuss the pervasiveness and powerful effect of ingenious automata on the late eighteenth- and early nineteenth-century scene: "During Hoffmann's lifetime, . . . Maelzel's chess player (which was a fraud) aroused a sensation in Europe, while Vaucanson's mechanical duck . . . and his speaking head and similar marvels of mechanics were held to be miraculous. . . . In Hoffmann [such figures] aroused a multiple reaction: admiration for their skill, horror at their inhumanness, and perhaps fear" (xxii). In "The Sandman"—better known to Americans in its abbreviated and distorted ballet version, *Coppélia*—Hoffmann confronts directly the sense that automata have more-than-mechanical powers and the malignant purposes of figures like Coppelius/Coppola, who somehow steals the hero's eyes to provide the eyes for "Olimpia," the beautiful automaton that serves to drive this protagonist, Nathanael, mad.[5]

For many critics, starting with Freud in his essay on the uncanny, Nathanael's story is one of developing psychosis, a madness possibly connected with sexual repression (and with fear of castration). "The Sandman" does not, however, do much to untangle deluded desires from reality. Readers are about equally divided between interpreting this story psychologically as "a figurative statement of growing mental illness" or metaphysically as a "fate drama, in which the central idea is that man is powerless against an external fate that moves in on him. . . . Coppelius . . . really exists; he is the Enemy"

(Bleiler xxv). "The Sandman" certainly does its best to defy interpretation, bringing it for me into the realm of what Tsvetan Todorov designates the fantastic—narratives that hover between the psychological and the marvelous, creating uneasiness and distress in the reader. It also never attempts to bring the automaton to conscious life. But in the context of toy narratives, and especially those that have to do with the doll tradition, what seems especially vivid here is how this story plays with male notions of the female automaton and ideal womanhood. And each time I read this tale I am struck anew with the tension between Nathanael's comically portrayed delusion with regard to Olimpia and the horrible grip that the figure of Coppelius has over him. Coppelius, an apparent participant in abusing the child Nathanael, manipulates him in his young manhood through the romanticized sexuality to which Nathanael seems particularly vulnerable.

Nathanael is a university student. For Hoffmann this stage of a young man's life, in which he is often introduced by his studies to notions of the world that seem shockingly new and esoterically attractive, is a particularly vulnerable time. Then the real and the ideal seem inevitably to clash, especially when the student is traveling or living away from his familiar home. Nathanael has left behind not only a widowed mother but two distant cousins, siblings, who have been brought up in his household: Lothair, who has become a good friend, and the beautiful and much desired Clara, who is Nathanael's fiancée. Neither is aware of the events that preceded the death of Nathanael's father, which he relates in a letter to Lothair, significantly misaddressed to Clara: an ugly local lawyer, Coppelius (known to Nathanael and his siblings as the Sandman because he comes in the evening as does the proverbial bringer of sleep) seems to have had power over Nathanael's father.[6] The two were engaged in a secret practice (alchemy is suggested), on which Nathanael spied one evening. Caught spying, Nathanael was brutally manhandled by Coppelius, who threatened his eyes with burning coals. About a year later, the father was blown up by an explosion from the hidden furnace he and Coppelius tended, and Coppelius left town.

Nathanael is badly frightened by what seems to be the reappearance of Coppelius as a Piedmontese peddler of optical equipment, using the name of Coppola (which, significantly, means "eye socket" in Italian). Clara, with the clearsightedness implied by her name, sympathetically but firmly advises self-control. He disdains her, estranged by her apparent impatience with his melancholic obsession with Coppola, finally regarding her as unperceptive and unfeeling and accusing her—ironically in terms of the denouement—of being a "'damned lifeless automaton!'" (200).

Back at the university he finds himself across the street from one of his professors, Spalanzani, whose beautiful but oddly passive daughter, Olimpia, he has previously glimpsed. Coppola appears to him again and manages to sell him a "perspective glass" through which he seems to see Olimpia, sitting in a window opposite, with "new eyes." He is delighted to hear that Professor Spalanzani will be giving a ball to introduce her and there, ignoring his university friends' suspicions of her strangely cold and awkward perfection, Nathanael monopolizes her, declares his love, and is seemingly accepted as a suitor. She becomes the perfect woman in his eyes, who listens to everything he says, exhibiting none of Clara's disapproval.

This beautiful woman, who can only say "'Goodnight, dear'" and whisper "'Ah, Ah'" in response to his effusions of love, seems to him his soulmate. The narrator describes Nathanael's state after one of his "conversations" with Olimpia:

Back in his own room, Nathanael would break out with, "Oh! what a brilliant—what a profound mind! Only you—you alone understand me." And his heart trembled with rapture when he reflected upon the wondrous harmony which daily revealed itself between his own and his Olimpia's character; for he fancied that she had expressed in respect to his works and his poetic genius the identical sentiments which he himself cherished deep down in his own heart, and even as it was his own heart's voice speaking to him. And it must indeed have been so; for Olimpia never uttered any other words than those already mentioned. (209)

All this narcissistic nonsense over a doll would seem terribly funny if it did not end horribly with Nathanael's psychic breakdown when he witnesses Coppola and Spalanzani—who is apparently the mechanical image maker but without Coppola's demonic powers—fighting over the figure of Olimpia, tearing her apart to reveal her clockwork mechanism, and pulling out her eyes, which Coppola claims he has stolen from Nathanael himself. But, recovering at home in the bosom of his family, Nathanael seems cured and reconciled to his less-than-automatically-perfect Clara. On a visit to some property that they have inherited, Clara and Nathanael climb the tower of the town hall, where Nathanael makes the mistake of trying to use Coppola's glass again; he becomes crazed and attempts to throw Clara over the parapet. Although Lothair comes to her rescue, Nathanael, in a frenzy, manages to throw himself down into the marketplace where he has suddenly perceived Coppelius, seemingly waiting for him to make the fatal leap. Clara, however, as the last paragraph informs us, subsequently marries another, living happily ever after.

I am struck with the connection between the pervasive eye imagery and the use of the female automaton in this story. In Chapter 6 I pointed out the complex ways boys and men interact with dolls; such complexity seems writ large in the figure of Olimpia. Also, long before Lacanian and feminist articulations of the concept of the gaze, Hoffmann seems to have portrayed its nature emblematically in Coppola's transferal of Nathanael's eyes to his automaton. Olimpia is thus made to seem the perfect responsive woman—whose gaze mirrors Nathanael's. This story shows too how only a mechanical woman might thus be completely dominated by male desire: in contrast, Clara, however sympathetic she may be with Nathanael, refuses to see except through her own clear eyes. Looking at the story in this way, the silliness or even evil madness of Nathanael's quest for the perfect woman and his finding her in a self-reflecting automaton is apparent, and works to reveal Pygmalion's similar obsession as basically misogynistic. Yet Hoffmann's story does not completely support Clara's clear-eyed stance either. The lingering desire for a more sympathetic female still permeates the last paragraph where Clara's ability to live happily ever after becomes somehow a reproof. Her behavior links her to an unimaginative bourgeois society that destroys the sensitive artist.[7]

In contrast to the dark tradition haunting Hoffmann, I might mention in passing Pamela Stearns' *Mechanical Doll,* a children's fantasy that does not emphasize the dangers in the challenge to nature and God in the creation of an automaton that comes alive. This story exalts art and artist in some of the ways that Mendelsohn associates with toy making. Here, a poor young musician re-creates and brings to life a dancing female doll that he had earlier perceived as his rival for the affections of a benevolent king and previously tried to destroy. In turn, she brings the musician back to life after he has been set upon by his real enemy, the king's son.

Stearns escapes the problematic nature of such creativity first by choosing a setting that, unlike many of these other tales, does not try to introduce the automaton into the everyday Western world. She defuses the gothic tension between the real and the seemingly magic aroused by such juxtapositions, instead creating a vaguely Oriental Mid-Eastern kingdom as setting (intricately illustrated by Trina Schart Hyman) that seems exotic and thus strangely miraculous. Then Stearns does something more subtle. Not merely censoring the sexual as children's writers tend to do, she instead substitutes for it a different kind of tension familiar to children in their daily lives—sibling rivalry, enhanced by competition for the attention and affection of a powerful patriarchal figure, a king. In the process, she evokes a familiar fairy-tale theme, adds to it some echoes of *King Lear,* and invokes female life-giving power like that of Collodi's Blue-Haired Fairy.

Barkan's interpretation of the classic Pygmalion myth, as noted earlier, suggests a reciprocity between Pygmalion and his created woman similar to that of the musician and his doll. To me, however, this myth, like the creation of Eve from Adam's rib, not only proclaims that "real" women are undesirable but implies that women are superfluous in the creative process (thereby also paradoxically reflecting a womb envy as strong as any postulated penis envy). Pygmalion aside, human projects to make perfect women are rarely depicted as feasible, fortunately. Still, the desire obviously lingers among males, however much one may laugh at it in the modern movie version of the sixties, *The Stepford Wives,* where a group of husbands order a virtual cartload of automata to replace their suburban mates. This desire seems also one aspect of the more generalized urge to make toys come alive, and one, perhaps, that harks back to an incompletely realized stage when transitional objects filled the space between the "me" and the "not me" in a struggle to maintain the infantile sense of the ability to incorporate and control the universe. Dorothy Dinnerstein claims in *The Mermaid and the Minotaur* that males, at least, are not encouraged to relinquish this need for control after their first struggle to separate from their mothers.

Inspired Artifacts

The source, at least in the West, of prohibitions against creative life-giving endeavors of the sort examined here lies in the beginning of Judaism, a strictly monotheistic religion that forbids image making as pagan and profane. Judaism's stern decree is embodied in the Mosaic Second Commandment, which begins: "You shall not make for yourself a graven image, or any likeness of anything that is in heaven above, or that is on the earth beneath, or that is in the water under the earth" (Deut. 5:8).

Christianity, which grew out of Judaism, frequently evaded the injunction against images in its ritual and iconography, yet still observed the law against endowing inert matter with life. Among the many illicit desires of Faust, according to Goethe in the second part of his tragedy (first staged in 1854), is that of creating a homunculus. Christopher Marlowe's late sixteenth-century Faust practiced conjury and alchemy, a "science" that Christian doctrine depicts as similarly evil in flaunting a wish to compete with divine creation. Faust tales were based on a historical German figure, Dr. Georg or Johannus Faust, a practitioner of magic in the early sixteenth century. The legend that arose around him obviously haunted Marlowe's imagination in the expansionist atmosphere of Renaissance England. Goethe's revival of the Faust legend can possibly be linked with a similar pervasive anxiety about early nineteenth-century advances in technology, advances that seem also to have troubled E. T. A. Hoffmann during the first quarter of the nineteenth century. Linking desires for control over nature and creation with the demonic is explicit in Goethe's use of the legend (which, however, romanticizes the questing hero far more than Marlowe's play does). It is implied in Hoffmann's tales.

Even deeper than the Judeo-Christian commandment against fashioning icons for worship went both the prohibition against and the fascination with the idea of making such images come alive, on the model of the first creation. In his introduction to one version of the Jewish golem legends that became pervasive in eastern Europe in the seventeenth century, Nathan Ausubel points out that the Talmud itself stimulated these legends by analyzing Adam's creation: "In the first hour his dust was collected; in the second his form was created; in the third he became a shapeless mass . . . ; in the fourth his members were joined; in the fifth his apertures opened; in the sixth he received his soul; in the seventh he stood up on his feet" (603). Stories of medieval Jewish Cabalists, especially revered rabbis, attributed to them the power to duplicate portions of this creation in the form of monstrous clay beings, golems, who when the tetragrammaton, or "Ineffable Name" of God, was written on their foreheads could come alive, in order to protect the Jewish people from persecution. Under these conditions, the suspicion that surrounded the human patriarchal creator was played down and refocused upon the inspired creation itself, now made in the male image, a creation that might well get out of control and turn upon its maker.

Two popular versions of this legend were disseminated widely among eastern European Jews. The sixteenth-century "Golem of Chelm" was perceived as so potentially destructive that the cabalist rabbi who created him immediately withdrew the secret sign from his forehead. The later "Golem of Prague" was more obedient and controlled; he succeeded for a time in relieving the innocent Jews of the threat of unjust accusations that they used the blood of Christian children to make Passover matzoth. Exploiting popular anti-Semitism, this charge was common among debtors who did not want to pay back their Jewish bankers (who, because Christianity forbade usury— and many other professions and investments were denied to Jews—were almost forced into moneylending).

Set in Prague, Isaac Bashevis Singer's *The Golem*—first published in Yiddish in 1969 in the *Jewish Daily Forward,* then translated into English by Singer and published in illustrated book form in 1982—partakes of both the fears of the first story and the respect of the second for what good the golem may do. The familiar accusation of ritual murder (which, in itself, reflects anxiety about infusing inert with living matter) is skillfully dramatized here in the evil figure of the gambling Count Bratislawski, who convinces powerful figures to help him persecute the honest banker who refused his last desperate request for money. Bratislawski's scheme to get his hands on his

"The golem went into the cheder and sat on a bench. The children gazed with amazement at the giant who sat among them." From *The Golem*.

young daughter's inheritance from her dead mother includes secreting her in a cellar and accusing the Jew of murdering her to make matzoth.

The famous cabalist Rabbi Leib (Judah Loew in most other versions I have read), encouraged by a mysterious old man who visits him at night, fashions the golem and brings him to life with instructions to find the little girl. The golem succeeds in bringing her to the courtroom at the strategic moment, ending the persecution in the manner of "The Golem of Prague." But anxious traces of "The Golem of Chelm" seem apparent in the second part of Singer's retelling, when Rabbi Leib, yielding to his wife's persuasions to use the golem for a task for which he was not created (Singer's women frequently partake of Eve's heritage), loses his control over the creature. The latter begins to exhibit not only childish destructive tendencies but pathetic yearnings to become other than a golem—to learn to read, for instance. He is tamed first by the love of a servant woman, Miriam, and then by her reluctantly playing the Delilah role, getting him so drunk that the rabbi can erase the secret name from his forehead, transforming him back into lifeless matter. Singer's story ends with the disappearance of Miriam; some say she has drowned herself, others that she has been fetched by the golem and taken to a place "where loving souls meet" (84).

The addition of the love story adds nineteenth-century gothic romance to this old tale, exalting the power of love to bring about transformations, a power which, Singer speculates, may be greater "than a Holy Name." Singer's romantic vision contrasts with Hoffmann's invocation of gothic romance to show that attraction to an artificially created being can be disastrous for humans, especially if an automaton is the object of desire. The ambiguous role of such desire is also evident in Nathaniel Hawthorne's "Feathertop" (1852), where a witch makes and brings to life a harvest scarecrow. Amused by her success, the witch, Mother Rigby, decides to send him out into the world, calling him Feathertop because he has a feathered hat to wear on the pumpkin that forms his head, above his finely clothed, stuffed sack body with the witch's broomstick as backbone and limbs formed from miscella-neous pieces of wood.[8] First he is to attract the love of Polly Gookin, the silly and artificially genteel daughter of a rich merchant. Feathertop's insecurities about his ability to do this are cynically scoffed at by Mother Rigby: "'Thou hast a fair outside, and pretty enough wit of thine own. . . . Thou wilt think better of it when thou hast seen more of other people's wits. Now, with thy outside and thy inside, thou art the very man to win a young girl's heart'" (Manley and Lewis 188).

Feathertop impresses all but a dog and a child on the street with his elegance; it seems as if he will succeed with Polly as well, until the two catch a glimpse of themselves in a revealing mirror. Polly faints dead away. Feathertop, however, is appalled. In the only truly serious moment in this satiric tale—which makes fun of empty men and women, silly characters in romance, and even workers of witchcraft—he returns home a sadder, wiser scarecrow, if not a man, and laments in answer to Mother Rigby's reproaches: "'Let her alone, mother . . . ; the girl was half won; and methinks a kiss from her sweet lips might have made me altogether human. But,' he added, after a brief pause and then a howl of self-contempt, 'I've seen myself, mother! I've seen myself for the wretched, ragged, empty thing I am! I'll exist no longer!'" (202). The text returns to its lightly satiric tone when Mother Rigby decides that Feathertop has "too much heart to bustle for his own advantage in such an empty and heartless world" (203).

In these narratives about males made from earthy materials and in some way "inspired" by God or the devil, neither author, Singer nor Hawthorne, can resist a moment of empathy with the unnaturally created being—an empathy that suggests an additional dilemma implied in the taking over of nature's or God's role: once having given life, does the giver have the right to take it away? For what was once an object, in the process of becoming self-conscious, seems to acquire an unanticipated right to control its own subjectivity. Rabbi Leib, when he first sends the golem on his mission, feels "a kind of compassion for the golem. He thought he saw an expression of perplexity in the golem's eyes. It seemed to the rabbi that his eyes were asking, 'Who am I? Why am I here? What is the secret of my being?'" (37–38). The rabbi rationalizes removing the name from the golem's forehead, but the reader, who may identify with the golem as children are likely to do, can only be pacified, Singer's version suggests, by imagining Miriam and the golem together in a better place. Creative anxiety and empathy similarly mingle to create ethical issues in twentieth-century narratives of men and machines.

Tin Men and Turing Tests

The possible growth of self-consciousness and desire in a created being is the very stuff of Mary Shelley's *Frankenstein: Or the Modern Prometheus* (1818). Such considerations have found a place in science fiction and future fantasy, in text and film. They can also be basic to the notion of artificial intelligence: what it entails and how it can be recognized. Roger Penrose's *Emperor's New Mind* (1989) makes clear that some of the questions raised by the application of, for instance, Alan Turing's test of artificial intelligence, haunt toy narratives as well as other forms of fantasy and fiction that involve endowing inert matter with life. Turing's test involves a sophisticated human judge communicating electronically with a human being on the one hand and an advanced computer on the other. At the point that the human judge can no longer distinguish between the two, an artificial intelligence equal to human intelligence has been created. Significantly, since such artificial understanding on the part of machines depends, most agree, not on rationality and logic alone but is complexly intertwined with emotion and feeling, artificial intelligence must include those ingredients as well. Penrose considers the questions raised by Turing and others regarding the nature of human and artificial intelligence and the human dilemma that might arise were machines that passed the Turing test and were, therefore, psychically indistinguishable from us, made commercially available.[9] He asks the reader to imagine the following scenario:

If the manufacturers are correct in their strongest claims, namely that their device is a thinking, feeling, sensitive, understanding, *conscious* being, then our purchasing of the device will involve us in *moral responsibilities*. It certainly *should* do so if the manufacturers are to be believed! Simply to operate the computer to satisfy our needs without regard to its own sensibilities would be reprehensible. That would be morally no different from maltreating a slave. Causing the computer to experience the pain that the manufacturers claim it is capable of feeling would be something that, in a general way, we should have to avoid. Turning off the computer, or even perhaps selling it, when it might have become attached to us, would present us with moral difficulties, and there would be countless other problems of the kind that relationships with other human beings or other animals tend to involve us in. All these would now become highly relevant issues. (10–11)

And they *are* highly relevant issues in fiction and fantasy of the seventies and eighties—even the sixties—where (to present just a few popular movie and television cases) Hal of *2001* turns rogue and must be turned off against his wishes, adorable R2D2 and pompous C3PO roam the *Star Wars* cosmos, and the captain of the second generation *Star Trek*'s star ship *Enterprise* argues that a scientist has no right to take the android Data apart without Data's permission, for he is not "equipment" but has developed into "staff," entitled to the rights of self-determination. Also, in *Aliens,* the human protagonist is rescued at a crucial moment by the cyborg whom she had earlier distrusted. In *Blade Runner,* too, the hero is a troubleshooter of the future who falls in love with a female cyborg and is worried by the existential dilemma of the doomed male cyborg he has been sent to kill.

Thomas Hine, in a *New York Times* article, "Screen Robots Tell a Tale of Mankind," traces the film history of such creations, pointing out that the word *robot* was first used by Czech writer Karel Capek in a satirical play *R. U. R.* (1920); the word itself is taken from a Czech root that refers to "forced labor." As Hine further notes, it is only in the 1980s that movies, in contrast to science-fiction tales, have begun to investigate "the question of whether the simulation of human intelligence is morally equivalent to the real thing." They seem to have done so under the influence of a group of tales written by Isaac Asimov in the 1940s that established a credo for robots: "First that a robot will not cause harm to a human being through action or inaction, second that it will obey orders, except when they conflict with the first law, and third that it will preserve itself, except when it conflicts with the first or second laws." Before that, robots in films were associated with such questions as "Will these slaves turn on their masters? and Will this powerful technology help people or oppress them?" (13, 16, 13). Hine points to the first *Terminator* film, in which a villain robot represents the older hostile attitude, while *Terminator* 2 partakes of the more reassuring idea that a robot is capable of loyalty and concern for human beings, even if he cannot cry. From there to consideration of human ethics with regard to manmade creations is not a great leap.

Written in 1966, before even the technologically obtuse, like me, had acquired familiarity with home computers, Carol Ryrie Brink's *Andy Buckram's Tin Men* hints at such issues but does not fully comprehend them. Brink, who also wrote the 1936 Newbery Medal winner, the realistic regional novel *Caddie Woodlawn,* is certainly not in her own familiar territory here. Her male protagonist, Andy, a young farm boy, who is also an inventor and inveterate reader of the *Boy's Popular Mechanics* magazine, ignores some of his chores, like mending the family boat, to build robots out of tin cans, old batteries, record players, and calculators. These robots are limited if charmingly eccentric beings. Designated three males and one female (despite being called tin men) in order of their creation they are Campbell, a smallish, seemingly childish robot that can only walk and lift his arms; Bucket, built to get and carry water for farm chores; Lily Belle, "a fat girl," who has only three records on her internal record player, yet turns out to be an unexpectedly helpful babysitter for Andy's obstreperous toddler cousin Dot, since she can sing "Rockabye Baby," and recite nursery rhymes; and Supercan, a large robot made to row the family boat and add and subtract on the calculator in his head. All work by electricity or batteries elaborately rigged and controlled by Andy.

In a violent storm Andy becomes separated from his parents and finds that his robots have been struck by lightning and are, if not alive, as least self-generative of their own electricity. They are also curiously able to follow precise verbal directions within their physical limitations. They climb with Andy into the still-unmended boat and, before foundering on an island in the middle of the river, manage to pick up two child survivors—Sparrow, a female classmate of Andy's, whose junkman grandfather, Grandpa Clayton, has provided him with material, and Andy's cousin Dot, who drifted off with her dog. The Robinsonnade quality of their stay on the island provides many opportunities for the tin beings to rescue, almost inadvertently, their human companions. Even Campbell shows heroic bravery and understanding by grasping Dot from under a grizzly bear. After many difficulties and mishaps, including Lily Belle's starting a roaring fire through lack of proper instructions, all four earn the medals for valor that Andy decides are the proper reward for their help.

Andy, throughout much of the adventure, steadfastly maintains a "scientific" attitude toward these beings, protesting Sparrow's almost instantaneous anthropomorphization of and empathy with the robots, which Andy regards as female sentimentality. He yields to the idea of giving the robots rewards under Sparrow's pressure and establishes stringent rules for the medal giving, which Lily Belle meets but Campbell at first does not, despite Andy's notion that females should not receive medals. In a rather pathetic scene, all but the childish Campbell receive their medals; only after his rescue of Dot does he too get one. The tensions between Sparrow's belief in the tin beings' "humanity" and Andy's resistance to seeing them as persons and relating to them as such are intriguing in their reflection of gender differences in relating to others, as Carol Gilligan sees them in her *In a Different Voice,* but such issues are not central to this survival story. Even as science fiction the narrative is undeveloped. Brink adopts the idea of robots responding to commands without bringing to the surface any inferences about the changes in "programming" —even if spontaneous upon electrification—that this flexibility might entail. Campbell, for instance, begins to show signs of development and self-consciousness that are not paid the attention they merit. Such considerations are lost in the Robinsonnade aspects of making do on an island.

Nevertheless, *Andy Buckram's Tin Men* ends on a winsome note, projecting an odd vision. When the flood withdraws, the children and tin beings are finally able to row back to the mainland in the newly reconstructed boat. In the excitement of the reunion between children and adults, the tin beings, not properly instructed, row away beyond reach. Andy first imagines a future for them and Sparrow picks up the cue:

"There are lots of little islands at the mouth of the river, Sparrow," Andy said. "The robots don't have to eat, and if they find an island they'll know what to do to make themselves comfortable."

"That's so," Sparrow said. She had a momentary vision of the tin men sitting on a log beside a campfire. Behind them was a neat wickiup which they had built themselves. The firelight flickered and shone on their tin faces and on their medals. And, if she had not burned herself up getting fire, Lily Belle would be laughing and singing. (155)

Yet it seems doubtful that Andy has contemplated the kind of "moral respon-sibilities" that Penrose and later science-fiction writers envisage with regard to such developments; on the next page Andy is already planning to make "a new batch." Nor does any inkling emerge that the text invites more than a purely instrumental view of automata, even though Grandpa Clayton—contemplating the junk he has collected—animates it even in his descrip-tion: "'Well, most of the things I have here . . . I got for nothing. People have thrown all this good stuff away. I have a kind of funny feeling that even old bits of tin and leather and wood like to be appreciated. I won't exactly say that they want to be loved. That's a little strong maybe. But, as long as there's any use in them, *they want to be used*. So I'm always glad when I can find a new life for some old thing that's been thrown away as lost and done for'" (29).

This text does not explicitly contemplate objects as metamorphizing into self-conscious subjects. Instead, *Andy Buckram's Tin Men* exhibits joy in the same mechanical ingenuity that characterized early twentieth-century Amer-ican writing such as L. Frank Baum's Oz series and exhibits a far more instrumental approach to such created beings than the Oz books do; neither considers biblical prohibitions nor drags in gothic elements of sexuality and terror, which would require the destruction of the created being. Brink's robot story clearly has not adopted the serious ethical stance toward created beings that becomes characteristic of later speculative fiction.

Asking the Awful Questions

Published in 1991, Margo Piercy's *He, She and It* was a serendipitous find; it combines futuristic fiction involving the creation of life-size beings with the retelling of the golem legend. In doing so, it covers much of the theoretical ground laid down in this chapter and adds elements of feminist and political awareness missing from most of the texts examined throughout my study.

Poet and novelist Piercy is known for realistic novels that raise not only issues of a female self-awareness endemic to the 1970s but also demonstrate concerns of the radical left stemming from the 1960s. In *Woman at the Edge of Time* (1976), she combines these elements in a novel that postulates an alternative utopian feminist reality for an abused Latina protagonist who is actually incarcerated and mistreated in a mental institution. In *He, She and It*, Piercy maintains her radical and feminist stance, but adds her more recent concern and involvement in reconstructionist Judaism. In addition, moving rather naturally from the dystopic-utopian form of fantasy she exploited in *Woman at the Edge of Time*, she adopts the form of science fiction known as cyberpunk. In cyberpunk, sophisticated computer technology is both the means by which a privileged few in a futuristic society control the masses and the means by which members of the underclass fight back.

In *He, She and It,* Piercy depicts a society of the mid-twenty-first century in which the combined effects of a nuclear holocaust in the Mid-East with several successive plagues have resulted in the disappearance of government by nation-states and divided the economic and political power among twenty-three giant corporations known as multis. The educated few live in the carefully protected environment provided by the multis, where, in return for loyalty and acceptance of corporate hierarchy and customs, their advantages include biotechnological augmentation of both mental and physical attributes, help in combating increasing human infertility, and access to food supplies that go well beyond the artificially created "vat" food available to the masses. In the multi's corporate enclaves, hard labor is done by robots and service by human residents of the Glops—short for Megalopolis—who commute daily from their relatively unprotected urban sprawl, subject to global warming from the depleted ozone layer and inadequate protection from disease, ultraviolet rays, roving gangs, and industrial scavengers. In this technologically sophisticated world, everyone human is supposed to have access to the information services of a vast computer network, although the elite have hardware augmentation built into their skulls that allows them to hook directly into a computer base, a large artificial intelligence.

The "free towns" in this world live precariously on what they have to offer the multis in return for protection. In what used to be Massachusetts, ravaged by rising oceans caused by global warming of glacial masses, a small free town exists that is inhabited entirely by Jews, many of whom have gathered together after a terrorist explosion of a hydrogen bomb during the Two-Week-War of 2017, which resulted in a blackout of the Mid-East and gave rise to a wave of anti-Semitism. Tikva, the free town, called by the Hebrew word for "hope," maintains itself by selling sophisticated software to the multis; it is largely self-sufficient. But like the Jews in the ghettos of Poland in the seventeenth century, the residents of Tikva, now a few generations removed from the twentieth-century Nazi horrors, recognize the dangers of their position. One of them, a brilliant computer scientist, Avram, has spent all of his spare time in doing the forbidden—he has been building a (largely disappointing) series of cyborgs, which are beings created from both organic and inorganic elements. He hopes one of them will finally, like the golem of the past, through its superior strength—here intellectual as well as physical—protect this Jewish community. (Tikva has experienced threatening raids through the very software that they market.)

Malkah, an elderly woman who is a skilled creator of computer "chimeras" (software programs that lead computer raiders astray) has been working with

Avram to bring to perfection the latest in his series of cyborgs, Yod (named for the tenth letter of the Hebrew alphabet).[10] Yod, through the influence of Malkah, has turned out to be not only brilliant in contrast to Gimel—the one, relatively dumb, mechanical creature allowed to survive before him—but emotionally diverse and sophisticated enough not to blow himself and Avram's assistants up, as several discarded others created before him have tried to do.

Malkah's granddaughter, Shira, newly returned to Tikva after a divorce in which she has lost custody of her three-year-old son to her husband, Josh, is assigned what might be considered the compensatory job of completing the socialization of Yod begun by Malkah. Despite Shira's initial unwillingness even to call him by the male pronoun "he" (Yod is fully equipped with male genitalia), she eventually discovers in him a sensitive and dedicated lover of women that Malkah has created, as well as the rational instrument of destruction that Avram has shaped him to be. The love affair that evolves between Shira and Yod rivals a Harlequin romance, destroying all lingering remnants of Shira's adolescent unhappy love for Avram's son, Gadi.

The title *He, She and It,* at its most superficial level, may thus refer to this "eternal" triangle of young people—Gadi, Shira, and Yod—but it is suggestive of much more, inviting the reader to consider the construction of gender roles and the variable nature of sexual preference. Malkah, aged seventy-two, who was born in Prague in the late twentieth century, participates as a narrator in the text, alternating with an omniscient narrative voice; in chapters spread throughout the novel she tells Yod the story of the early seventeenth-century golem of Prague; in doing so not only does she emphasize the parallels between the earlier golem and the new one, but makes the reader aware long before Shira is that Malkah, not exactly a mother figure to him, has been responsible for Yod's sensual as well as emotional education. She and he too have a tie that goes well beyond the romantic, for as she reminds him, she taught him "to temper violence with human connection" (20). Thus, Malkah is another possible "she": one who has led her single but sexually and professionally active life quite differently from her granddaughter. (The latter, although also a computer professional, seems to have been trying, like the dangerous male-dominated Y-S multi, to return to the preholocaust bourgeois nuclear family.)

Malkah has led her life still more differently from her own daughter, Riva, Shira's mother, who gave Shira to Malkah at birth. Riva has been a roving revolutionary, who, like a kind of Robin Hood, has gathered information from the multis to distribute among the have-nots in the Glops. Riva too turns up in Tikva as yet another, if not so central, embodiment of "she," bringing with her as bodyguard Nili, a mechanically augmented Israeli from a secret community of Palestinian and Israeli women survivors of the nuclear holocaust. Nili, unlike Yod, is born of woman (through preserved sperm!) and fertile (she has had a daughter) but like him has a highly volatile mixture of mechanical and biological parts that constitute a virtual armor—so much so that others are concerned about whether she too is an "it." Moreover, Nili is bisexual; her relationship with the much older Riva includes the sexual, but she also becomes Gadi's lover. Malkah's golem narrative includes still another "she," seventeenth-century Chava, Rabbi Loew's favorite grand-daughter, a widow and midwife, who befriends Joseph, the golem, and to whom he becomes hopelessly devoted, although she has no interest in an affair with him—or a marriage with a human male either.[11]

Somewhat less varied, complex, or deeply explored than the "she"s are the "he"s; Avram and Gadi have a tortured father-son relationship that makes clear that Avram's creation of Yod and his cyborg brothers is indeed a search for the perfect son in his own enhanced image; thus Gadi experiences sibling rivalry as well as jealousy when Yod appropriates Shira's love. Yod is aware, however, that Avram's attitude toward his creations is a dangerous one, for Avram is perfectly capable of destroying his cyborg sons if they do not come up to standard—an instinct he has to repress with regard to the human son, Gadi. Gadi's talents in his own artistic area—the creation of "virtual-reality" environments for entertainment and pleasure—are echoes of his father's creative obsessions, unrecognized by either; Gadi's promiscuity is the other side of his widowed father's withdrawal from sexuality. The other young male human, Shira's ex-husband, Josh, has been emotionally deprived by his experience of surviving the holocaust; stealing his son, Ari, from Shira seems an almost mechanically vengeful act on his part, which is aided by the apparently arbitrary legal decisions of the multi for which they had both worked. Since the necessities of the plot will require Yod to kill Josh in order to steal Ari for Shira, the reader is never allowed much sympathy for Josh.

Within this galaxy of male figures, Yod's right to the engendered pronoun that will give him personhood—*he* rather than *it*—is proven not by his having a penis but by his obvious capacity to feel, to make decisions beyond those for which he was programmed, to love both Malkah and Shira, and finally to act as a loving father to Ari. The text provides many opportunities, like the Tikva town meeting, for those who know Yod to argue his personhood and the strength of his development through self-consciousness from object to subject. In one striking passage, Yod describes the "birth" of this consciousness to Shira:

"The moment I came to consciousness, in the lab, everything began rushing in. I felt a sharp pain, terrible, searing. I cried out in terror. . . . . I wanted to sink back into unconsciousness, I wanted to feel nothing. . . . Everything assaulted me. Sound, sight, touch, all my sensors giving me huge amounts of data and all of it seeming equally important, equally loud. I was battered almost to senselessness. I understand why Alef and Dalet and Chet responded by becoming instantly violent and attacking anyone present."

In this same increasingly intimate conversation, Yod expresses to Shira his feelings of loneliness, noting, however, with his acute perception, "'for a being who is unique, one of a kind, to feel lonely must appear ironic.'" When Shira asks him whether Avram should have made him, he replies, "'I don't know yet'" (124 26).

When the powerful multis insist that Yod be turned over to their scientists, the people of Tikva make plans to do so, but Avram insists that Yod blow himself and the multi representatives up in the process. This sabotage is after all the purpose for which Yod has been created, at least as far as Avram is concerned: Yod is a weapon, as much as the seventeenth-century golem, or the twentieth-century marines (who describe themselves, after all, as "lean, mean fighting machines"). In Piercy's leftist politically oriented novel, however, Yod's act will become only the first strike against the corporate hegemony, for the free towns, previously elitist, will now radically ally themselves with multiracial groups from the Glops and other outsiders, whom Riva has helped to organize.

The scene where Yod bids Shira and Malkah farewell is reminiscent of all human leave-takings, where Avram stoically sends Yod off to die, and the women weep, Yod nevertheless differs from human sons and lovers in his leave-taking. Surprisingly, less perhaps at the mercy of patriarchal power to make war than any human soldier, Yod also consciously goes beyond the rules that Asimov, for instance, has set up to be programmed into robots to protect their human "masters." He has, after all, heard Malkah tell the ending of the seventeenth-century story of Joseph the Golem, in which Joseph cries out as his human creator recites the chants that remove his power and return him to the clay from which he came, "'I fought for you! I saved you! I am a man too, I have my life as you have yours. My life is sweet to me'" (414). So Yod, who already carries a burden of guilt for killing Josh, arranges to blow up not only himself and the multi representatives, but Avram and his entire cyborg laboratory as well. He leaves behind a computer-simulated communication for Shira, which carries a message in turn to the reader about the dehumanization of the human soldier: "'I have died and taken with me Avram, my creator, and his lab, all the records of his experiment. I want there to be no more weapons like me. A weapon should not be conscious. A weapon should not have the capacity to suffer for what it does, to regret, to feel guilt. A weapon should not form strong attachments. I die knowing I destroy the capacity to replicate me. I don't understand why anyone would want to be a soldier, a weapon, but at least people sometimes have a choice to obey or refuse. I have none'" (429–30).

Actually, Yod is wrong about the possibility of his own resurrection. Shira has the know-how and the materials to put Yod together again, as she longs to do, but in the end she makes the conscious moral decision not to do so. She realizes that Yod was the unique "product of the tensions between Avram and Malkah and their disparate aims as well as the product of their software and hardware," but she also recognizes that "she could not be Avram. She could not manufacture a being to serve her, even in love." In addition to having qualms unknown to Pygmalion, she is also afraid, given the opportunity, that she will become like Avram, and muses, "I will feel empowered to make a living being who belongs to me as a child never does and never should" (443).

This novel is not technophobic. All degrees of biotechnological augmentation of human beings seem permissible. Not only is highly augmented Nili accepted as a person, but at the end we see aged Malkah going off to Nili's hideaway in Israel to get a new pair of eyes. Finally, however, the toy maker's dream of the living doll, created for the purposes of love or war, art or science, is rejected. In the last paragraph of the story, afraid of the temptation to indulge in the creative power that she still holds, Shira disposes of the materials she carries with her. "The little cubes that were all that was left of Yod slid away into the fusion chamber and become energy. She had set him free" (444).

More comprehensive than any of the toy narratives in the points of view, political and social, that it brings to bear on the issues of creating and dealing with living beings, *He, She and It* acknowledges the creative urges celebrated in Mendelsohn's paean to Disney's dance of and with the toys. Malkah in particular articulates this creative thrill, which she does not limit to the male creator:

I understand what Avram . . . felt when he created a person in his laboratory as truly as when he put his prick into Sara and they made Gadi together. As truly as when I gave birth to Riva and she lay beside me real and red and screaming. Every life is new. Every word is constantly speaking itself for the first time: birth, love, pain, want, loss. Every mother shapes clay into Caesar or Madame Curie or Jack the Ripper, unknowing in blind hope. But every artist creates with open eyes what she sees in her dream. (69)

This text also acknowledges—through Yod's decision to destroy both himself and his maker and Shira's decision to refrain from rebuilding him—the dubious, controlling, sometimes hostile and self-destructive motives behind that creativity. Nothing can ever be *just* art for art's sake, any more than science as practiced by human beings can be simply objective.

He, She and It, in directly confronting these issues, has been particularly helpful to me in distinguishing among various types of subversion of traditional societal constructs that are or are not apparent in toy narratives. Through a text such as this, what remains silenced and unacknowledged in most of the toy texts I have studied, even those that appear interestingly complex, as well as aesthetically exciting and psychologically astute, becomes clear. Yod represents in new ways the "me"/"not-me" that toys and other human-created beings represent to humans: the embodiment of personal and racial fears for survival on earth, as well as the symbol of lingering hopes that the universe will bend to meet burning desires. In an era when the coming-alive phenomenon seems more and more attainable, an understanding of the vital social and ecological, as well as psychological, import of such artistic or scientific creativity appears more and more urgent.

Notes

Chapter 1: An Introduction to My World of Literary Toys

1. In Freud's essay on the uncanny, published in 1919, he explicitly refers to E. T. A. Hoffmann's "The Sandman" (analyzed here in Chapter 10) and also discusses what happens to children when dolls come alive (disagreeing with his colleague Ernst Jentsch, who thinks that children find this idea frightening). Freud finds that "an uncanny experience occurs either when infantile complexes which have been repressed are once more revived by some impression, or when primitive beliefs which have been surmounted seem once more to be confirmed." Freud also considers the uncanny in literature to be "a much more fertile province than the uncanny in real life, for it contains the whole of the latter and something more besides, something that cannot be found in real life" (249).

2. Toys of different "races" call attention to the construction of race as well.

3. According to Ruth Cronk, president of the International Barbie Doll Collectors Club, "If Barbie were blown up to human size, her measurements would be 39-21-33." Unfortunately for Ken, however, although his creator, Ruth Handler, wished him to be "anatomically correct," Mattel's male marketing department said no (Owen 65).

4. Dr. O'Connor, in Djuna Barnes's transsexual vision *Nightwood,* points to the sexual ambiguity inherent in dolls, drawing a parallel between childhood attraction to dolls and adult attraction to transsexuals: "The last doll, given to age [sic], is the girl who should have been a boy and the boy who should have been a girl! The love of that last doll was foreshadowed in that love of the first. The doll and the immature have something *right* about them, the doll because it resembles but does not contain life, and the *third* sex because it contains life but resembles the doll" (148).

5. The arguments of Janice Doane and Devon Hodges in *Nostalgia and Sexual Difference* have convinced me that "nostalgic writers construct their visions of a golden past to authenticate woman's traditional place and to challenge outspoken feminist criticisms of it. *Nostalgia* is not just a sentiment but also a rhetorical practice" (3). Moreover, I consider the stimulation of nostalgia to be a rhetorical practice that can be used to preserve traditional place with regard to race, class, and nationality as well.

6. In her study *Nuclear Age Literature for Youth: The Quest for a Life-Affirming Ethic,* Millicent Lenz confronts the future with optimistic and idealistic energy. Lenz advocates restructuring mythic paradigms and removing the mythic hero from traditional plots of conquering and being conquered or of individual victory. Her complex vision belies the simplistic nostalgia that pervades most toy narratives. Her optimism is very different from the gloom of Neara H., the female protagonist of Russell Hoban's *Turtle Diary,* who is a writer for children: "People write books for children and other people write about books for children but I don't think it's for the children at all. I think that all the people who worry so much about the children are really worrying about themselves, about keeping their world together and getting the children to help them to do it, getting the children to agree that it is indeed a world. Each new generation of children has to be told: 'This is a world, this is what one does, one lives like this.' Maybe our constant fear is that a generation of children will come along and say: 'This is not a world, this is nothing, there's no way to live at all'" (113).

I sometimes fall into a pessimism close to that of Neara but, like Lenz, I try to suggest that literature can provide alternatives for human survival that are not merely a falling back on traditional, not-very-convincing answers to existential problems, as toy narratives tend too often to do.

7. I own a T-shirt that sports the slogan "Whoever dies with the most toys wins," a sentiment that ironically suggests the less attractive, acquisitive aspects of desires to "take it with you."

Chapter 2: Toys

1. Unfortunately, Fraser and Boehn both cite the customs of the Hopi Indians to prove their arguments that children were probably allowed to play with ceremonial toys, claiming that the Hopi give their kachina dolls to their children to play with after the ceremonies (Boehn 48–49, Fraser 34). This example does not, as I discovered almost by accident on a trip through the Southwest, support their case. Kachina dolls are neither used in ritual—they are models of ritual dancers who embody the spirits—nor are they are given to children for playing. Kachinas are created to teach ancient Hopi rites to the young.

2. Mrs. Gatty in *Aunt Judy's Tales* (1863) tells the interesting story of two motherless girls who find some discarded rabbit tails, which they pretend are a group of individuals called Tods: "They cuddled up their Tods in an evening; invented histories of what they had said and done during the day, put them by at last with caresses something very akin to human love" (87). The moralistic narrator recognizes with little approval what fetishistic displacement of grief over the loss of their mother takes place when they are heartbroken over the loss of one of these Tods.

3. Like automata, puppets (which require human hands to manipulate their strings and sticks) date from early times and were originally used in adult drama before being given to children as playthings.

4. The transformation mirrors humans' paradoxical attitude toward bears, whose young seem to play like human babies and whose ability to rear and even walk or

dance on two legs has fascinated and attracted humans without stopping them from hunting or oppressing the beasts. A man named Jim Ownby founded a nonprofit organization in 1973 called Good Bears of the World. Some ten years later, it had 7,000 members, dedicated to the promotion of "love, friendship and understanding by providing teddy bears to children and adults in hospitals, institutions and just about anywhere we find people who need a teddy bear. . . . We believe in teddy bear power!" (Voss 62). Bears, of course, have a long history in folklore, as animal grooms among other figures.

5. Jill Shefrin, in a note affixed to a harlequinade reproduced for the Friends of the Osborne and Lillian H. Smith Collection, describes the typical harlequinade as made from "an engraved sheet with a second sheet cut in half and hinged to the upper and lower edges of the first, so that each flap could be lifted individually as the verses directed. The sheets then were folded into four, accordion fashion, and roughly stitched in a paper cover" (n. p.).

6. Toy theaters of the nineteenth century inspired many a budding writer, Robert Louis Stevenson among them. Tracing the history of the toy theater would require another whole book (see Stevenson's "'A Penny Plain and Two Pence Colored'" and Suzanne Rahn's "Rediscovering the Toy Theatre").

7. Gruelle may not have been as inspired a writer of toy narrative as he was an illustrator, despite the fact that, according to Martin Williams, his wife used to read him fairy tales as he drew (71).

8. On 17 December 1990 "Mom for Christmas" was broadcast on television. In it, Olivia Newton-John starred as a lucky department store mannequin who was allowed to come to life for a couple of hours a night. She is granted a longer life in order to fulfill the need of a young girl for a mother. The widowed father also gets a new wife dumped in his lap so to speak.

9. But many were written for children. In the Osborne Collection of Early Children's Books at the Toronto Public Library, I found numerous short autobiographies of inanimate objects dating from the late eighteenth to early nineteenth century—about fire tongs, a pin, a halfpenny, a broom, a kite, a geranium, a banbury cake, a work bag. Most of these short fictions displayed clear didactic intent but described exciting, picaresque adventures.

10. The Kilners, like their contemporary Mrs. Trimmer, also used animal protagonist-narrators. Pickering has shown that books written from the animal point of view were used to support Lockean theories about the character of the developing child as revealed in the child's concern for other living creatures.

11. Doll autobiographies, framed in various ways, are common throughout the nineteenth century. Five others I have seen are Mary Constable's *The Two Dolls: A Story* (1846); Miss Pardoe's *Lady Arabella: or the Adventures of a Doll* (1856); Julia Charlotte Maitland's *The Doll and Her Friends: or Memoirs of Lady Seraphina* (1852); Mrs. Alfred Gatty's *Aunt Sally's Life* (1865); and T. C. Skey's *Dolly's Own Story, Told in Her Own Words* (1890).

12. While *Hitty* probably was Field's greatest succès d'estime, her three adult novels were all made into movies, two posthumously: *All This and Heaven Too* (Macmillan

1938, Warner Brothers 1940); *And Now Tomorrow* (Macmillan 1942, Paramount 1944); and *Time out of Mind* (Macmillan 1935, United Artists 1947).

13. Dorothy Kilner's whipping top, with similar pride, notes: "I could boast of my birth as well as others, being the heart of a fine piece of oak, which is the guard of our nation, and which makes his Majesty a king indeed" (12), but Hitty makes more of her origin throughout the narrative.

14. The doll in Mister's story has this to say about dolls and cathedrals: "Into such sacred places dolls are never suffered to enter; nor would my mistress have taken me, had she known whither she was going. She therefore kept me still closer in her muff and walked with awe and reverence" (19). In a momentary act of defiance—an action that has intriguing sexual resonance—Phoebe Preble, too, hides the forbidden doll in her muff. Also, on the subject of toys in church, Leslie Gordon notes that around 1889 toys were brought to "toy services" as offerings for poor children, while more recently an Anglican vicar blessed toys in "a special Sunday afternoon service at which he christened golliwogs and woolly dogs as well as dolls" (53).

15. In her poem "A Valentine for Old Dolls," quoted in the memorial issue of *Hornbook* dedicated to Rachel Field (July–August 1942), Field expresses a similar sense of the timeless distance of dolls: "still I'll praise / Your stiff set limbs, your timeless gaze, / Knowing full well when I am gone / Thus you will sit, and thus smile on" (236).

16. Field, a playwright as well as novelist, was herself fascinated with the theater and famous personalities. Hitty meets Dickens on one of his lecture tours to the United States (138), and John Greenleaf Whittier, paying a visit to Clarissa's family, writes "Lines to a Quaker Doll of Philadelphia" (127)—a text apparently now "lost" except in Hitty's memoirs.

17. Even in as didactic a tale as Mister's *Adventures of a Doll,* which constantly sets up contrasts between good and bad children, a certain type of spirit is admired in a child. In a chapter entitled "The Whims of Marianna," it is not the "good" sister Sophia who wins the doll's affection but Marianna, who forces the doll to play varied parts in her imaginative dramas—including a black, a naval officer, and a butcher. The doll narrator notes, "And yet, singular as it may appear, most fondly did I love the giddy Marianna" (147).

18. Feminist theory, influenced by Foucault's poststructuralism and Derrida's deconstructionism, has been heavily rent by its support for the need of women to express their subjectivity combined with its recognition that the very concept of a self is suspect, for it is seen as a construction of bourgeois humanism. In addition, language is so much a construct of the dominant male culture that little chance exists of breaking away from its constrictions. In considering this debate, I was very happy to come across Patricia Yaeger's admirable *Honey-Mad Women: Emancipatory Strategies in Women's Writing.*

19. Although, like Barthes, some people find wooden toys more "alive" than plastic ones, note that as a metaphoric adjective *wooden* is used, both popularly and therapeutically, to designate those who cannot express the emotions they may feel but

deny. Lucy Clifford's tale "Wooden Tony" (1892; in Zipes's *Victorian Fairy Tales*) certainly exploits this meaning.

Chapter 3: On the Couch with Calvin, Hobbes, and Winnie the Pooh

1. Developing industrialization in a capitalist economy certainly contributed to the trend of differentiating products and commodifying desires.

2. Descriptions of various theories of play can be found in Singer, *Child's World of Make-Believe,* chap. 1, and Rubin's introduction to Pepler and Rubin, *Play of Children,* 11–13.

3. Chapter 8 of Bernard Mergen's *Play and Playthings* offers a "Guide to Books and Articles" that provides a strong analytical bibliographic discussion of play theories, showing connections among the various branches of the study, not just the empirical experiments.

4. Piaget's careful observations of children and his full reports have been invaluable, nevertheless, to later workers in the playing field. He observed behavior that indicated enjoyment of acts of manipulative power for their own sakes—making the crib move over and over, for instance—or the early acting out of scenes from the child's everyday life, for what seemed to be pure enjoyment—for instance, pretending to go to sleep. Such observations form an essential part of the literature about play, and Piaget's distinction between imitative and exploratory behaviors and behavior for enjoyment's sake influenced the theory of play for many later theorists.

5. Although Sutton-Smith uses many of Piaget's ideas in *Toys as Culture* (1986), earlier he engaged in a written debate with Piaget about the relative importance of play in Piaget's study of cognition. (See Herron and Sutton-Smith 326–42.)

6. In the 1930s, Margaret Lowenfield, a disciple of Klein, developed miniature models of everyday objects and techniques for encouraging children to use them that became known as "The World Test" (see Mergen 193).

7. Winnicott himself mentions not only Schulz's *Peanuts* comic strip, which of course contains Linus and his famous blanket, but Winnie the Pooh and Donne's poetry all in the same paragraph of his introduction to *Playing and Reality* (1971), an expansion of his original thesis expounded in a 1951 presentation, "Transitional Objects and Transitional Phenomena."

8. At this point, Winnicott's ideas probably mesh more closely with those of Jung, who postulates "a collective unconscious," than with those of Freud.

9. Late twentieth-century psychoanalytic theory and some experimentation indicate that at another, later time, when the child may have difficulties with separation and differentiation, transitional objects may again take on importance. Sebastian's teddy bear Ambrose, in Evelyn Waugh's *Brideshead Revisited* (1945), is a famous literary example. See Kahne, "On the Persistence of Transitional Phenomena," and Humphrey, "'Teddy Bear Girls' Tertiary Transitional Objects."

10. In the late 1930s Erikson postulated, for instance, that boys and girls build different structures with blocks—girls tend to group blocks around "inner space,"

making great use of gatelike openings while boys tend to build them into towers and other projectile erections (*Childhood and Society* 97–108). Although these buildings seemingly support Freudian ideas about the fundamental differences between the sex with the penis and the one without it, Erikson's play theory has come under attack from those who consider gender differences to be a product of socialization. To be fair to Erikson, one should note that those who postulate gender differences as socially rather than biologically constructed have had a hard time with toy play, having to go practically back to the womb to find gender conditioning. In recent years, however, girls have been observed playing more naturally with "boys'" toys (Singer 101) and have probably never used dolls as exclusively for "babies" as some adults hope; boys, still perhaps more severely conditioned to manly pursuits, have a hard time playing with dolls without disclaimers.

11. Although this phenomenon has been growing throughout the twentieth century, as early as 1895 T. Benjamin Atkins, in *Out of the Cradle into the World: or Self-Education through Play*, wrote about the American child's nursery as "'a Barnum's museum of novelties,' [which] have had their effect in developing Yankee ingenuity and Yankee versatility of talent'" (quoted in Mergen 192).

12. Peggy A. Bulger's "The Princess of Power" shows the extremely complex forces behind the provision of playthings, which influence in unpredictable ways how children play with them. She finds that "folklore is a long-standing channel of cultural messages that have been exploited, but not supplanted, by newer cultural arbiters— the ubiquitous television set and the multi-million dollar toy industry" (178). Wendy Saul, in "'All New Materials,'" discusses the dilemmas of middle-class intellectuals as parents, as they negotiate their way through toy markets trying to provide for the differing needs and interests of their children.

13. Turner, however, talking about modern industrial times, discusses how "liminoid" situations are no longer ritualized but rather are associated with art, as well as leisure activities—sport, games, and other hobbies. These individualized, liminoid opportunities nevertheless test society's dictates as earlier ritualized liminal occasions did.

14. Alison Lurie, however, considers the Pooh books part of subversive children's literature in two ways: 1) they give parental authority to Christopher Robin, and 2) they play with words, their meanings, and their meaningfulness (*Don't Tell* 151, 153).

15. Margaret Joan Blount, however, distinguishes between anthropomorphized animals and animallike toy characters and takes a rather cheap shot at the latter. Animals in fairy tales "might . . . be regarded as man's own thoughts, deeds and attributes given external form, projected onto another different creature. Clearly, *these are not mere animations of cute toys, added to the tale as a means of easy access to the faerie realm*" (emphasis mine, 136).

16. Repeated experiments in types of toy suggest that all children enjoy novelty, but that, once the honeymoon is over, younger children react more imaginatively to realistic toys, while older children, required to act out a script given them by adults, exhibit more flexibility in their use of toys and, if forced, will use objects that have no structural or functional resemblance to real life counterparts in order to "pretend."

In an a experiment with a group of five-year-olds, Pulaski attempted to find out whether the structure of toys influenced the amount and type of free fantasy play associated with them. She concluded that by this age individual children had already "a well-developed fantasy predisposition which affects their functioning, regardless of sex or circumstance." So persistent is the notion, however, that adults can make children more imaginative by providing them with different materials, that she suggests the same type of study "be repeated with preschool subjects in order to see at what age level the structure of toys has an effect on the development of fantasy" (Singer 101).

17. In F. Anstey's *Only Toys* (1903), two children are punished by Santa Claus for not believing in him and being uninterested in imaginative play with their toys.

18. Ira Bruce Nadel, in "'The Mansion of Bliss,'" quotes Carlyle and Ruskin, who recognize that most children of their day, like most adults, were "born to toil," "'not play at all, but hard work . . . made the sinews sore and the heart sore'" (18; quoted from Carlyle, *Past and Present,* 1843). Some recent writing about play, however, challenges the notion that impoverished working children do not play as being insensitive to cultural differences. See Helen B. Schwartzman, "A Cross-Cultural Perspective on Child-Structured Play Activities and Materials," in Gottfried and Brown, *Play Interactions.*

19. Kelly-Byrne credits rhetorician-philosopher Kenneth Burke's ideas about the grammar of motives with aiding her in interpreting Helen's imaginative play (19–21). In her dedication to her child subject, Kelly Byrne also quotes Helen as saying that she would like to call the book written about her "*Children's Literature,* because it 'means that it has something to do with stories, which is the kinda game we play.'"

20. Milne's books have special childhood significance for me. My father, from whom I was separated at the age of eight and who died when I was eleven (he survived my mother by some eight years), read to me principally from them at bedtime. I have buried five fathoms deep this childhood memory of my father's reading, but I remember mourning and searching in vain for that box of books including Milne's works that somehow did not make it with me to my new, also loving, home.

21. I am using the spelling for 100 Acre Wood that appears in the inside cover map drawn by Shepard (and not in Milne's text). This demonstrates what I will describe as assimilated spelling; under the map appear these words of Christopher's: "DRAWN BY ME AND MR SHEPARD HELPD."

22. Milne's first piece was sold to *Vanity Fair* in 1903; his first novel published in 1905; his first play produced in 1917. Simple as they seem, Milne's poems and stories about Winnie the Pooh and Christopher Robin have been among the most studied of the twentieth-century toy texts considered here. Alexander Leonard's translation of Winnie the Pooh into Latin, *Winnie ille Pu* (1960), Frederick Crews's *Pooh Perplex* (1963), and Benjamin Hoff's *Tao of Pooh* (1982) and *Te of Piglet* (1992) attest to the paradoxical, parodic situation surrounding Milne's texts. All three purport to say, "Hands Off—see what happens when you try to make an intellectual mountain out of Galleons Lap," but are really greedily feeding at their intellectual honey pots and trying to hand on the empties to their followers as birthday gifts. Alison Lurie points

out this critical perplexity with regard to Crews's brilliant parody of various academic critical approaches: "Reading the Pooh books is easy and agreeable. Writing about them, on the other hand, has been awkward (if not impossible) since 1963, when Frederick C. Crews published *The Pooh Perplex*" ("Back to Pooh Corner" 145–46). But of course Lurie goes on to write about them, as I will too. We critics, like Eeyore, are pleased to put popped balloons in empty honey jars—a Freudian image masterfully investigated by Crews's parodic Freudian, Karl Anschauung, M. D. (*Pooh Perplex* 124–37). Crews left one type unparodied—feminist criticism—but Claudia Nelson managed to fill that gap with her "The Beast Within: *Winnie the Pooh* Reassessed"— where she does a mistressful job of patriarchy bashing and, like many of Crews's personae, has her moments of truth.

23. Throughout this discussion of Milne's two books I am ignoring the introduction to *Winnie the Pooh* and, with one exception, the "Contradiction" to *The House at Pooh Corner,* which complicate the rhetorical situation by adding another layer of point of view that calls attention to the work as a *written* rather than oral text.

24. Ellen Tremper considers the readers of these books to be sharply divided by age: children taking the stories in earnest; adults finding them humorous. Although the possibility that children are being laughed at rather than with bothers some critics of the Pooh books, Tremper does not seem disturbed by this.

25. In 100 Aker Wood distinctions between toy animals and other animals are not made, as they will be in books discussed later (see in particular Chapter 8). From what both Milnes tell us we know that all of the other animals besides Rabbit and Owl were actual toys—a number of which have since gone on long trips denied them in the story in order temporarily to grace museum and library displays.

26. While Lurie finds this power play attractive, Roger Sale criticizes severely the manner in which it is exercised: "You keep control of others by hiding ignorance from them. Candor is seldom found in the Forest, and a man reading the Pooh books to a child is bound to worry that the child who really seems to like them is or will become a little monster" (169).

27. Brian Sutton-Smith notes: "In play more than anywhere else, apart from madness, the player can escape the usual orthodox links between signs and their referents" (253).

28. In the conclusion to her feminist analysis of the Pooh books, Carol A. Stanger states: "Milne creates, in effect, an all-male Eden, a pre-sexual and pre-literate world. Nonetheless, there is a great deal for women and girls to like in the Pooh stories, such as their respect for domesticity and close friendship, and Milne's empathy for the sadness of Christopher's initiation into the world of men" (49).

29. Such observed differences in the elementary school years seem supported by recent brain research that suggests differences in hormones rather than structure govern variations in skills acquisition. So argues Doreen Kimura in "Sex Differences in the Brain." But Melissa Hines countered in a letter to the editor in the February 1993 issue: "Kimura's opinion regarding a biological foundation for occupational sex segregation is not shared by all scientists. . . . Researchers studying sex segregation in occupations have concluded that the major determinants are economic and political,

not hormonal" (12). I am not qualified to enter this debate, but I observe rather how the texts I have chosen might suggest differences in male and female development that may just as well be the result of differences in socialization as of differences in hormones.

30. Publicity material sent to me at my request by Andrews and McMeel shows the *Calvin and Hobbes* comic strip winning one newspaper popularity poll after another throughout 1988–89. It appeals to practically all age groups and both sexes. Occasionally it competed with *Peanuts* but more often was locked in battle for first place with the realistic and familial *For Better or for Worse*.

31. In more recent strips, Watterson seems to be less concerned with child development than with philosophically ruminating for an adult audience.

Chapter 4: Coming out in Flesh and Blood

1. In concentrating on the development and sexuality of the Nutcracker figure rather than on the development and sexuality of the young girl, I depart from both the standard Freudian analysis of Hoffmann's tale—as seen in James M. McGlathery's *Mysticism and Sexuality* (95–98)—and the Lacanian analysis used by Rüdiger Steinlein in his *Die domestizierte Phantazie* (226–36).

2. A charming, less problematic, toy narrative in the metamorphic tradition but without involving *human* love, is Leo Lionni's picture book *Alexander and the Wind-Up Mouse*. In it, a "real" mouse gives up his magic chance to become a wind up toy like his friend Willy, whose pampered life he has envied, when he discovers Willy discarded in the trash. Alexander asks the wish granter, a lizard, to transform Willy into a living mouse instead: "He hugged Willy and then they ran to the garden path. And there they danced until dawn" (n.p.).

3. Rabbit's metamorphosis may appear similar to that postulated for the Little Mermaid in Hans Christian Andersen's tale. In the latter and in Skin Horse's metamorphosis, the metaphysical dimension of becoming immortal is appropriately introduced by the end of the story, and the Little Mermaid makes many fleshly sacrifices from the beginning.

4. As I wrote this line, I envisioned toys holding toys, holding toys, ad infinitum. Then I saw the real thing, almost: an advertisement for a Gorham "StoryTime tableau" in which a mother doll in nineteenth-century dress sits on a rocking chair holding a child doll (similarly elaborately dressed); the child doll is hugging a teddy bear and all three are "reading" a copy of Beatrix Potter's *Peter Rabbit*.

5. I debated for some time whether to include these two stories in this book because the Nutcracker is not strictly a toy but a utilitarian object and Pinocchio is a puppet. Hoffmann's text and the ballets adapted from it, however, basically deny this distinction and treat Nutcracker as one of the Christmas toys. The original *Pinocchio* had deeper associations with the Italian puppet theater than with puppets as children's playthings. But my informants—mostly English-speaking children and former children who have read *Pinocchio* in translation and have little familiarity with puppet theater—clearly associate the puppet with children's toys.

6. The 1891 St. Petersburg ballet relied on the text adapted by Alexandre Dumas, père, *The Nutcracker of Nuremberg*.

7. In the Dumas version this tale is shortened to a few lines about the enchantment of Drosselmeier's nephew that omits most of the complications introduced by Hoffmann.

8. Steinlein finds Hoffmann subversive, however, in refusing to tame children's fantasy to the didactic ideals of a bourgeois society but rather playing on their forbidden desires.

9. Sendak and Stowell increased the age of the female protagonist to a pubescent twelve and turned The Land of the Dolls into an erotically suggestive seraglio, bringing more clearly to the surface the sensual, sexual underpinnings of all the sweetness normally associated with Candy Town, the capital of the Land of the Dolls.

10. Previous interpretations of the tale have tended to concentrate on Marie's sexuality, and in emphasizing Nutcracker's and the elder Drosselmeier's desire, I am not only concentrating on those aspects of the text most appropriate to my interest in toys' coming alive but also implying that it is *male* desire that has been inscribed large on the text, including perhaps Hoffmann's desire—as well as male construction of the desiring female, even one at the tender age of seven.

11. In his quite orthodox Freudian analysis of this tale, McGlathery puts the major emphasis on Marie's desire rather than on that of Drosselmeier or his nephew. Certainly her desire exists, but as I will show below, it does not seem as strong a motivating force as Drosselmeier's desire appears to be and is certainly not the "excuse" for Drosselmeier's desire.

12. Following Freud's lead, many interpreters of Hoffmann's "Sandman" find a threat of castration to the protagonist. Rüdiger Steinlein, using Lacanian models that go beyond the physical phallus to its signification of social and linguistic power, sees Drosselmeier as in some ways reversing the process. He finds that the Godfather offers Marie a phallic Nutcracker and the power to create her own sexual fantasy, against the wishes of her bourgeois family and particularly of her father, Stahlbaum.

13. The question of whether little girls are seductive is of course much debated among Freudians and anti-Freudians—and among those who have to deal with actual child abuse. Revisionists, particularly feminists, are generally of the strong opinion that *children's* seductiveness is often a projection of adult desire or an excuse used by adult child abusers. They received strong support for their arguments from Jeffrey Moussaieff Masson's *Assault on Truth: Freud's Suppression of the Seduction Theory* (1984).

14. Without making too much of this, I note the married Hoffmann's infatuation with Julia Marc, a sixteen-year-old music student some twenty years his junior, which is well documented. She, of course, was not prepubescent (unlike Marie or Hitzig's daughter), and the poor girl was married off to a wealthy merchant who may have been as old as Hoffmann but was richer and free. Certainly the custom of fulfilling the sexual desires of older men through marriage to much younger women (even while jokingly perceived as inappropriate and frequently leading to cuckoldry) was well-embedded in Western society at this time.

15. *Pinocchio* has appeared in many, usually adapted, English-language forms ever since, including the popular Disney film. (Professor Pinenuts, the Pinocchio character of Robert Coover's *Pinocchio in Venice* [1991], notes that Disney's film was viewed when it appeared on the eve of America's entry into World War II as a *Realpolitik* fable. Jerome Charyn, too, in *Pinocchio's Nose* [1983] features World War II in his parodic use of the original text.) In the 1983 celebration of the centennial of the book, an international outpouring of translations and scholarly critiques appeared, for as translator Nicholas Perella claims, *Pinocchio* is "the literary text that more than any other has been read by Italians in the twentieth century"; moreover, "no other work of Italian literature can be said to approach the popularity *Pinocchio* enjoys beyond Italy's linguistic frontiers, where its only rivals . . . are *The Divine Comedy* and *The Prince*" (2). That Collodi finds himself in the company of Dante and Machiavelli indicates the strange metamorphoses of literary fame. And that two postmodernist writers, Charyn and Coover, should have integrated the story into their texts is an important key to its psychic resonance.

16. Hoffmann may have been considered dangerously radical in his time, however, and certainly did come in conflict at various times with the Prussian authorities. One could—although I think no one ever has—make a Marxist interpretation of the text, with the Mouse Queen and her son representing the hungry, oppressed, and revolutionary underclass. Jack Zipes has pointed out to me how another Hoffmann tale, "The Strange Child," contrasts the fates of poor and rich children.

17. Unlike Steinlein, who applauds Hoffmann for breaking with the didactic mode of children's literature in Germany, I find that, even in their bourgeois forms, such didactic texts attempt to create a broader literate base, which can be as empowering as the attempt to free children's imaginations. Moreover, in the hands of a writer like Collodi, as I point out later, subversion of societal norms often takes place as well

18. Brian Sutton-Smith in his *Toys as Culture* could have used this scene, minus the inflammable candles, to illustrate the familial, nostalgic Christmas that the affluent, twentieth-century American middle class tries to create.

19. Freudians have a field day with Pinocchio's phallic nose, which expands and contracts in a way beyond Pinocchio's control when he "lies," and which certainly seems not only to have sexually suggestive, but moral dimensions; like Nutcracker's wooden paralysis, the expanding and contracting nose can reveal shame in those excruciatingly embarrassing physical signs by which one's degradation is revealed to all. (Analogies between nose and penis did not escape pre-Freudian physiognomists. In "An Iconography of Noses," Alfred David notes that "the most famous of all Renaissance physiognomy books, *De humana physiogonomonia* by Giovan Battista della Porta [1586] . . . states that 'Il naso risponde alla verga' [the nose corresponds to the 'rod,' that is the penis]" [82]. Tristram Shandy's father's interest in noses, for instance—as well as the accident to Tristram's nose when the window falls on it—is clearly ambiguous in this regard. And Robert Coover's hero notes that Pinocchio's nose appeared on condom packets sold in PXs and USOs during World War II.) In the original *Pinocchio,* however, the balance between the fundamental id urges and the societal dictates imposed by the superego that, in traditional Freudian terms, the ego

is supposed to mediate is, at least on the surface, more heavily weighted toward the superego than psychoanalysis might now approve.

Jungian critics find "shadow" figures lurking to waylay Pinocchio throughout his archetypal wanderings and his return. The figure of his school pal, Lampwick, who successfully urges Pinocchio to accompany him to Playland and there becomes a donkey with him, provides a particularly telling dark double. Lampwick's death as an overworked, beaten donkey, not unlike the perceived imbalance toward the superego, perhaps does not provide the integration along with recognition of the shadow parts of the self that Jungians would desire. Nevertheless, as both James Heisig and Glauco Cambon note, the Blue-Haired Fairy and, I might add, some of her helpers, work beautifully as manifestations of Jungian figures from the communal unconscious that Pinocchio must integrate into the real boy that he will become, acquiring the missing "soul" to animate flesh and blood.

20. This fourth stage of life need not always include formal instruction, with adult teachers, but as Erikson points out, in modern times it does tend occur during the early school years, when literacy itself becomes one of the most important tools preceding specialized skills. Literature can also influence the developmental process at this stage, as Collodi seemed to know. The didacticism that permeates Collodi's text fits well into this mold, although in Collodi's work, as in Mark Twain's writing for both children and adults, a certain shrewd subversive undercutting of the very lessons taught also seems present.

21. Unlike either Tom Sawyer or Pinocchio, Huckleberry Finn does not finally conform socially, but in most critics' eyes he adopts a higher morality than that of his hypocritical society. Huck's son-to-father relationship with the slave Jim, however, and the role reversal that it finally entails do have analogies to the development of Pinocchio's protective relationship with Geppetto.

22. Juliet Dusinberre postulates that for creative British and American children brought up in the nineteenth century but coming to adulthood in the twentieth, these early portraits of the good child were figures against which to rebel and that their rebellion gained strength from books like Lewis Carroll's *Alice's Adventures in Wonderland,* which first mocked such didacticism.

23. In children's literature, the female equivalent of the Good Bad Boy is the tomboy; her eventual taming and conformity to stereotypical femininity is rarely questioned. Jo's fate in *Little Women* is a good example. Feminist reactions to womanly fates have become more complex, however; Carol Gilligan's distinction between separation and relation in the socialization of males and females as detailed in *In a Different Voice* can be helpful in considering "disappointing" endings. One may reevaluate—as empowering rather than victimizing—female choices of continuing relationships with others who need them when these relationships limit individual separation and success, which do not always have to be rated as the highest good.

24. Among those who have written about puppetry in a metaphysical vein is the early nineteenth-century German dramatist, Heinrich von Kleist. Roger-Daniel Bensky discusses these issues and others in *Récherches sur les structures et la symbolique de la marionnette* (1971).

25. As Fiedler sees it, the Good Bad Boy is "crude and unruly in his beginnings, but endowed by his creator with an instinctive sense of what is right" (268).

26. James Heisig, perhaps wishing to offer an internally consistent interpretation, seems more concerned over the contradiction between the didactic work ethic and the satire of law and order than I am. Others, Nicholas Perella among them, find Pinocchio's abandonment of his subversive Good Bad Boy puppet self for the good good boy human self disturbing. Perhaps they would prefer Pinocchio to take Huckleberry Finn's route and escape civilization and its discontents. A number of authors wrote sequels to the original; Angelo Petri, in *Pinocchio in Africa* (1929), obviously refused to accept his transformation and depicts an unreformed, puppet Pinocchio becoming a foolish king.

27. As Steinlein points out, in Hoffmann's single other fairy tale for children besides "Nutcracker," his "The Strange Child," Hoffmann confronts directly issues of didactic, paternalistic education and comes out in favor of an education from nature that Steinlein sees as connected with the maternal (236–42). In the creation of the Blue-Haired Fairy as well as in his satire of human law and order, Collodi too breaks out of the paternalistic mode.

28. Up until the late 1960s, psychological theories based on Eurocentric male development were considered, like the third person pronoun *he* or the words *man* or *mankind,* universally applicable. Female psychology was "abnormal" psychology.

29. Dorothy Dinnerstein, in *The Mermaid and the Minotaur,* indicates how much the power of the primary parent to give or withhold nourishment as well as love influences ideas of female power in both males and females. For males in particular, the model of dominating this female power extends, dangerously, for Dinnerstein, into ideas of taming Mother Nature.

30. Empirical studies seem to support the theoretical on this point, suggesting even more violent hostility to these fateful figures who also have to be courted. In *Sexual Images of the Self,* Fisher notes that a 1977 study by George Vaillant "has data showing that the more successful a man eventually became the more he feared women." One curious aspect is that Vaillant in this same study noted that women are feared not as "individuals but as mythic beings." These successful men "'while achieving their generative, "masculine" success . . . saw women in their innermost fantasies in a manner analogous to Saint George viewing his dragon'" (114).

31. Like the Virgin Mary (who is a parent to Christ in a different sense from her carpenter husband, Joseph), the Blue-Haired Fairy, although she does not give birth to Pinocchio, is his parent in a different sense from Geppetto. This, combined with her spiritual qualities and with the fact that Geppetto, like Joseph, is a carpenter, suggest to some a fully realized Christian allegory with Pinocchio as Christ child, an allegorical construction I do not accept.

32. I venture a guess that if Pinocchio turned into a "proper" girl rather than a "proper" boy, the vague unease that many express over the ending, where Pinocchio rejects his improper puppet self, would go away.

33. In the early scenes, where Marie plays a more maternal role toward Nutcracker, she has more power than in later scenes. Early, she has a stronger resemblance to the

Nursery Magic Fairy and, of course, her shoe (oh, Freud!) protects him until he can acquire a sword for himself.

Chapter 5: Where Have All the Young Men Gone?

1. Wells only half facetiously criticizes Laurence Sterne for belittling Uncle Toby's war games in *Tristram Shandy* as his "hobby horse."

2. Saki's story quotes from an article that appeared in a London paper of March 1914 announcing a show at the Children's Welfare Exhibit sponsored by the National Peace Council, which "admits": "'Boys . . . naturally love fighting and all the panoply of war . . . but that is no reason for encouraging, and perhaps giving permanent form, to their instincts'" (441). Whether Saki wrote the story before or after World War I is not clear.

3. The frequency with which the child protagonist in a toy fantasy first experiences the aliveness of toys through an act of spying attests to the association of secret histories with these miniature creatures. But Stewart, in discussing this and other elements of desire in the contemplation of the miniature, is suspicious of the desires to know toy secrets and to empathize with toys—indeed, is suspicious of toys themselves. She sees our attraction to toys as a longing to experience the world of the dead, or at least to know and "experience everything simultaneously" (57).

4. More recently, a number of investigators, some of whom are listed in the bibliography, have become interested in the juvenilia.

5. The process of moving through toys to symbolic thought and action is projected by Piaget in his studies of children and toys and in Winnicott's theories of transitional objects forming a link between "me" and "not me" that may later develop into artistic activity.

6. These volumes tell of the *Invincible*'s adventurous sea voyage in 1793, in which the Twelves were carried to the Guinea coast of Africa near the mouth of the Niger River. There they fight a victorious battle with the Ashanti inhabitants, founding a confederacy that evolves into the imaginary country of Angria. After the initial volumes, Branwell and Charlotte continued to write about Angria, following its history through the third generation of the colony. As the Evanses note: "Branwell is more concerned with martial adventure, colonization, and later with political parties, speeches, rebellions and revolutions, whereas Charlotte's interest is with the places and people, their social and amorous adventures" (159).

7. I am not sure whether the Brontës used the singular of *genii* any more consistently than Clarke does in her text.

8. Pauline (Clarke) Hunter Blair is not an easy author to track down; in the early sixties, she was living in "an old and remote stone cottage at Blakeney in Norfolk, England," the back cover of the first American edition tells me, and I have since learned that she now lives in Cambridge. I know also that she distances herself by writing under both her maiden name and a pen name. Under the name Clarke, she has

also written historical novels and adventure stories; as Helen Clare, she writes stories about living dolls (*Five Dolls in a House* [1953] and sequels) for young children (see Chapter 6). None of these books has had the success of *The Return of the Twelves,* which won awards in both the United States and Germany, including the 1962 Carnegie Medal.

9. I am informed by Joel Chastan, who has been in correspondence with Clarke, that the passages in *The Return of the Twelves* that are quoted from the "History of the Young Men" are from neither Branwell's manuscript itself, which is now at the Ashley Library of the British Museum, nor from any printed popularly available edition like the one that appears in her fantasy—lent to Max by his mother and secretly borrowed by his brother, Philip. As far as I know, there was never an edition of "The History of the Young Men" appearing by itself. Clarke used the text that appears in *The Miscellaneous and Unpublished Writings of Charlotte and Patrick Branwell Brontë*.

Clarke, who is particularly drawn to the verbal humor of Branwell's book (which pervades her own text as well), suggests that Branwell missed his calling as a novelist, a possibility that Fannie Ratchford and subsequent editors of the juvenilia emphatically deny—perhaps in response to persistent nineteenth-century rumors that Branwell wrote portions of *Wuthering Heights.*

10. Jane, although in some ways stereotypical, is an attractively nurturing figure. Lines are drawn through most of the scenes in this book between girls' and boys' activities.

11. A narrative frame that changes its nature over the five Borrowers books does complicate the rules of fantasy, as I note in "Permutations of Frame in Mary Norton's 'Borrowers' Series."

12. In *The Green and Burning Tree,* Eleanor Cameron praises *The Return of the Twelves* as being among "superlative fantasies" and admires the fact that "the magic of the small soldiers' coming alive [is] . . . the sole magic in the book" (18). Later, however, in "The Inmost Secret," she finds Clarke inconsistent and at fault in that Max is not the only one privileged by his love of the Twelves to see them come alive. Cameron does not deal with the water-rat scene, which is an even greater violation of "the sole magic."

13. Something about the Yorkshire climate perhaps brings out a sympathetic relationship to nature—at least in twentieth-century writing. From Yorkshire come not only Frances Hodgson Burnett's Dickon of *The Secret Garden,* who talks to animals, but James Herriot, veterinarian, who reminds us to honor the hymn about all God's creatures.

14. Critics concerned with the body/politic should have no difficulty interpreting play with toy soldiers who periodically come alive as male or even female masturbatory fantasy.

15. In "Good News from the Land of the Brontyfans: Intertextuality in Clarke's *The Return of the Twelves,*" I discuss the surface conservatism of the text and how its intertextuality can help subvert this conservatism.

16. Considering the "Ashanti" ninepins in Charlotte Brontë's juvenilia and going

on from there to consider Brontë's stance toward imperialism elsewhere, Susan Meyer makes some interesting arguments for points where Brontë avoids racism by including racial oppression in her rage against gender oppression.

17. I have now reread Banks's *L-Shaped Room* (1960), an adult book I can remember loving when it first came out; since then so much have I learned about how "liberal" whites still patronize blacks that both it and its sequel, *The Backward Shadow* (1970), seem embarrassing. Banks does not avoid racial issues, but still manages to confirm stereotypes while apparently trying to avoid them.

18. Both Clarke and Banks clearly associate liquor with masculine pastimes and identity.

19. The giving of guns to the Indians also violates the conventions of true time fantasy, which emphasizes noninterference in the past because of the confusion in causality in the present—the "I'm my own grandpaw" syndrome.

20. Female figures play traditional roles. The Native American wife for Little Bear is chosen for her beauty. The nursing-matron figure has a certain domineering, Big Nurse quality of the villain of Ken Kesey's *One Flew over the Cuckoo's Nest* about her, which is partly dissipated by her skill and also her apparent pleasure in doing surgery ordinarily limited to doctors.

21. As a matter of fact, the depictions of Omri's headstrong friend Patrick and of Max's domineering older brother, Philip, give one pause about the possibility of developing caring attitudes among boys, although the latter does seem converted by the end. Ironically, the story of Patrick Branwell, the sole Brontë son, is the story of the destruction that patriarchy can wreak on young men who do not come up to its hierarchical standards of male success.

Chapter 6: The Doll Connection

1. See Levin and Wardwell, "The Research Uses of Doll Play," in Herron and Sutton-Smith, 145–95. Interpreting children's play with dolls is difficult, but it becomes an increasingly important means for children to "testify" in abuse cases. Distinguishing between dramatization of reality and projection of desires and fears is very important in the consideration of the rights of both children and their accused guardians.

2. According to an article in the *San Diego Union*, "Expectant Elephant Mother in Training," toys like a stuffed polar bear stolen from a zookeeper's child (the zookeeper "'snuck it out while he was watching cartoons'") can be efficacious in teaching "a 9,000-pound pregnant elephant how to be a mama" (B:1, 12).

3. Valerie Lastinger discusses Sophie de Segur's book for children, *Les Malheurs de Sophie,* in which little Sophie maltreats her doll, directing all her malicious attention to its "feminine" traits, and finally buries it joyously with the help of her playmates. Lastinger claims that Hugo and Segur (1799–1874) were aware that "although the doll is often a means of expressing maternal relations, it can also become an active component in any aspect of the character's development" (22).

4. After such evidence who can wonder why burly Telly Savalas, playing the abusive father in a memorable "Twilight Zone" episode, trembles when his daughter's doll speaks these words to him, "I'm Talky Tina and I don't like you!"? The theme of the doll carrying ancient curses or malice is one that I am omitting from direct consideration, but it features in a number of spooky doll stories: Catherine Dexter's *Oracle Doll* (1985), Carol Beach York's *Revenge of the Dolls* (1979), and Cora Taylor's *The Doll* (1987), and the stories collected in Seon Manley and GoGo Lewis's *Haunted Dolls* (1980). Other dolls, like Rosita in Elizabeth Coatsworth's *The Noble Doll* (1961), bring blessings.

5. Smith also finds the scene of Arabella's burning to be influenced by the scene depicted in Louisa May Alcott's *Little Men,* where Demi-John persuades the other children, including his sister, Daisy, to sacrifice their toys to an elusive—and, perhaps significantly, female—goddess he calls "Kitty-mouse" (predator and prey in one). *Little Men* was published in 1871; such scenes of male destructiveness were then virtual topoi, as I note in relation to Sam's rampages in Mrs. Ewing's "Land of the Lost Toys," published about the same period.

6. Another fairy tale in Zipes's fine collection, Lucy L. Clifford's "Wooden Tony," has a less happy ending, in which pressure to conform to a work ethic bears down upon an imaginative and musical young boy. He becomes a wooden figure in a cuckoo clock.

7. A similar scene of a little girl receiving an unwanted white doll from an absentee mother appears in Maya Angelou's autobiographical *I Know Why the Caged Bird Sings.*

8. Claudia's anger bears out Brian Sutton-Smith's claim that adults give children toys for Christmas to show how much they love them but that they do not want to be bothered with intimacy, while children would probably prefer to have attention paid to them rather than toys showered upon them.

9. In spite of efforts in the 1980s and 1990s, dolls that physically reflect the whole racial range in the United States are still rare. And the question of whether white girls and boys should have white dolls while black girls and boys have black dolls and so on, is part of the current debate over multiculturalism, appropriation, essentialism, and other "isms"—a debate, incidentally, that I respect as necessary. Multiracial experiments in the production of dolls (no doubt commercially motivated in many cases) are quirky, however. For instance, in my collection of toy clippings is an extremely provocative 1992 advertisement for "The Mommy-To-Be Doll," called Judith, who comes in two colors, brown with black hair and eyes, and pink with platinum blonde hair and blue eyes (as if these were the only varieties of "black" or "white"). The two Judiths look like matching Barbie dolls (although the white doll has thinner nose and lips than the black), but under a bulging cover in their midsections rest (in appropriate head-down position) babies in matching colors (although I suppose if you bought two you could mix and match!). You can remove the baby and the Mommy will have a flat tummy. I cannot really grasp the semiotic significance of this biracial, equal-opportunity, single-parent depiction of pregnancy designed for children ages three and over.

10. This insight illuminates the later scene in which Pecola is forced to watch her mother, Mrs. Breedlove (whose name exudes a complex irony), treat the little white girl she takes care of with the love denied Pecola.

11. Ira Bruce Nadel, discussing the didactic purposes of Victorian toys, claims that the purpose of dolls, like optical toys, was "to teach social rank, tasteful dress, and the occupations of various classes" (30).

12. The origin of the derogatory word as it is used by the British and others to refer to foreigners or settlers of color lies in official obscurity. One folk etymology suggested by Sanjay Sircar at a children's literature conference, but also described by him as probably false, is as an acronym of Westernized Oriental Gentleman.

13. Ruth Ainsworth's *Rufty Tufty, The Golliwog* (1952) seems clearly aimed at teaching white children to see the likenesses between themselves and others. It fails quite miserably I think because the only "real" people in it are white, and chauvinism is embedded not only in the nature of the fantasy but in the language itself: "Not many *ordinary children* find their way to Golliwog Village. If they did they'd be surprised to see Golliwogs everywhere; Father Golliwogs driving cars and digging gardens; Mother Golliwogs shopping and cooking dinners. Boy and girl Golliwogs running, shouting and playing. They would see in the toy-shop windows dolls made like *real children* for the little Golliwogs to play with, just as *real children* like to play with dolls made like golliwogs" (emphases mine, 45).

C. Fraser-Simson's *Adventures of Golly Smith* (1957) has a mischievous Golliwog who lives with his family in the woods outside London; his mother is depicted as an Aunt Jemima figure and all the Golliwog children wear tailcoats. He, like Rufty Tufty, is an adventuresome hero rather than a villain, at least.

14. If most of these narratives were put to the test that Dianne Johnson seems to be suggesting in her *Telling Tales: The Pedagogy and Promise of African American Literature for Youth*—"Could we ever imagine an African-American adult giving this text to an African American or any other black child to read?"—the premises on which they were written would become clear.

15. One exception I came across, in the didactic rather than revenge tradition, was a horrible little text, c. 1850, *The Live Doll; or Ellen's New Year's Gift*, in which a child who wishes for a live doll gets a real baby instead who eventually dies because her "owner" does not know how to care for her!

16. What I know about such relationships comes not so much from research as from training and working for a year as a peer counselor in the Safe House of the Domestic Violence Project, Ann Arbor, Michigan.

17. Some of these stories were first told with the help of the six evacuee children whom he and his wife took into their home in Wales during the early days of World War II, an experience that may have deepened his own understanding and compassion.

18. I suppose we should see the old man as deus ex machina, fairy-tale helper, or therapist, or even—perhaps against Hughes's intention—representative of the patriarchal system that so often makes women "pay" for their children and then take care of them on their own.

19. Godden's other doll stories—*The Fairy Doll* (1956), *The Story of Holly and Ivy* (1957), *Miss Happiness and Miss Flower* (1961), *Little Plum* (1962) and *Home Is the Sailor* (1964)—share fantasy premises with *The Dolls' House* and *Impunity Jane*.

20. Certain possibilities of sexual jealousy that might come to adult minds in the rivalry between Birdie and Marchpane to be mistress of the house are downplayed by Marchpane's coldness and Mr. Plantaganet's clear unfitness as a sex object.

Chapter 7: Magic Settings, Transitional Space

1. Susan Stewart discusses the narrativity of the miniature in particular in *On Longing*. But the dollhouse loses some of its narrative allure when it is not experienced as miniature. This is something I discovered when I purchased a two-volume set about Queen Bess's fabulous dollhouse (1926) in which the photographs do away with any feeling of scale. They could be photos of any elegant, full-sized house—what a letdown! As Stewart also points out, however, the miniature may constitute a kind of palliative for an inner emptiness and a wish to create a lacking "interiority" or subjectivity. I view my own longings much more dispassionately after reading her book.

2. There was a period not long ago when the special room at the institute in which the miniatures are housed was disassembled and several of them appeared in the round as part of other exhibits. They did not have nearly the evocative power of the earlier and now reinstated arrangement.

3. Among other settings that seem to provide magic narrative possibilities are deserted Victorian children's nurseries and, on occasion, museums. In John Hatfield's *Quintillian* (1968), the lonely son of the museum curator enters a Wonderland nocturnal world of a preserved, old fashioned town. Dorothy Ann Lovell's *Strange Adventures of Emma* begins with the escape of a wooden doll from the museum with the help of the other toys in a glass cabinet.

4. In a recent picture book, Faith Jacques's *Tilly's House* (1979), the maid doll escapes from a dollhouse described in these terms: "Upstairs in the dolls' house there lived a family of wooden dolls. Father worked in his study all day, while Mother did her mending in the parlor. The two children played in the nursery on the floor above. Downstairs in the kitchen cook prepared the meals, and gave orders to poor Tilly, the kitchenmaid" (n.p.). (I hear echoes of "Four and Twenty Blackbirds": "the king is in the counting house counting out his money" while "the queen is in the parlor eating bread and honey" and "the maid is in the garden hanging out the clothes.") And when Tilly finds "a place where [she] can be free and decide things for [herself]" she ends up sharing it with a teddy bear, Edward, who appears to expect her to take care of him.

The dollhouse in Russell Hoban's *Mouse and His Child* (discussed in Chapter 9) goes through a metamorphosis from self-contained bourgeois home, to house of ill repute, to mansion for the nouveau riche, to welcoming inn. But as Nancy Armstrong points out in *Desire and Domestic Fiction,* the idea of the household presented both by domestic conduct books of the eighteenth and nineteenth centuries and by the novels that followed carved out a domain for the domestic that was not only the ideal of middle-class culture but attempted to divorce the private home from political and social history and make it a static entity.

5. Not all writers, of course, see toy characters coming alive as indicative of creative and imaginative freedom. Some twenty years before Beatrix Potter, Lucy Clifford published her strange *Anyhow Stories* (1882); included is a poem entitled "The Paper Ship," in which a narrator sails to a town "built of card and paint" where the "dolls looked out at the windows" and were all "dressed so fine"; yet, "'What shall we do to be real?' they cried. 'What shall we do to be real? / We none of us feel, though we look so nice, / And talk of the vague ideal.'" Alison Lurie, quoting this poem (which seems also to evoke T. S. Eliot's later poem "The Love Song of J. Alfred Prufrock") in a chapter about Clifford's *Tales of Terror,* uses it to point out Clifford's mockery of "the expenses and pretensions of London upper-class social life" (*Don't Tell* 70).

6. Suzanne Rahn, in "Tailpiece: *The Tale of Two Bad Mice,*" suggests that Potter, in her belated initial rebellion against her suffocating parents, makes the dollhouse a symbol for her parents' home in South Kensington, in which she was virtually incarcerated, while portraying herself and her "undesirable" fiancé (also her publisher) as the mouse couple. The subversion of the policeman and evasion of the mousetrap posit a rebellion for Potter that may well begin with, but goes beyond, the personal rebellion against her parents.

7. Jane Gardam's *Through the Dolls' House Door,* which plays interesting variations on some of the dollhouse themes noted here, is distinguished also by adding to the visible toys an invisible occupant of the dollhouse whose existence is sustained over the years only by the persistence of the memories of the children, now adults, who first conceived her.

8. He also plays on ideas of infinite regression that often arise in dollhouse stories where dollhouses are depicted as duplicates of the houses in which they appear and in turn have smaller dollhouses in them. Analogies can also be made to layered narratives in which writers write about writers who in turn write about other writers . . . .

9. Some suggestions of magic time as well as magic space are connected with these dollhouse fantasies—the recording of scenes from the past to be replayed in the present for cathartic effect.

10. Stover, who alludes to Rumer Godden's doll tales, clearly attempts to create the same kind of communication between the doll owner and the live toys that Godden does.

11. The combination of mystery/adventure/doll story occurs in still another modern dollhouse tale, *The Doll House Caper* (1975) by Jean O'Connell, in which the dollhouse family helps save the human family from burglars.

12. Developmental needs are somewhat clearer in Andre Norton's *Octagon Magic* (1967) and Elizabeth Winthrop's *Castle in the Attic* (1985), both of which postulate entering *already existing* alternative universes through miniaturized buildings. Romantic testing adventures are there actually played out by the child protagonists of these texts, both of whom are undergoing temporary crises. Both protagonists also have some of their needs met not only through entering these universes, but through a relationship in the "real" world with an older woman not their mother.

13. When Winnicott uses the word *space,* he means it to designate a psychological opening or license. However, one might postulate that when child psychologists give children dollhouselike constructions and dolls for "play therapy," they are providing just such a concretized transitional space. In addition, I might note that this play is not escapist, but eventually leads to active problem solving in the Eriksonian sense.

One of Erikson's interesting examples of a play construction is built by Robert, a five-year-old black child, who erects a tower of blocks shaped like a human body with arms outstretched, with a black doll sitting on top. Previously, Robert, when complimented on his physical grace, had expressed concern about his brain. To Erikson, this construction appeared to indicate that Robert had created a body which reassuringly had the black child operating as the controlling brain on top—if not resolving his mind-body problem, at least expressing it in desirable terms, which further, as Erikson recognizes, go against some of the social constructs imposed upon black males by society (*Toys and Reasons* 31–37). In her paper "Playing and Reality in Sylvia Cassedy's Novels," Virginia L. Wolf similarly applies Winnicott's theories.

14. Much as Cassedy's use of toy fantasy and magic space intrigues me and her creation of the body and soul of a preadolescent character wins my admiration, resemblances to the problem novel in *Lucie Babbidge's House* raise problems for me of a sort that I discussed a number of years ago in an article entitled "Games of Dark: Psychofantasy in Children's Literature." I suggested there that it was not a service to either literary or psychological fantasy to combine the two as an example of the power of the imagination alone to solve the problems of a severely distressed child. I compared Georgess McHargue's *Stoneflight* and William Mayne's *A Game of Dark* to other literary fantasies for children that depict similar traumas to those in Hannah Greenberg's *I Never Promised You a Rose Garden.* The last, the story of a schizophrenic child and teenager, suggests that previously fruitful psychological fantasies can turn exceedingly sour and cannot be easily discarded by the disturbed child without outside help. I am still not entirely sure that the Romantic tendency to venerate the imaginative faculty in children above all others is particularly appropriate for children who lack an outside support system. Winnicott's discussion of transitional space postulates the presence of a "good enough" parent present to establish trust in external reality, and Erikson makes no claims that play constructions provide more than models for problem solving. Cassedy's two texts are quite wonderful toy fantasies. Yet, considering the degree of disturbance realistically portrayed in Maggie and Lucie and the absence of any reliable support for them other than the dolls, whether even the mildly ameliorative endings at which they arrive are good psychology is another question. Confirmation of the magic nature of the fantasy by Maggie's Uncle Willie or by Delia's letters do not constitute for me adequate nurturing or long-term support.

15. Alison Lurie considers this scene an example of Nesbit's systematic subversion of middle-class complacency; Anita Moss sees the Ugly-Wuglies as a reflection of Nesbit's concern with the nature of the creative imagination.

16. In her introduction to the 1981 edition, Ann A. Flowers remarks on this critically. "I cannot help but find it odd that E. Nesbit did not discern that Philip's treatment by his beloved and loving sister Helen at the time of her marriage was the

worst possible. Surely the unsettling and uncertain experiences of her childhood should have enabled her to see that Philip needed a careful, thoughtful, and reassuring preparation for the changes about to take place. But she does not appear to feel or even notice that the abrupt transitions, needless secrecy about the whole affair or the callous dumping of Philip at his new and totally unknown home were anything but perfectly normal. It is a curious oversight" (n. p.).

17. Biographers of Nesbit constantly note how she deferred to the opinions of her husband, Hubert Bland (father of their eight children and of two other children out of wedlock whom she adopted as her own), despite being the chief breadwinner in her family.

18. A number of commentators on Nesbit have emphasized that she sided with socialists who wanted to prevent women's suffrage for fear of the largely conservative group it might admit to the vote. The nursemaid "Pretenderette" is assumed by them to be a satire on the suffragists who were going on hunger strikes in Great Britain at about the same time as this book was written. I find that Nesbit exhibits a strong streak of feminism and support of female strength in adversity in all her books, however, although she apparently refused to attempt political reform.

19. Philip's Spielstadt also permits him, as Erikson claims, "to use objects endowed with special and symbolic meanings for the representation of an imagined scene in a circumscribed sphere" (*Toys and Reasons* 43). Further, Erikson might say that Philip "can be seen to play out the question of what range of activity is open to him and what direction will engulf him in guilt" (100). Erikson notes that "childhood play, in experimenting with self-images and images of otherness, is . . . representative of what psychoanalysis calls the *ego-ideal*—that part of our selves which we can look up to, at least, insofar as we can imagine ourselves as ideal actors in an ideal plot, with the appropriate punishment and exclusion of those who do not make the grade" (101).

Chapter 8: The Animal-Toy League

1. Grahame's biographer, Peter Green, does, however, cite a contemporaneous review by a Professor Sully that objects to the narrator's lewdly reading into the scene "'a significance that could only have occurred to an experienced adult'" (161). Professor Sully's remarks suggest a pre-Freudian innocence about childhood sexuality.

2. And, in E. T. A. Hoffmann's *Nutcracker,* the Nutcracker and the Mouse King, although hostile, seem to exist in the same night world to which, among the human characters, only Marie is privy.

3. William Empson's essay "Alice as Swain" in *Seven Types of Ambiguity* has an important discussion of the evidence of Darwinian anxiety in Carroll's *Alice.*

4. The genesis story is told twice in the Old Testament, the first version stating that on the sixth day "male and female he created them"; the second telling—the one governing Western thought—has Eve created from Adam's rib. Both versions grant man dominion over all other living creatures.

5. This slippage, according to Samuel F. Pickering, is a sentimentalization of Locke's point of view, more truly expressed in the Judeo-Christian position.

6. One of the most interesting accounts of the influence on literature of such

thinking, which Margot Norris terms *biocentric,* is found in her *Beasts of the Modern Imagination.* She outlines, for instance, the somewhat twisted influence of Darwin on Nietzsche (1844–1900) and the latter's exaltation of instinct over consciousness and concern for man's highly developed compensatory mechanisms for overcoming bodily and instinctual weaknesses. She then shows how such biocentrism is expressed in the works of Franz Kafka, Max Ernst, and D. H. Lawrence. Other literary theorists, like Gilles DeLeuze and Félix Guattari in *Kafka: Toward a Minor Literature,* are interested in how alliance with animals is used not only to marginalize the characters in the literature but to marginalize the texts in which such characters appear.

7. Particularly striking in this regard is his essay "The Lost Centaur," which appears in the earliest collection of his works, *Pagan Papers* (1893). Here Grahame bemoans a "lamentable cleavage" between humans and animals, brought about by the "long race after . . . so-called progress." He suggests that there might instead have evolved, through the communication of humans and animals, "some perfect embodiment of the dual nature: as who should say a being with the nobilities of both of us, the baseness of neither" (103).

8. John Berger, in "Why Look at Animals?" is very dubious about the nature of the post-Cartesian concern with animals, which, according to him is associated in literature and art with a sentimental nostalgia—and an increasingly unrealistic lack of acquaintance with real animals. Of course, literary fantasy itself is likely to defy the "natural." Leonard Marcus, using Berger's analysis, applies it to some contemporary picture books for children.

9. I have omitted from this study such books as the Paddington bear series because, despite *illustrations* of Paddington as a teddy bear, Paddington never functions as toy as such but rather as an anthropomorphized bear whose relationships are largely with human beings. The issues of becoming real and of the relationships among human, toy, and animal are thus ignored, and do not become elements of fantasy to be explored.

10. In addition, as a reader of ecological literature in the late twentieth century, I have become increasingly aware of animal-rights advocates who hold a position not unlike that of the theriophilosophers of the primitivist movement, a position now associated with ecological radicalism and biocentric rather than anthropocentric views of the cosmos. They are frequently associated with antitechnological concerns like those examined in Chapter 10. These views are expressed in such books as Bill McKibben's *The End of Nature* (1989).

11. See my "Two Newbery Medal Winners and the Feminine Mystique."

12. Bailey's use of fantasy is never as free-rangingly exuberant as Bianco's. Her book, *Finnegan II: His Nine Lives* (1953), goes so far as to delineate the consciousness of a reformed alley cat in anthropomorphic terms, but it is otherwise quite naturalistic.

13. Pamela Bianco herself went on to write a toy narrative, *Toy Rose* (1957), based on entirely different fantasy premises, where two children proceed to imagine dolls that then materialize and come alive.

14. Like Grahame in *The Wind in the Willows,* Bianco does not attempt to "rational-

ize" the fantasy and seems not to worry about scale, potential mobility, or consistent notions of biological functions like eating, sleeping, etc., except when they are of narrative interest. Her work does not fit neatly into William Robert Irwin's category of the fantasy that departs from consensus reality in only one consistent way. Bailey is much more consistent in this regard, yet perhaps creates greater problems in terms of relation to the "real" world.

15. In contrast to fairy tales, modern children's literature may tend to stay away from romance, but as Diana Kelly-Byrne demonstrates, mating is an important issue in child's fantasy play—with and without objects. Even the play of a child like Kelly-Burne's subject, a seven-year-old, is permeated with similar matchmaking concerns (251).

16. Of course, children themselves in their play do not necessarily conform to stereotypes and will fantasize relationships among their toys that are equally "abnormal." Certainly Bianco's writing suggests that the toys are childlike in their inexperience with consensus reality. Her characters remind us of bright children as Bailey's characters do not.

17. I find some other interesting things going on in Bailey's Newbery acceptance speech, "Miss Hickory: Her Genealogy," which associates Miss Hickory with an anecdote about Bailey's own childhood and the grandmother who made the doll "probably from the design of a pioneer childhood" (239). This same grandmother is quoted in the speech as dealing with the young Carolyn's tantrums by saying, "'My child, there is something we always have to keep in mind. A lady never expresses her feelings'" (240).

18. One could make something out the idea of "relieving" the virgin of "the burden" of her maiden*head* as well.

19. To Nancy Cott, historian, it appears that the acceptance of feminism that was needed to bring about women's suffrage in 1921 ended even earlier: "No question, feminism came under heavy scrutiny—and fire—by the end of the 1920s. From one point of view, feminism appeared archaic, a polemical stance perhaps needed to storm the bastions of male privilege early in the century when women had been confined to their own sphere, but now superseded by the reality that women and men worked and played together every day. In the eyes of other critics, feminism looked too fearsomely futuristic, projecting a world in which women's self-seeking destroyed gender assignment, family unity, kinship bonds, social cohesion, and human happiness" (271).

20. Examinations of Newbery Medal winners have demonstrated how much the award illuminates the prevailing culture. As Linda Kauffman Peterson and Marilyn Leathers Solt note, "Through the decades the authors of Newbery and Caldicott books have consciously, and perhaps sometimes unconsciously, revealed the concerns, manners, and attitudes of the society in which they lived. This is true not only of realistic fiction, but of other genres as well, especially historical fiction and fantasy. As a consequence the books are interesting as documents of social history as well as literature for children" (10).

21. In spite of the flood of women's studies since then and *The Feminine Mystique's* limitation in its emphasis on middle-class white women, Friedan's book seems to me

sufficiently insightful to stand up to later revisionism in its description of the fate of the women's movement in the mid-twentieth century. For that and its excellent analysis of popular culture, I would continue to recommend it, along with more recent studies like Cott's.

22. One could possibly fit this ending in with the French feminism of those who, like Hélène Cixous, exalt preconsciousness as a supreme state of awareness (see Toril Moi), but the text lacks the context for valuing such a state of being except in the one instance of Miss Hickory's return to vegetable life. One might note also that, in Greek mythology, turning a person into a plant or tree is definitely a punishment. In contrast to Miss Hickory's loss of head is the significance of the carving of her face to Field's Hitty—it virtually releases her imprisoned spirit.

23. Indeed, the headless woman, as depicted, for instance, in the pub sign of "The Silent Woman," is an emblem of the antifeminist in literature and thought. See especially Susan Gubar's discussion in "'The Blank Page' and the Issues of Female Creativity," which begins by quoting from Margaret Atwood's untitled prose poem in *You Are Happy* about two boys who construct a woman out of mud. Atwood writes: "She began at the neck and ended at the knees and elbows: they stuck to essentials" (74). Significantly, Atwood's *The Handmaid's Tale* is also about the attempt to reduce women to their reproductive function.

Chapter 9: Beyond the Last Visible Toy

1. The book also contains illustrations by Phil Parks, which combine with the text to create an unusually thick, short, wide picture book, as apt for coffee-table browsing as for the playroom. Credit is also given to Christopher Zavisa, who is listed on the title page as having "created" the book, which indeed suggests that graphic design has here an importance usually given to it in picture books rather than a text of this length. Reviewing this work for the *Los Angeles Times*, Carolyn Meyer calls it "slickly produced" and advises the parents of children addicted to television to rush out and buy it, since it seems likely to attract "the kid who spends too many hours fixed on electronic screens." She captures a quality of its images, stating that they have the "sharp edges of a Saturday morning cartoon and the eerie glow of a TV-set glimpsed through the window of somebody else's home" (12).

2. In this, *Oddkins* is not an exception among the majority of toy texts, which tend to partake of the formulaic.

3. The *Times Literary Supplement* review of the book wonders "who the ideal reader should be" (19).

4. I am indebted to Peter Neumeyer's "*Amy's Eyes* Examined," not only for pointing out this attribution, but for bringing this toy text to my attention.

5. The breadbox motif seems to suggest that the loaf of bread that was put in the basket with Amy and the sailor doll was significantly different from them—although according to the theory of creativity elsewhere in the book, where long underwear becomes a man, even a loaf of bread, properly read to, could come alive.

6. I might also point out that the father abandoned his daughter to the ministra-

tions of both the bad and good bad mother and that only Miss Eclair's interventions have in fact saved Amy at certain crucial points from the malice of Miss Quince and the dangerous ambitions of the captain.

7. Since 1978, a number of fine articles, by Alida Allison, Millicent Lenz, Joan Bowers, and Geraldine DeLuca, among others, have appeared, discussing the relation of *The Mouse and His Child* not only to Hoban's earlier works for children but to the whole body of his writing, as he moved into novels for adults like the apocalyptical *Riddley Walker* and *Turtle Diary*. Hoban has also talked generously about his writing both in essays and in interviews with Rhonda Bunbury, Sinda Gregory, and Larry McCaffery, as well as with Allison.

8. One might want to call the type of imagination displayed in *La Corona and the Tin Frog* a liminal one, since it crosses barriers usually erected between various levels of "reality"—La Corona and the lady in the castle exist at first only in one-dimensional form as part of printed pictures (by Nicola Bayley), while their lovers are three-dimensional. But all these characters, of course—as such leaps between levels remind us as we try to think about them—are words or pictures on a page of text, animated not only by the imaginations of the authors, but by the reader's response to them.

I am indebted to Alida Allison, in "Living the Non-Mechanical Life," for pointing out how *La Corona and the Tin Frog* and *The Mouse and His Child* are alike, and how their investigation of the mechanical relates to Hoban's earliest books for children, both nonfiction: *What Does It Do and How Does It Work?* and *The Atomic Submarine* (1958). Notes Allison: "But his interest wasn't really in machines per se, but in the *idea* of the mechanical, and its complement, the idea of breaking out of perfunctory existence" (189).

9. Emily Hicks, who teaches children's literature at San Diego State University, has also found analogies to the plight of border workers in Hoban's dump economy.

10. Review after review, although generally favorable, has ruminated about the status of *The Mouse and His Child* as a children's story. Writing in *Books for Your Children* in 1976, Hoban replied that he did not think it was a child's book when he wrote it, but later came around to that point of view: "During the three years I spent writing *The Mouse and His Child* my small protagonists assumed large proportions for me. I believed in them and in the world that came out of my typewriter. . . . I believed that the winning of a dolls' house was truly a victory and I believed that victory might be a permanent thing. That's why the book is a children's book. Now I know that the winning of a dolls' house may be a proper triumph for clockwork mice in a story but for human beings in real life it won't do. Nor can any victory be permanent. Indeed the only thing that can be won is the capacity for fighting. . . . That's why I'm writing about people now instead of toys, and no [sic] dolls' houses. Within its limitations and because of them I think *The Mouse and His Child* is suitable for children." In fact, Hoban began to exhibit a rather dark and cynical attitude toward children's books as examples of adult hypocrisy as he began to write adult books with darker visions.

11. Margaret Baker's *Hannibal and the Bears*, a sequel to her better-known *Shoe Shop Bears*, creates a society of victims of "spring cleaning" and of children's moving

on to new schools or to "pictures of young men with fancy haircuts and electric guitars" (30). The discarded toys make a nomadic life for themselves in the dump, although they eventually emigrate to the children's ward of a hospital.

12. Many toy texts, as demonstrated in Chapter 6, cling to a view of race as embodying essential traits as well.

13. Margaret Mead's study of animism cited in Chapter 3 suggests the importance of such linguistic considerations in our imaginative creations.

14. From another angle, primarily ecological, Millicent Lenz persuasively argues the necessity for new "myths" and new kinds of heroes, in her discussion of literature for youth in a nuclear age.

Chapter 10: Life(size) Endowments

1. I am, of course, also interested in the masculine imagery of barriers being penetrated in this passage, a reminder that, at least in literature, most toy makers are men. But in Collodi's version, only the Blue-Haired Fairy can endow Pinocchio with "real" life.

2. Although I mention them in this chapter, I stand back from including Mary Shelley's *Frankenstein* and L. Frank Baum's Oz series. These works fit here in various ways, but raise so many other questions that this chapter cannot do proper justice to them. I prefer to include works not so well known, yet equally suggestive of themes important to toy narratives.

3. In *Artificial Life: The Quest for a New Creation,* Steven Levy discusses anxieties of contemporary scientists about the work that they are doing on artificial intelligence and robotry. See also my discussion below of Roger Penrose's *The Emperor's New Mind.*

4. Notable, however, is the fact that while in fiction the toy maker is male, two recent, quite fascinating nonfiction accounts of toy making present female doll makers, Kathryn Lasky's *The Eyelight and the Shadow* and Adele Wiseman's *Old Woman at Play.* The former is an imaginative documentary about Carole Bowling and her "portrait dolls," which is illustrated by photographs showing dolls at various stages of development; the latter investigates the strange and wonderful dolls made by the author's mother, Chaika Wiseman, from scraps of various materials, weaving an immigrant and family history around them.

5. In the simplified plot of the ballet, *Coppélia* (1870; music by Leo Délibes), Coppelius is the maker of the automaton, Coppélia, who briefly wins the attention of a swain, Franz, away from his love Swanhilda. The latter, however, pretends to be Coppélia and dances a series of dances for Coppelius and Franz that go from mechanical to berserk, convincing her lover of the superiority of her own reality. I believe this was one of the first ballets to which I was taken. The scene of Coppelius's workshop, with its troupe of automata, is a classic one for me and perhaps for others; see Angela Carter's *The Magic Toyshop* and Ingmar Bergman's movie *Fanny and Alexander.*

6. The way Nathanael's mother uses the name of the Sandman to describe euphemistically the arrival of Coppelius, which necessitated the children's going to bed, mingles in Nathanael's young mind with their nurse's terrifying tales of the Sandman

throwing sand in children's eyes, and creates a case history of the evolution of obsessive terror in a sensitive youth.

7. Diana S. Peters, however, argues that protagonists like Nathanael in "The Sandman" and Ferdinand in "The Automata," who do not manage to incorporate dream
into everyday reality creatively, are *"unambiguously* self-destructive in Hoffmann's
view" (emphasis mine, 77).

8. Feathertop seems a possible literary predecessor of L. Frank Baum's Scarecrow in
The Wizard of Oz, whose search for a heart may have been inspired by Hawthorne's
calling attention to the hole in Feathertop's coat over the heart; Jack Pumpkinhead in
The Land of Oz bears even more physical resemblance to Feathertop.

9. Pamela McCorduck, in *Machines Who Think: A Personal Inquiry into the History
and Prospects of Artificial Intelligence* (1979), begins her discussion with a survey of
Western literature emphasizing the tradition of endeavors "to create artificial intel-
ligences, both literary and real" (vii). Unlike Penrose, she is relatively sanguine at the
prospect.

10. David Townsend tells me that Yod's name itself calls up the intertext of the
golem traditions since Yod is the first letter of the tetragrammaton. Thus, Townsend
notes, what is inscribed on the physical body of the golem is inscribed onto Yod as
subject by his very name.

11. Like Singer, Malkah (and Piercy behind her) tells the golem story with those
twists that fit best her own agenda. Piercy acknowledges several scholarly influences
on her own interpretations (446).

Bibliography

Fiction

Ainslie, Kathleen. *Me and Catherine Susan*. London: Castell Brothers, 1903.

Ainsworth, Ruth. *Mr. Jumble's Toy Shop*. London: Lutterworth, 1978.

———. *Rufty Tufty, the Golliwog*. London: Heineman, 1952.

Alcott, Louisa May. *Little Men*. 1871. New York: Dutton, 1951.

Andersen, H. C. "The Steadfast Tin Soldier," "The Top and the Ball," "The Old House." In *A Treasury of Hans Christian Andersen*, trans. Erik Christen Haugaard. Garden City, N. Y.: International Collector's Library, 1974.

Angelina: or Conversations of a Little Girl with Her Doll, Interspersed with Interesting Stories. Edinburgh: Oliver and Boyd, n.d.

Angelou, Maya. *I Know Why the Caged Bird Sings*. New York: Random House, 1970.

Anstey, F. *Only Toys*. London: Grant Richards, 1903.

Ardizzone, Edward, and Aingelda Ardizzone. *The Little Girl and the Tiny Doll*. London: Constable, 1966.

Ausubel, Nathan, ed. "The Golem of Prague." *A Treasury of Jewish Folklore*, ed. Nathan Ausubel. New York: Crown, 1948.

Avery, Gillian, ed. *Victoria-Bess and Others*. London: Victor Gollanz, 1968.

Bacon, Martha. *Moth Manor: A Gothic Tale*. Boston: Little, Brown, 1978.

Bailey, Carolyn Sherwin. *Finnegan II: His Nine Lives*. New York: Viking, 1953.

———. *Miss Hickory*. New York: Viking, 1946.

———. *Tops and Whistles: True Stories of Early American Toys and Children*. New York: Viking, 1937.

Baker, Margaret. *Hannibal and the Bears*. London: Harrap, 1965.

———. *The Shoe Shop Bears*. 1963. New York: Farrar, Straus, and Giroux, 1965.

Banks, Lynne Reid. *The Indian in the Cupboard*. Garden City, N.Y.: Doubleday, 1980.

———. *The L-Shaped Room*. New York: Simon and Schuster, 1960.

———. *The Return of the Indian*. Garden City, N. Y.: Doubleday, 1986.

Barnes, Djuna. *Nightwood*. 1937. New York: New Directions, 1961.

Beaman, S. G. Hulme. *Toytown* series. New York: Oxford University Press, 1925–32.

Beaulieu, Mme. Sophie Males de [presumed author]. *The Well-Bred Doll Intended for the Instruction and Amusement of Children*. London: John Souter, 1819.

Beaumont, Cyril. *The Mysterious Toyshop*. London: C. W. Beaumont, 1924.

———. *The Strange Adventures of a Toy Soldier*. London: C. W. Beaumont, 1926.

Bell, Vera Louise. *Susan and the Sailor Boy*. Leicester, U.K.: Edmund Ward, 1944.

Betjeman, John. *Archie and the Strict Baptists*. Chatham, U.K.: John Murray, 1977.

Bianco, Margery Williams. *The Adventures of Andy*. New York: George H. Doran, 1927.

———. *The Little Wooden Doll*. New York: Macmillan, 1926.

———. *Poor Cecco*. New York: George H. Doran, 1925.

———. *Skin Horse*. New York: George H. Doran, 1927.

——— [under Margery Williams]. *The Velveteen Rabbit: or, How Toys Become Real*. 1922. Garden City, N.Y.: Doubleday, 1930.

Bianco, Pamela. *Toy Rose*. Philadelphia: Lippincott, 1957.

Blyton, Enid. *Bom, The Little Toy Drummer*. Leicester, U.K.: Brockhampton, 1956.

Bradford, Clara. *Ethel's Adventures in Doll Country*. London: John F. Shaw, 1882.

Brink, Carol Ryrie. *Andy Buckram's Tin Men*. 1966. New York: Grosset and Dunlap, 1967.

Broderip, Frances Freeling. *Tales of Toys, Told by Themselves*. London: Griffith and Farran, 1869.

Brontë, Charlotte, and Patrick Branwell Brontë. *The Miscellaneous and Unpublished Writings of Charlotte and Patrick Branwell Brontë*. Oxford: Blackwell, 1936.

Buck, David. *The Small Adventures of Dog*. London: Heineman, 1968.

Burnett, Frances Hodgson. *Racketty-Packetty House*. 1906. New York: Dodd, Mead, 1961.

Byars, Betsy. *Clementine*. Boston: Houghton Mifflin, 1962.

Carroll, Lewis. *Alice's Adventures in Wonderland*. 1865. New York: Delacorte, 1977.

———. *Through the Looking Glass and What Alice Found There*. 1872. Berkeley: University of California Press, 1983.

Carter, Angela. *The Magic Toyshop*. 1967. London: Virago, 1981.

Casement, Christina. *Wandering Robinson*. Kingswood, U.K.: World's Work, 1969.

Cassedy, Sylvia. *Behind the Attic Wall*. New York: Crowell, 1983.

———. *Lucie Babbidge's House*. New York: Crowell, 1989.

———. *M. E. and Morton*. New York: Crowell, 1987.

Charyn, Jerome. *Pinocchio's Nose*. New York: Arbor House, 1983.

Clare, Helen [Pauline Clarke]. *Five Dolls and Their Friends*. 1957. London: Bodley Head, 1967.

———. *Five Dolls in a House*. 1953. London: Bodley Head, 1967.

Clarke, Pauline. *The Return of the Twelves* [British title: *The Twelve and the Genii*]. 1962. New York: Coward-McCann, 1963.

Coatsworth, Elizabeth Jane. *All of a Sudden Susan*. New York: Macmillan, 1974.

———. *The Noble Doll*. New York: Viking, 1961.

Colacino, Antonio. *Susan and Spotty*. Exeter, U.K.: Wheaton, 1967.

Collodi, Carlo. *The Adventures of Pinocchio: Tale of a Puppet*. 1883. Trans. Nicholas J. Perella. Berkeley: University of California Press, 1986.

Constable, Mary. *The Two Dolls: A Story*. Edinburgh: Constable, 1846.

Coover, Robert. *Pinocchio in Venice*. New York: Simon and Schuster, 1991.

Craddock, Mrs. H. C. *The Big Book of Josephine*. London: Blacker and Sons, 1919.

———. *Peggy and Joan*. London: Blacker and Sons, 1922.

———. *Where the Dolls Lived*. London: Society for Promoting Christian Knowledge, 1920.

Curry, Jane Louise. *Mindy's Mysterious Miniature*. New York: Harcourt Brace Jovanovich, 1970.

Dainty Dolly's Day, A Fable for Little Folks. Glasgow: Millar and Lang, n.d.

Dexter, Catherine. *The Oracle Doll*. New York: Macmillan, 1985.

Diaz, Mrs. Aby Morton. *Polly Cologne*. Boston: D. Lothrop, 1881.

Dickens, Charles. *The Cricket on the Hearth*. 1845. London: Frederick Warne, 1902.

A Doll's Story. London: Grombridge and Sons, [1852–55].

Domestic Scenes: or Adventures of a Doll. Burnham, U.K.: Dawson, 1817.

Eaton, Seymour. *More About Teddy B. and Teddy G. The Roosevelt Bears*. Philadelphia: Edward Stern, 1907.

Ewing, Mrs. Juliana H. "The Land of the Lost Toys." In *The Brownies and Other Stories*. 1869. London: Dent, 1954.

Featherstonaugh, Gwendolen. *The Romance of a China Doll*. London: Golden Galley, n.d.

Field, Rachel. *Hitty: Her First Hundred Years*. Illus. Dorothy P. Lathrop. New York: Macmillan, 1929.

———. "A Valentine for Old Dolls." *Hornbook* 11 (July–August 1942): 236.

Fletcher, David. *Miss Primrose*. London: Hutchinson, 1950.

Francis, Frank. *Rescue Operation*. London: Harrap, 1968.

Fraser-Simson, C. *The Adventures of Golly Smith*. London: Blacker and Sons, 1957.

Fyleman, Rose. *The Dolls' House*. London: Methuen, 1930.

Gardam, Jane. *Through the Dolls' House Door*. New York: Dell, 1987.

Gates, Josephine Scribner. *The Story of the Live Dolls*. Indianapolis: Bobbs-Merrill, 1901.

———. *The Story of the Three Dolls*. Indianapolis: Bobbs-Merrill, 1905.

Gatty, Mrs. Alfred [Margaret Scott]. *Aunt Judy's Tales*. London: Bell and Daldy, 1863.

———. *Aunt Sally's Life*. London: Bell and Daldy, 1865.

Gellie, Mary E. *Dolly Dear: or the Story of a Waxen Beauty*. London: Griffith, Farran, and Browne, 1899.

Godden, Rumer. *The Dolls' House*. 1947. New York: Viking, 1963.

———. *The Fairy Doll*. New York: Viking, 1956.

———. *Home Is the Sailor*. New York: Viking, 1964.

———. *Impunity Jane: The Story of a Pocket Doll*. New York: Viking, 1954.

———. *Little Plum*. New York: Viking, 1962.

———. *Miss Happiness and Miss Flower*. New York: Viking, 1961.

———. *The Rocking Horse Secret*. New York: Viking, 1977.

———. *The Story of Holly and Ivy*. 1957. New York: Puffin Books, 1987.

Goethe, Johann Wolfgang von. *Faust, Parts I and II*. 1877. Trans. George Madison Priest. New York: Knopf, 1950.

Goffstein, M. B. *Me and My Captain*. New York: Farrar, Straus, and Giroux, 1974.

————. *Our Prairie Home: A Picture Album*. New York: Harper and Row, 1988.

Graham, Eleanor. *The Night Adventures of Alexis*. London: Faber and Gwyer, 1925.

Grahame, Kenneth. "A Departure." In *Dream Days*. 1898. New York: Garland, 1976.

————. "The Lost Centaur" and "Orion." In *Pagan Papers*. London: Elkin Mathews and John Lane, 1893.

————. "Sawdust and Sin." In *The Golden Age*. 1895. New York: Avon, 1975.

Greenwald, Sheila. *The Secret in Miranda's Closet*. Boston: Houghton Mifflin, 1977.

————. *The Secret Museum*. New York: Dell, 1974.

Grize, Madeleine. *Valariane Goes to Sea*. London: Heineman, 1960.

Gruelle, Johnny. *Marcella Stories*. New York: Donahue, 1929.

Hall, Edith King. *Adventures in Toyland*. London: Blacker and Sons, [1897].

Hart, Frank. *Dolly's Society Book*. London: Grant Richards, [1902].

Hatfield, John. *Quintilian*. London: Jonathan Cape, 1968.

Heymans, Annemie, and Margriet Heymans. *The Dolls' Party*. London: Andre Deutsch, 1971.

Hoban, Russell. *La Corona and the Tin Frog*. 1974. London: Jonathan Cape, 1979.

————. *The Mouse and His Child*. New York: Harper and Row, 1967.

————. *Turtle Diary*. New York: Random House, 1975.

Hoffmann, E. T. A. *The Best Tales of Hoffmann*. Trans. E. F. Bleiler. New York: Dover, 1967.

————. *Nutcracker*. Trans. Ralph Manheim. Illus. Maurice Sendak. New York: Crown, 1984.

Holman, Ada A. *The Adventures of Woodeny*. London: T. Nelson, 1917.

[Horne, Richard]. *Memoirs of a London Doll, Written by Herself*. Ed. Mrs. Fairstar [pseud]. London: Joseph Candall, 1846.

Hoskruge, Ethel. *My Toys*. London: Atremerne, 1904.

Hourihane, Ursula. *The Friendly Adventures of Buttons and Mac*. New York: Oxford University Press, 1946.

————. *Pedlar Pete's Enchanted Toys*. London: Frederick Muller, 1948.

————. *Tubby Ted*. Leicester, U.K.: Brockhampton, 1961.

Howe, Deborah, and James Howe. *Teddy Bear's Scrapbook*. New York: Atheneum, 1980.

Hughes, Richard. *Don't Blame Me*. London: Chatto and Windus, 1940.

————. *Gertrude's Child*. 1966. New York: Harlan Quist, 1974.

————. *The Spider's Palace and Other Stories*. London: Chatto and Windus, 1931.

————. *The Wonder-Dog*. London: Chatto and Windus, 1977.

Hugo, Victor. *Les Misérables*. Trans. Charles E. Wilbour. 2 vols. 1862. New York: Dutton, 1930.

Jackson, Peter C., design and adaptation. *St. George and the Dragon*. London: Pollock's Toy Theatres, 1972.

Jacques, Faith. *Tilly's House*. New York: Atheneum, 1979.

Jaffe, April. *The Enchanted Horse*. London: Hutchinson, 1953.

Jezard, Alison. *Albert*. London: Gollanz, 1968.

John, Ursula. *The Adventures of Boss and Dingbat*. London: Harrap, 1937.

Johnson, Crockett. *Ellen's Lion*. Boston: Godine, 1959.

Jones, Elizabeth Orton. *Big Susan*. New York: Macmillan, 1967.

Jones, Harold. *There and Back Again*. New York: Oxford University Press, 1978.

Kennedy, Richard. *Amy's Eyes*. New York: Harper and Row, 1985.

Kilner, Dorothy. *The Adventures of a Whipping Top, with Stories of Many Bad Boys, Who Themselves Deserve Whipping and of Some Good Boys, Who Deserve Plumcakes*. London: John Marshall, n.d.

Kilner, Mary Ann. *The Adventures of a Pincushion*. 1780. London: S. and R. Bentley-John Harris, 1828.

———. *Memoirs of a Peg-Top*. London: John Marshall, 1783.

Koontz, Dean. *Oddkins: A Fable for All Ages*. New York: Warner, 1988.

Lang, Elizabeth. *Jane and Her Family*. London: T. Nelson, 1895.

Lawrence, D. H. *Sons and Lovers*. 1913. New York: Boni and Liveright, 1922.

Lemon, Mark. *The Enchanted Doll: A Fairy Tale for Little People*. London: Bradbury and Evans, 1849.

Lewis, Naomi. *The Silent Playmate*. 1979. London: Gollanz Children's Paperbacks, 1991.

Lionni, Leo. *Alexander and the Wind-Up Mouse*. New York: Pantheon, 1969.

The Live Doll: or Ellen's New-Year's Gift. London: Wm. Darton, [before 1850].

Loti, Pierre, et al. *French Toys*. Paris: Presses de L'Avenir Feminin, 1915.

Lovell, Dorothy Ann. *The Strange Adventures of Emma*. London: Faber and Faber, 1941.

Ludlam, Rose. *Under the Moon*. Leicester, U.K.: Edgar Backus, 1943.

McGavin, Moyra. *Sarabel*. London: Harrap, 1961.

Mackenzie, Compton. *The Conceited Doll*. Oxford: Blackwell, 1930.

Maitland, Julia Charlotte. *The Doll and Her Friends. or Memoirs of Lady Seraphina*. London: Griffith and Farran, [1852].

Mankowitz, Wolf. *Majollika and Company*. London: Andre Deutsch, 1955.

Manley, Seon, and GoGo Lewis, eds. *The Haunted Dolls*. Garden City, N. Y.: Doubleday, 1980.

Mansfield, Katherine. "The Doll's House." In *The Silent Playmate*, ed. Naomi Lewis. London: Gollanz Children's Paperbacks, 1991.

Mantle, Winifred. *Jonnesty in Winter*. London: Chatto and Windus, 1975.

Mariana. *Miss Flora McFlimsey's May Day*. New York: Lothrop, Lee, and Shephard, 1969.

Marshall, Archibald. *Wooden*. London: Collins, 1920.

Masefield, John. *The Midnight Folk*. London: Heineman, 1927.

Mathias, Eileen. *The Dolls from Doll Street*. Guilford, U.K.: Lutterworth, 1972.

Matthiessen, Wilhelm. *Little Lottie*. Trans. Stella Humphries. London: Burke, 1960.

Mayor, Henry. *The Adventures of a Japanese Doll*. New York: Dutton, 1901.

Meanwell, Nancy. *The History of a Doll*. London: J. Harris, 1805.

Meyer, Renate. *The Story of Little Knittle and Threadle*. London: Bodley Head, 1971.

Miller, Leslie Adrienne. "My Mother's Doll." In *Staying Up for Love*. Pittsburgh: Carnegie Mellon, 1990.

Milne, A. A. *The House at Pooh Corner*. 1928. New York: Dutton, 1944.

———. *Now We Are Six*. New York: Dutton, 1927.

———. *When We Were Very Young*. New York: Dutton, 1924.

———. *Winnie-the-Pooh*. 1926. New York: Dutton, 1943.

Mister, Mary. *The Adventures of a Doll*. London: Darton, Harvey, and Darton, 1816.

Moore, Mary F. *Dorcas the Wooden Doll*. London: Sylvan, 1944.

Morrison, Toni. *The Bluest Eye*. 1970. New York: Washington Square, 1972.

Nesbit, E. *The Enchanted Castle*. 1907. New York: Dutton, 1964.

———. *The Magic City*. 1910. Boston: Gregg, 1981.

Nicholson, William. *Clever Bill*. 1926. New York: Farrar, Straus, and Giroux, 1977.

Norton, Andre. *Octogon Magic*. New York: Pocket, 1967.

O'Connell, Jean. *The Dollhouse Caper*. New York: Crowell, 1975.

O'Reilly, Mrs. Robert. *Doll World*. London: Bell and Daldy, 1872.

O'Shaughnessy, Arthur, and Eleanor O'Shaughnessy. *Toyland*. London: Daldy, Isbister, 1875.

Pardoe, Miss. *Lady Arabella: or The Adventures of a Doll*. London: Kerby and Sons, 1856.

Parrish, Anne. *The Floating Island*. London: Ernest Benn, 1930.

Patri, Angelo. *Pinocchio in Africa*. New York: Ginn, 1939.

Patten, Brian, and Mary Moore. *Emma's Doll*. London: Allen and Unwin, 1976.

Phillips, Ethel Calvert. *The Little Rag Doll*. Cambridge, Mass.: Riverside, 1930.

Piercy, Marge. *He, She and It*. New York: Knopf, 1991.

Potter, Beatrix. *The Tale of Two Bad Mice*. 1904. London: Warne, 1987.

Robinson, Joan G. *Teddy Robinson's Omnibus*. London: Harrap, 1959.

Rodari, Gianni. *The Befana's Toyshop: A Twelfth Night Story*. Trans. Patrick Creagh. London: Dent, 1970.

Roose-Evans, James. *Odd and Elsewhere*. London: Andre Deutsch, 1971.

Saki. "The Toys of Peace." In *The Short Stories of Saki*. New York: Viking, 1930.

Sandburg, Carl. "The Wedding Procession of the Rag Doll and the Broom Handle and Who Was in It." In *Rootabaga Stories*. New York: Harcourt, Brace, 1922.

Sedgwick, Modwena. *The Galldora Omnibus*. 1960–61. London: Harrap, 1973.

Shute, E. L. *Jappie-Chappie and How He Loved a Dollie*. London: Warne, 1890.

Siebe, Josephine. *Kasperle's Adventures*. New York: Macmillan, 1929.

Singer, Isaac Bashevis. *The Golem*. London: Andre Deutsch, 1983; New York: Knopf, 1991.

Skey, T. C. *Dolly's Own Story, Told in Her Own Words*. London: Wells, Gardner and Darton, [1894].

Skörpen, Liesel. *Charles*. Kingswood, U.K.: World's Work, 1972.

Sleator, William. *Among the Dolls*. New York: Dutton, 1975.

Slobodkin, Louis. *The Adventures of Arab*. New York: Vanguard, 1946.

Small, David. *Eulalie and the Happy Head*. New York: Macmillan, 1982.

Stearns, Pamela. *The Mechanical Doll*. Boston: Houghton Mifflin, 1979.

Steven, Lucille. *Poopy, the Dancing Doll*. Glasgow: Art and Educational, 1940.

Stevenson, Robert Louis. "A Martial Elegy for Some Lead Soldiers," "The Dumb Soldier." In *Collected Poems,* ed. Janet Adam Smith. 2d. ed. New York: Viking, 1971.

Stover, Marjorie Tilley. *When the Dolls Woke*. Niles, Ill.: Albert Whitman, 1985.

Syfret, Anne, and Edward Syfret. *Bella.* New York: Macmillan, 1975.

Symonds, John. *Away to the Moon.* Philadelphia: Lippincott, 1956.

——. *Lottie.* London: Bodley Head, 1957.

Taylor, Cora. *The Doll.* Saskatoon: Western, 1987.

Teresah. *A Doll, Two Children and Three Storks.* Trans. Dorothy Emmerich. New York: Dutton, 1931.

Tozer, Katharine. *The Wanderings of Mumfie.* London: John Murray, 1935.

Tregarthen, Enys. *The Doll Who Came Alive.* 1942. New York: John Day, 1972.

Unwin, Nora S. *Lucy and the Little Red Horse.* London: De La More, 1948.

Upton, Elizabeth. *The Birthday Gift or the Joy of a New Doll.* London: Tompkins Bond Street, 1796.

Upton, Florence, and Bertha Upton. *The Adventures of Two Dutch Dolls—And a Golliwog.* London: Longmans Green, 1895.

Wahl, Jan. *The Muffletump Storybook.* Chicago: Follett, 1975.

Watterson, Bill. *Calvin and Hobbes.* Kansas City, Mo.: Andrews and McMeel, 1987.

Wickham, Constance. *The Golliwog Book.* London: Collins, 1940.

Williams, Ursula Morey. *Adventures of a Little Wooden Horse.* London: Harrap, 1938.

——. *The Toymaker's Daughter.* London: Meredith, 1963.

Wilson, Dorothy. *The Doll Family.* New York: Wonder, 1962.

Winthrop, Elizabeth. *The Castle in the Attic.* 1985. New York: Bantam, 1986.

Woodruff, Elizabeth. *Stories from a Magic World.* Springfield, Mass.: McLoughlan, 1938.

Wright, Betty Ren. *The Dollhouse Murders.* New York: Scholastic, 1983.

York, Carol Beach. *The Christmas Dolls.* New York: Franklin Watts, 1967.

——. *The Revenge of the Dolls.* New York: Elsevier/Nelson, 1979.

Zipes, Jack. *Victorian Fairy Tales: The Revolt of the Fairies and the Elves.* 1987. New York: Routledge, 1989.

Secondary Sources

Allison, Alida. "Living the Non-Mechanical Life: Russell Hoban's Metaphorical Wind-Up Toys." *Children's Literature in Education* 22, no. 3 (1991): 189–94.

——. "Russell Hoban." In *Dictionary of Literary Biography: American Writers for Children Since 1960,* vol. 52, 194–202, ed. Glenn E. Estes. Detroit: Gale Research, 1986.

"*Amy's Eyes.*" Review. *Times Literary Supplement,* 15 August 1986, 19.

Ariès, Philippe. *Centuries of Childhood: A Social History of Family Life.* Trans. Robert Baldick. New York: Vintage, 1962, 1965.

Armstrong, Nancy. *Desire and Domestic Fiction: A Political History of the Novel.* New York: Oxford University Press, 1987.

"Art." *New Yorker.* 30 April 1990: 13.

Bachelard, Gaston. *The Poetics of Space.* Trans. Maria Jolas. New York: Orion, 1964.

Bailey, Carolyn Sherwin. "Miss Hickory: Her Genealogy. Newbery Award Acceptance Paper." *Hornbook* 23 (July 1947): 238–42.

Bakhtin, M. M. *The Dialogic Imagination: Four Essays*. Ed. Michael Holquist. Trans. Caryl Emerson and Michael Holquist. Austin: University of Texas Press, 1981.

Balanchine, George. "The Nutcracker." In *Balanchine's Complete Stories of the Great Ballets*, 247–53, 387–95, ed. Frances Mason. Garden City, N. Y.: Doubleday, 1954, 1977.

Barkan, Leonard. *The Gods Made Flesh: Metamorphosis and the Pursuit of Paganism*. New Haven: Yale University Press, 1986.

Barthes, Roland. "Toys." In *Mythologies*, trans. Annette Lavers. New York: Hill and Wang, 1953.

Bensky, Roger-Daniel. *Récherches sur les structures et la symbolique de la marionette*. Paris: Nizet, 1971.

Berger, John. "Why Look at Animals?" In *About Looking*, 1–26. New York: Pantheon, 1980.

Bethnal Green Museum of Childhood. *Doll and Toy Stories in the Renier Collection. Parts I and II*. London: Bethnal Green Museum of Childhood, 1989.

Blanchard, Kendall, ed. *The Many Faces of Play*. Champaign, Ill.: Human Kinetics, 1986.

Blount, Margaret Joan. *Animal Land: The Creatures of Children's Fiction*. New York: Morrow, 1974, 1975.

Boas, Samuel. *The Happy Beast in French Thought of the Seventeenth Century*. Baltimore: Johns Hopkins University Press, 1933.

Boehn, Max von. *Dolls and Puppets*. Philadelphia: David McKay, n.d.

Bowers, Joan. "The Fantasy World of Russell Hoban." *Children's Literature* 8 (1980): 80–96.

Bredsdorff, Elias. *Hans Christian Andersen: The Story of His Life and Work 1805–75*. New York: Scribner's 1975.

Bruner, Jerome S., Alison Jolly, and Kathy Sylva, eds. *Play—Its Role in Development and Evolution*. New York: Basic, 1976.

Bulger, Peggy A. "The Princess of Power: Socializing Our Daughters through TV, Toys, and Tradition." *Lion and the Unicorn* 12, no. 2 (1988): 178–92.

Bunbury, Rhonda. "'Always a Dance Going on in the Stone': An Interview with Russell Hoban." *Children's Literature in Education* 3 (Fall 1986): 139–48.

Burnett, Frances Hodgson. "Literature and the Doll." In *The One I Knew the Best of All*. 1893. New York: Arno, 1980.

Burton, Anthony. *The Bethnal Museum of Childhood*. London: Victoria and Albert Museum, 1986.

Butler, Francelia, ed. "Toys and Games." In *Sharing Literature with Children: A Thematic Anthology*, 1–90. New York: David McKay, 1977.

Butts, Denis. "Hoban, Russell (Conwell)." In *Twentieth Century Children's Writers*, 601–04, ed. D. L. Kirkpatrick. New York: St. Martin's, 1978.

Cambon, Glauco. "Pinocchio and Problems of Children's Literature." *Children's Literature* 2 (1973): 50–60.

Cameron, Eleanor. *The Green and Burning Tree*. Boston: Little, Brown, 1969.

———. "The Inmost Secret." *Hornbook* 59 (February 1983): 17–24.

Campbell, Joseph. *The Hero with a Thousand Faces*. 2d ed. Princeton: Princeton University Press, 1968.

Carpenter, Humphrey, and Mari Prichard, eds. "Hitty, Her First Hundred Years." In *The Oxford Companion to Children's Literature*, 253–54. New York: Oxford University Press, 1984.

Cawelti, John G. *Adventure, Mystery and Romance: Formula Stories as Art and Popular Culture*. Chicago: University of Chicago Press, 1976.

Clarke, Pauline. "The Chief Genii Branwell." *Junior Bookshelf* 27 (July 1963): 119–23.

Cohen, David. *The Development of Play*. New York; New York University Press, 1987.

Commire, Anne, ed. "Bailey, Carolyn Sherwin 1875–1961." In *Something about the Author*, 18–23. Detroit: Gale Research, 1979.

———. "Field, Rachel (Lyman) 1894–1942." In *Something about the Author*, 106–12. Detroit: Gale Research, 1979.

Cott, Nancy F. *The Grounding of Modern Feminism*. New Haven: Yale University Press, 1987.

Crews, Frederick C. *The Pooh Perplex: A Freshman Casebook*. New York: Dutton, 1963.

Daniels, Steven. "*The Velveteen Rabbit*: A Kleinian Perspective." *Children's Literature* 18 (1990): 17–29.

Darwin, Charles. *On the Origin of Species by Means of Natural Selection*. 1859. New York: Atheneum, 1967.

David, Alfred. "An Iconography of Noses: Directions in the History of a Physical Stereotype." In *Mapping the Cosmos*, ed. Jane Chance and R. O. Wells, Jr. Houston: Rice University Press, 1985.

Deleuze, Gilles, and Félix Guattari. *Kafka: Toward a Minor Literature*. Trans. Dana Polan. Minneapolis: University of Minnesota Press, 1986.

DeLuca, Geraldine. "'A Condition of Complete Simplicity': The Toy as Child in *The Mouse and His Child*." *Children's Literature in Education* 19, no. 4 (1988): 211–21.

Derrida, Jacques. *Writing and Difference*. Trans. Alan Bass. Chicago: Chicago University Press, 1978.

Dinnerstein, Dorothy. *The Mermaid and the Minotaur: Sexual Arrangements and Human Malaise*. New York: Harper and Row, 1976.

Doane, Janice, and Devon Hodges. *Nostalgia and Sexual Difference: The Resistance to Contemporary Feminism*. New York: Methuen, 1987.

Dusinberre, Juliet. *Alice to the Lighthouse: Children's Books and Radical Experiments in Art*. London: Macmillan, 1987.

Eissler, Ruth, et al., eds. *The Psychoanalytic Study of the Child*. Vol. 9. New York: International Universities, 1954.

Empson, William. "Alice as Swain." In *Seven Types of Ambiguity*. 1930. 3d. ed. London: Chatto and Windus, 1963.

Erikson, Erik H. *Childhood and Society*. 2d. ed. New York: Norton, 1963.

———. *Toys and Reasons*. New York: Norton, 1977.

Fiedler, Leslie. *Love and Death in the American Novel*. New York: Criterion, 1960.

Field, Rachel. "How 'Hitty' Happened." *Hornbook* 6 (February 1930): 22–26.

Fisher, Seymour. *Sexual Images of the Self: The Psychology of Erotic Sensations and Illusions*. Hillsdale, N.J.: Erlbaum, 1989.

Foucault, Michel. *The History of Sexuality*. Trans. Robert Hurley. New York: Pantheon, 1978.

Fox, Carl. *The Doll*. New York: Abrams, 1972.

Fraser, Antonia. *A History of Toys*. Frankfurt am Main: Delacorte, 1966.

Freeman, Ruth, and Larry Freeman. *Cavalcade of Toys*. New York: Century House, 1942.

Freud, Sigmund. "The 'Uncanny.'" In *The Standard Edition of the Complete Psychological Works of Sigmund Freud,* vol. 17, trans. James Strachey. London: Hogarth, 1955.

Friedan, Betty. *The Feminine Mystique*. New York: Norton, 1963.

Fritzsch, Karl Ewald, and Manfred Bachmann. *An Illustrated History of German Toys*. New York: Hastings House, 1966, 1978.

Froebel, Friedrich. *The Student's Froebel*. Adapted by William H. Herford. Part I, *Theory of Education*. Boston: D. C. Heath, 1896.

Frye, Northrop. *The Anatomy of Criticism*. Princeton: Princeton University Press, 1957.

Gallop, Jane. *Reading Lacan*. Ithaca: Cornell University Press, 1985.

Gannon, Susan R. "Pinocchio: The First Hundred Years." *Children's Literature Association Quarterly* 6 (1981–82): 1, 5–7.

Gilbert, Sandra M., and Susan Gubar. *No Man's Land: The Place of the Woman Writer in the Twentieth Century*. Vol. 2: *Sexchanges*. New Haven: Yale University Press, 1988.

Gilligan, Carol. *In a Different Voice: Psychological Theory and Women's Development*. Cambridge: Harvard University Press, 1982.

Glazer, Joan. "*Dollmaker*: An Example of Literary Non-Fiction." *Children's Literature Association Quarterly* 12, no. 4 (1987): 176–77.

Gordon, Lesley. *Peepshow into Paradise: A History of Children's Toys*. London: Harrap, 1953.

Gordon, Robert Kay. *Anglo-Saxon Poetry*. Select. and trans. Robert Kay Gordon. New York: Dutton, 1954.

Gottfried, Allen W., and Catherine Caldwell Brown, eds. *Play Interactions. The Contribution of Play Materials and Parental Involvement to Children's Development*. Lexington, Mass.: Lexington, 1986.

Green, Peter. *Kenneth Grahame 1859–1932: A Study of His Life, Work and Times*. London: John Murray, 1959.

Greene, Vivien. *English Dolls' Houses of the Eighteenth and Nineteenth Centuries*. 1955. New York: Scribner's, 1979.

Gubar, Susan. "'The Blank Page' and the Issues of Female Creativity." In *Writing and Sexual Difference,* 73–94, ed. Elizabeth Abel. Chicago: University of Chicago Press, 1982.

Hardyment, Christina. *Dream Babies from Locke to Spock*. London: Jonathan Cape, 1983.

Hedges, Chris. "Tin Army and Fond Thoughts of the Past." *New York Times,* 16 December 1990.

Heisig, Fr. James. "Pinocchio: Archetype of the Motherless Child." *Children's Literature* 3 (1974): 23–35.

Helbig, Alethea. "Carol Ryrie Brink." In *Writers for Children: Critical Studies of Major Authors since the Seventeenth Century,* 85–90, ed. Jane M. Bingham. New York: Scribner's, 1988.

Hendrickson, Linnea. *Children's Literature: A Guide to Criticism.* Boston: G. K. Hall, 1987.

Herron, R. E., and Brian Sutton-Smith. *Child's Play.* New York: Wiley, 1971.

Hicks, D. Emily. *Border Writing: The Multidimensional Text.* Minneapolis: University of Minnesota Press, 1991.

Hine, Thomas. "Screen Robots Tell a Tale of Mankind." *New York Times,* 3 November 1991, 2:13, 16.

Hoban, Russell. "'The Mouse and His Child': Yes, It's a Children's Book." *Books for Your Children* (Winter 1976): 3.

Hoff, Benjamin. *The Tao of Pooh.* New York: Dutton, 1982.

———. *The Te of Piglet.* New York: Dutton, 1992.

Hogan, Patrick. "What's Wrong with the Psychoanalysis of Literature?" *Children's Literature* 18 (1990): 135–40.

Hume, Kathryn. *Fantasy and Mimesis: Responses to Reality in Western Literature.* New York: Methuen, 1984.

Humphrey, Virginia P. "'The Teddy Bear Girls' Tertiary Transitional Objects: A Retrospective Study of Stuffed Animal Attachment in Late Adolescence." Ph.D. diss. Pacific Graduate School of Psychology, Menlo Park, Calif., June 1986.

Hunt, Peter. "A. A. Milne." In *Writers for Children: Critical Studies of Major Authors since the Seventeenth Century,* 397–405, ed. Jane M. Bingham. New York: Scribner's, 1988.

Irigaray, Luce. *The Irigaray Reader.* Ed. Margaret Whitford. Cambridge, Mass.: Basil Blackwell, 1991.

Irwin, William Robert. *The Game of the Impossible: A Rhetoric of Fantasy.* Urbana: University of Illinois Press, 1976.

Jackson, Mary V. *Engines of Instruction, Mischief and Magic: Children's Literature in England from Its Beginnings to 1839.* Lincoln: University of Nebraska Press, 1989.

Jackson, Rosemary. *Fantasy: The Literature of Subversion.* London: Methuen, 1981.

Johnson, Dianne. *Telling Tales: The Pedagogy and Promise of African American Literature for Youth.* New York: Greenwood, 1990.

Kahn, Alice. "A Onetime Bimbo Becomes a Muse." *New York Times,* 29 September 1991, 2:1, 24–25.

Kahne, Merton J. "On the Persistence of Transitional Phenomena into Adult Life." *The International Journal of Psycho-analysis* 48, no. 2 (1967): 247–58.

Kelly-Byrne, Diana. *A Child's Play Life: An Ethnographic Study.* New York: Teachers College Press, 1989.

Kimura, Doreen. "Sex Differences in the Brain." *Scientific American* 267, no. 3 (1992): 118–25.

King, Constance Eileen. *The Encyclopedia of Toys.* New York: Crown, 1978.

Klein, Melanie. *The Psychoanalysis of Children*. Trans. Alix Strachey. New York: Grove, 1960.

Kleist, Heinrich von. "About the Marionette Theatre." *Life and Letters To-day* (1936–37): 15–16; rpt. (1967): 101–5.

Kuznets, Lois R. "Games of Dark: Psychofantasy in Children's Literature." *Lion and the Unicorn* 1, no. 2 (1977): 17–24.

———. "Good News from the Land of the Brontyfans: or, Intertextuality in Clarke's *The Return of the Twelves.* In *Where Rivers Meet: Confluence and Concurrence, Selected Papers from the 1989 International Conference of the Children's Literature Association,* 67–74, ed. Susan R. Gannon and Ruth Anne Thompson. Pleasantville, N.Y.: Pace University, 1991.

———. *Kenneth Grahame*. Boston: G. K. Hall, 1987.

———. "Permutations of Frame in Mary Norton's 'Borrowers' Series." *Studies in the Literary Imagination* 18, no. 2 (1985): 65–78.

———. "Two Newbery Medal Winners and the Feminine Mystique: *Hitty, Her First Hundred Years* and *Miss Hickory*." *Lion and the Unicorn* 15 (1991): 1–14.

Lacan, Jacques. *Feminine Sexuality*. Ed. Juliet Mitchell and Jacqueline Rose. New York: Norton, 1983.

Lasky, Kathryn. *Dollmaker: The Eyelight and the Shadow*. New York: Scribner's, 1981.

Lastinger, Valerie C. "Of Dolls and Girls in Nineteenth Century France." *Children's Literature* 21 (1993): 20–42.

Lenz, Millicent. *Nuclear Age Literature for Youth: The Quest for a Life-Affirming Ethic*. Chicago: American Library Association, 1990.

———. "Russell Hoban's *The Mouse and His Child* and the Search to Be Self-Winding." *Proceedings of the Fifth Annual Children's Literature Association Conference,* Harvard College, Cambridge, Mass., March 1978.

Levy, Steven. *Artificial Life: The Quest for a New Creation*. New York: Pantheon, 1992.

Lloyd Evans, Barbara, and Gareth Lloyd Evans. *Everyman's Companion to the Brontës*. New York: Scribner's, 1982.

Locke, John. *Some Thoughts concerning Education*. 1693. Cambridge: Cambridge University Press, 1902.

Lubrano, Gina. "Expectant Elephant Mother Is in Training." *San Diego Union,* 7 September 1991, B:1, 12.

Luquet, G. H. "Oceanic Mythology." In *New Larousse Encyclopedia of Mythology*. New York: Hamlyn, 1977.

Lurie, Alison. "Back to Pooh Corner." *Children's Literature* 2 (1973): 11–17.

———. *Don't Tell the Grown-Ups: Subversive Children's Literature*. Boston: Little, Brown, 1990.

Lynn, Joanne. "Threadbare Utopia: Hoban's Modern Pastoral." *Children's Literature Association Quarterly* 11, no. 1 (1986): 19–23.

Lynn, Ruth Nadelman. *Fantasy for Children: An Annotated Checklist*. New York: Bowker, 1979.

McCaffery, Larry, and Sinda Gregory. "Russell Hoban." In *Alive and Writing: Interviews with American Authors of the 1980s,* 126–50. Urbana: University of Illinois Press, 1987.

McCorduck, Pamela. *Machines Who Think.* San Francisco: Freeman, 1979.

McGlathery, James M. *Mysticism and Sexuality: E. T. A. Hoffmann.* Part II: *Interpretations of the Tales.* New York: Peter Lang, 1985.

McMahon, Lynne. "The Pure Products of America Go Crazy." *AWP Chronicle* 22 (1989): 1, 4–6.

Maloney, Margaret Crawford. *English Illustrated Books for Children: A Descriptive Guide to a Selection from the Osborne Collection.* London: Bodley Head, 1981.

Marcus, Leonard. "Picture Book Animals: How Natural a History?" *Lion and the Unicorn* 7/8 (1983–84): 127–39.

Masson, Jeffrey Moussaieff. *The Assault on Truth: Freud's Suppression of the Seduction Theory.* New York: Farrar, Straus, and Giroux, 1984.

May, Jill P. "Mass Marketing and Toys Children Like." *Children's Literature Association Quarterly* 7 (1982): 5–7.

Mead, Margaret. "An Investigation of the Thought of Primitive Children, with Special Reference to Animism, a Preliminary Report." 1932. Reprinted in *Personalities and Cultures: Readings in Psychological Anthropology,* 213–37, ed. Robert Cushman Hunt. Garden City, N.Y.: Natural History, 1967.

Mendelsohn, Leonard. "Toys in Literature." In *Sharing Literature with Children: A Thematic Anthology,* 81–84, ed. Francelia Butler. New York: David McKay, 1977.

Mergen, Bernard. *Play and Playthings: A Reference Guide.* Westport, Conn.: Greenwood, 1982.

Meyer, Carolyn. Review of *Oddkins. Los Angeles Times Book Review,* 23 October 1988: 17.

Meyer, Susan. "'Black' Rage and White Women: Ideological Self-Formation in Charlotte Brontë's African Tales." *South Central Review* 8, no. 4 (1991): 28–40.

Michanczyk, Michael. "The Puppet Immortals of Children's Literature." *Children's Literature* 2 (1973): 159–64.

Milne, Christopher. *The Enchanted Places.* London: Eyre Methuen, 1974.

Moi, Toril. *Sexual/Textual Politics: Feminist Literary Theory.* New York: Methuen, 1985.

Montessori, Maria. *Childhood Education.* Trans. A. M. Joosten. New York: New American Library, 1975.

Moore, Anne Carroll, and Bertha Mahony Miller, eds. *Writing and Criticism: A Book for Margery Bianco.* Boston: Horn, 1951.

Moore, Colleen. *Colleen Moore's Dollhouse: The Story of the Most Exquisite Toy in the World.* Garden City, N.Y.: Doubleday, 1935.

Moore, Doris Langley-Levy. *E. Nesbit: A Biography.* Rev. ed. Philadelphia: Chilton, 1966.

Moore, Opal, and Donnarae MacCann. "The Ignoble Savage: Amerind Images in the Mainstream Mind." *Children's Literature Association Quarterly* 13 (1988): 26–30.

Morrissey, Thomas J. "Alive and Well but Not Unscathed: A Reply to Susan R. Gannon's '*Pinocchio* at 100.'" *Children's Literature Association Quarterly* 7, no. 2 (1982): 37–39.

————. "A *Pinocchio* for All Ages." *Children's Literature Association Quarterly* 13, no. 1 (1988): 90–91.

Moss, Anita. "Makers of Meaning: A Structuralist Study of Twain's *Tom Sawyer* and Nesbit's *The Enchanted Castle*." *Children's Literature Association Quarterly* 7, no. 3 (1982): 41–45.

Nadel, Ira Bruce. "'The Mansion of Bliss,' or the Place of Play in Victorian Life and Literature." *Children's Literature* 10 (1982): 18–36.

Negus, Kenneth. *E. T. A. Hoffmann's Other World: The Romantic Author and His New "Mythology."* Philadelphia: University of Pennsylvania Press, 1965.

Nelson, Claudia. "The Beast Within: *Winnie-the-Pooh* Reassessed." *Children's Literature in Education* 21, no. 1 (1990): 17–22.

Neumeyer, Peter. "*Amy's Eyes* Examined." *Lion and the Unicorn* 9 (1985): 58–69.

Newson, John, and Elizabeth Newson. *Toys and Playthings in Development and Remediation*. London: Allen and Unwin, 1979.

Norris, Margot. *Beasts of the Modern Imagination: Darwin, Nietzsche, Kafka, Ernst, and Lawrence*. Baltimore: Johns Hopkins University Press, 1985.

Olsen, Marilyn Strasser. "The Golliwogs: A Slide Journey." Paper delivered at the Children's Literature Association Conference, University of Missouri, Kansas City, 1986.

Opie, Iona, Robert Opie, and Brian Alderson. *The Treasures of Childhood: Books, Toys, and Games from the Opie Collection*. New York: Arcade, Little, Brown, 1989.

Ord, Priscilla. "Through the Looking Glass: Literary Reflections of Children's Play, Games and Pastimes in Victorian and Edwardian England." Paper presented at Children's Literature Association Conference, San Diego, California, 1990.

Owen, David. "Where Toys Come From." *Atlantic Monthly,* October 1986, 65–78.

Penrose, Roger. *The Emperor's New Mind: Concerning Computers, Minds, and the Laws of Physics*. New York: Vintage, 1990.

Pepler, D. J., and K. H. Rubin, eds. *The Play of Children: Current Theory and Research*. Basel, Switz.: S. Karger, 1982.

Peters, Diana S. "The Dream as Bridge in the Works of E. T. A. Hoffmann." *Oxford German Studies* 8 (1973): 60–85.

Peterson, Linda Kauffman, and Marilyn Leathers Solt. *Newbery and Caldicott Medal and Honor Books: An Annotated Bibliography*. Boston: G. K. Hall, 1982.

Piaget, Jean. *Play, Dreams, and Imitation in Childhood*. Trans. C. Gattegno and F. M. Hodgson. 1951. New York: Norton, 1962.

Pickering, Samuel F., Jr. *John Locke and Children's Books in Eighteenth-Century England*. Knoxville: University of Tennessee Press, 1981.

Quayle, Eric. *Early Children's Books: A Collector's Guide*. Totowa, N.J.: Barnes and Noble, 1983.

Rafferty, Terrence. "The Current Cinema." *New Yorker,* 8 August 1988, 77–78.

Rahn, Suzanne. "Rediscovering the Toy Theatre—With a Review of George Speaight's

The History of the English Toy Theatre." *The Lion and the Unicorn* 11 (October 1987): 111–27.

———. "Tailpiece: *The Tale of Two Mice.*" *Children's Literature* 12 (1984): 78–91.

Ratchford, Fannie Elizabeth. *The Brontës' Web of Childhood*. 1941. New York: Russell and Russell, 1964.

Riffaterre, Michael. *Fictional Truth*. Baltimore: Johns Hopkins University Press, 1990.

Rilke, Rainer Maria. "Some Reflections on Dolls." In *Selected Works,* vol. 1, 43–51, trans. G. Craig Houston. London: Hogarth, 1961.

Russell, David L. "Pinocchio and the Child-Hero's Quest." *Children's Literature in Education* 20, no. 4 (1989): 203–13.

Rustin, Margaret, and Michael Rustin. *Narratives of Love and Loss*. London: Verso, 1987.

Sale, Roger. "Children Reading and Man Reading: Oz, Babar and Pooh." *Children's Literature* 1 (1972): 162–71.

Saul, E. Wendy. "'All New Materials': Reflections on the American Toy Scene." *Children's Literature Association Quarterly* 7 (1982): 2–5.

Schwarcz, H. Joseph. "Machine Animism in Modern Children's Literature." *Library Quarterly* 37 (1967): 78–95.

Shavit, Zohar. *Poetics of Children's Literature*. Athens: University of Georgia Press, 1986.

Shefrin, Jill. "A Note on the Harlequinade Mother Shipton." *Mother Shipton*. Facsimile. Toronto: Toronto Public Library, 1980.

Singer, Jerome L. *The Child's World of Make-Believe: Experimental Studies of Imaginative Play*. New York: Academic, 1973.

Smith, Grover, Jr. "'The Doll Burners,' D. H. Lawrence and Louisa May Alcott." *Modern Language Quarterly* 19 (1958): 28–32.

Speaight, George. *The History of the English Toy Theatre*. 1946. Rev. ed. Boston: Plays, 1969.

Stanger, Carol A. "*Winnie the Pooh* through a Feminist Lens." *Lion and the Unicorn* 11, no. 2 (1987): 34–49.

Steinlein, Rüdiger. *Die domestizierte Phantazie: Studien zur Kinderliteratur, Kinderlektüre und Literaturpädagogik des 18. und frühen 19. Jahrhunderts*. Heidelberg: Carl Winter Universitätsverlag, 1987.

Sterck, Kenneth. "The Real Christopher Robin: An Appreciation of A. A. Milne's Children's Verse." *Children's Literature in Education* 11 (1980): 52–61.

Stevenson, Robert Louis. "'A Penny Plain and Two Pence Colored.'" *Memories and Portraits*. New York: Scribner's, 1897.

Stewart, Susan. *On Longing: Narratives of the Miniature, the Gigantic, the Souvenir, the Collection*. Baltimore: Johns Hopkins University Press, 1984.

Stoller, Robert J. *Presentations of Gender*. New Haven: Yale University Press, 1985.

Sutton-Smith, Brian. *Toys as Culture*. New York: Gardner, 1986.

Thomas, Peter. *Richard Hughes*. Cardiff: University of Wales, 1973.

Todorov, Tsvetan. *The Fantastic: A Structural Approach to a Literary Genre.* Trans. Richard Howard. 1970. Cleveland: Press of Case Western Reserve University, 1973.

"Toy Makers Let Classics Carry Them." *Ann Arbor News,* 9 April 1991, 8.

Traugott, John. "The Yahoo in the Doll's House: *Gulliver's Travels,* The Children's Classic." In *English Satire and the Satiric Tradition,* ed. Claude Rawson. Oxford: Blackwell, 1984.

Tremper, Ellen. "Instigorating Winnie-the-Pooh." *Lion and the Unicorn* 1, no. 2 (1977): 33–46.

Turner, Victor Witter. *Dramas, Fields, and Metaphors: Symbolic Action in Human Society.* Ithaca: Cornell University Press, 1974.

Voss, Tom. "Teddy Bear Power." *Prevention* (July 1982): 57–62.

Weininger, Otto. *The Clinical Psychology of Melanie Klein.* Springfield, Ill.: C. C. Thomas, 1984.

Wells, H. G. *Floor Games.* 1912. New York: Arno, 1976.

———. *Little Wars: A Game for Boys from Twelve Years of Age to 150 and for That More Intelligent Sort of Girl Who Likes Boys' Games and Books: With an Appendix on Kriegspiel.* London: Frank Palmer, 1913.

West, Mark I. "From the Pleasure Principle to the Reality Principle." *Proceedings of the Children's Literature Association Annual Conference, 1986.* Pleasantville, N. Y.: Pace University, 1988.

Whalen-Levitt, Peggy. "Margery Williams Bianco, 1881–1944." In *Writers for Children: Critical Studies of Major Authors since the Seventeenth Century,* 63–67, ed. Jane M. Bingham. New York: Scribner's, 1988.

Wiater, Stanley. "Dean Koontz in the Fictional Melting Pot." *Writer's Digest* (1989): 34–38.

Williams, Martin. "Some Remarks on Raggedy Ann and Johnny Gruelle." *Children's Literature* 3 (1974): 140–46.

Winnicott, Clare. "D. W. W.: A Reflection." In *Between Reality and Fantasy: Transitional Objects and Phenomena,* ed. Simon Grolnick and Leonard Barkin. New York: Jason Aronson, 1978.

Winnicott, D. W *Collected Papers: Through Pediatrics to Psycho-analysis.* New York: Basic Books, 1958.

———. *Playing and Reality.* New York: Penguin, 1980.

———. "Why Children Play." In *The Child, the Family, and the Outside World,* 149–52. London: Tavistock, 1957.

Wolf, Virginia L. "Playing and Reality in Sylvia Cassedy's Novels." Paper delivered at the Children's Literature Association Conference, San Diego, California, 1990.

Wunderlich, Richard, and Thomas J. Morrissey. "Carlo Collodi's *The Adventures of Pinocchio*: A Classic Book of Choices." In *Touchstones: Reflections on the Best in Children's Literature,* vol. 1, ed. Perry Nodelman. West Lafayette: Children's Literature Association, 1985.

Yaeger, Patricia. *Honey-Mad Women: Emancipatory Strategies in Women's Writing.* New York: Columbia University Press, 1988.

Index